Gift of

The
SEARCH FOR LOVE

Sketch of George Sand, by Alfred de Musset, made before their trip to Italy

George Sand
The Search for Love

By

Marie Jenney Howe

New York
The John Day Company
1927

PRINTED IN THE U. S. A.

FOR THE JOHN DAY COMPANY, INC.

BY THE QUINN & BODEN COMPANY, RAHWAY, N. J.

To
ROSE YOUNG

ABOUT THE AUTHOR

MARIE JENNEY HOWE was born in Syracuse, New York. She studied for the ministry at Meadville Theological School, Meadville, Pennsylvania, where she received the degree of Bachelor of Divinity. She was for some time minister of the First Unitarian Church in Des Moines. After her marriage to Frederic C. Howe she was identified with many phases of the woman movement. In campaigns for woman suffrage and on behalf of professional and working women, she has taken a prominent part as speaker and organizer.

In preparing the material for "George Sand: The Search for Love," Mrs. Howe spent two years in Paris doing research work. She visited Nohant, George Sand's home in the center of France, where she became acquainted with George Sand's grand-daughter, Madam Aurore Sand. Mrs. Howe is on the governing board of the French Société des Amis de George Sand.

CONTENTS

LIST OF ILLUSTRATIONS

The bas-relief of George Sand on the binding case and title page is from the medallion by David d'Angers, 1833, now in the Louvre, Paris.

PREFACE

OFTEN, after reading the biography of an important man or woman, I have laid down the book with a sense of frustration. I wanted to know the inner life of the famous person. What did he think and feel? I found myself asking.

Alas, famous men and women do not, as a rule, leave confidential letters and journals that would justify a conscientious biographer in an attempt to satisfy our intimate interest. But this rule was broken by the woman who came to be known as George Sand. In following her voluminous correspondence, it seems as though everyone to whom she had ever written, saved her letters and, in course of time, published them. In connection with each of her love affairs she confided a series of letters to a trusted friend. Often she added as a postscript, "Burn this letter," whereupon that letter was guarded with particular care and preserved for an inquisitive posterity. The biographer of George Sand has, therefore, what most biographers miss,—all the letters that ought to have been burned.

More revelatory than letters, George Sand wrote an occasional confession in which she laid bare her heart with a frankness as shocking to others as it was merciless to herself. The confession, intended for the eyes of one alone, was always shared with others and eventually given to the public. In one instance such a confession was used as evidence in a law suit. In still another, a self-condemnatory journal was handed over to her worst enemy who used it to injure her reputation.

But George Sand herself was most to blame for the intimate material left to posterity. She was incurably trustful toward friends and lovers. Whenever she was betrayed, deceived or slandered, she forgot and forgave and trusted again. "In her mental attitude," says George Brandes, "she was almost a prodigy. There was not a trace of narrow-mindedness in her." She seemed to feel that she lived in a world peopled by disinterested men and women who were seeking the truth about human nature, and that anyone who offered himself for analysis was a valuable specimen for the laboratory of psychical research. She submitted her experience in the hope that others would profit thereby. "I would be willing to tell or publish all the facts of my life," she wrote to Sainte-Beuve, "if I thought they would prove useful to others."

By means of her own generous self-revelations, I have tried in this biography to throw light on George Sand's inner life, to explain the secret of her suffering, the reasons for her loneliness, and the unprecedented situation which has made her the most misunderstood woman in the history of literature. *The Search for Love* is an effort to see George Sand's life through her own eyes and, as far as possible, to follow her stream of consciousness from childhood to old age.

Such an effort would be presumptuous were it not for the wealth of material available.

In addition to letters, journals and confessions, George Sand wrote the history of her own life up to fifty years of age. If anything of importance was omitted from this autobiography, it has been supplied by Wladimir Karénine, who is accepted as the authoritative biographer of George Sand.

Madame Karénine's *George Sand, Sa Vie et ses Œuvres,* will doubtless remain a source book for lesser biographers, as only a devoted Sandist would undertake to thoroughly peruse these four volumes of detailed information. They are based on hitherto unpublished documents given Madame Karénine by the family and friends of George Sand.

The Search for Love is not fictionized biography. It is history told with as near an approach to story form as authentic records permit. Wherever in her autobiography George Sand describes conversations, brief dialogues have been abridged from the long conversations she narrates. Where the only historical material is her correspondence, the story form is necessarily restricted to a narrative constructed from the letters at hand.

In this biography there are no guesses and no bold assumptions. Paragraph after paragraph consist of writings from the hand of George Sand. These are left unquoted, either because they are given a free translation or because they are greatly condensed. Often the material is reassembled but it is never invented. Imagination has been used, as it must always be used in interpretive biography, to touch up details of a faded background, but not to alter a line of the portrait.

For those who like to refer to authentic records, the following sources will be found to have supplied the historical material used in each phase of this history of George Sand's life. The bibliography at the back of this volume gives the book titles here rendered into English.

In Chapters I and II, the story of childhood and young womanhood is taken from George Sand's autobiography corrected by Madame Karénine's more accurate compilation of facts and dates. Instead of a chapter on genealogy the ancestral history goes into the story as it was given to the heroine, at the age when she actually heard it and with the effect she describes.

In Chapter III the description of marriage and early life in Paris, relies on Madame Karénine for main outlines while several anecdotes have been introduced from George Sand's biography by Séché and Bertaud. The Sèze romance is from the Sand-Sèze correspondence published by Aurore Sand last year. For lack of material the Sèze romance has necessarily been omitted from all previous biographies of George Sand.

Chapter IV, the Sand-Musset love story, has been built from the Sand-Musset correspondence and Pagello's journal, although several other sources have been drawn upon and credit given. No other biography of George Sand has been written since the publication of Alfred de Musset's letters to George Sand in 1904.

Madame Karénine's volume including this romance appeared in 1899.

For Chapter V, the Michel of Bourges friendship is related in great detail in George Sand's autobiography. For the love affair the main source is George Sand's letters to Michel published anonymously as *The Letters of a Woman*. Other sources are her *Letters to Everard* and her *Intimate Journal*.

Chapter VI is compiled from the published correspondence covering this period.

In Chapter VII the sources for the early romance with Chopin are George Sand's autobiography and her *Winter at Majorca*. The end of the Chopin episode is constructed almost wholly from Madame Karénine's third volume published in 1912. There is no material of any importance for the Sand-Chopin misunderstanding outside of Karénine's book. To read the new Chopin biographies on the last ten years of Chopin's life is merely to reread as much of Karénine as the great composer's admirers are willing to accept.

The last five chapters of *The Search for Love* have drawn upon Lovenjoul, Caro, René Doumic, Houssinville, Séché and Bertaud, Aurore Sand's article on her memories of childhood, Sarah Bernhardt's autobiography and, most of all, upon Karénine's fourth volume published in 1926.

Considerable new material on George Sand appeared during the year 1926. Madame Karénine's fourth volume is the most important new contribution. It covers the period of the last twenty-eight years of George Sand's life. George Sand's *Journal Intime*, with an introduction by her granddaughter Aurore Sand, is also important. The Sand-Sèze letters edited by Aurore Sand comprise the first information given to the public on this six-year romance. Three hitherto unpublished letters from George Sand to Dr. Pagello appeared in *Candide* and are an interesting addition to the three-cornered love affair.

Therefore *The Search for Love* adds to previous biographies of

George Sand: the Sèze romance; the truth derived from Alfred de Musset's letters and from George Sand's three letters to Dr. Pagello; information on George Sand's old age as presented in Madame Karénine's final volume; and self-revelatory material contained in George Sand's *Journal Intime*.

GEORGE SAND

GEORGE SAND was the greatest feminine genius known to literature. No woman has ever matched her in creative power and none has approached her in productivity. Her works fill one hundred and ten volumes. Beginning with romantic fiction, she turned to novels of social reform and rounded out her forty-five years of writing with pastoral tales that have become classic literature. Her success was sensational. The popularity she enjoyed during her lifetime has never been surpassed by any writer in any age. In the words of Vicomte d'Haussonville, she "wielded an intellectual royalty that no other woman has ever attained," she "saw her works pass from the aristocracy to the working-class" and she "spoke a language which appealed equally to the passions of men, the hearts of women and the imagination of children."

Her many-sidedness was remarkable. All that any woman has ever felt or dreamed or suffered is summed up in the life of George Sand. Incurably domestic, she was also the most public-spirited woman of her day. Profoundly maternal, she became self-supporting and achieved what seemed to her contemporaries a man's place in the world. Made, as her friends explained, to be the good wife of a good man, she was called a vampire and accused of breaking men's hearts. She was every sort of woman except the courtesan. She never gave her love for anything except love in return.

George Sand was a modern woman born one hundred years

too soon. But it was not alone as a herald of the new womanhood that she made history. Heine said, "She set the world on fire." In a period that was monarchist, she was republican. In a society that was orthodox, she stood outside the church. Living under the harsh code of Napoleon, she fought to reform laws that seemed to her oppressive. Victor Hugo said, "Beings like George Sand are public benefactors." He wrote to her, "I thank you for being so great a soul."

To one who follows the course of her long life, George Sand seems as contradictory and inconsistent as any woman would appear if all her letters and journals, written from school days until she was a grandmother, could be read. What seems right at twenty appears to the ripe age of thirty as youthful ignorance and the defiant ethics of thirty may again seem crudely mistaken at philosophic fifty. So it was with George Sand. She ruined her life several times but always crawled out from the débris and built up a new existence, until in the end she learned to adjust herself to life as it is and people as they are.

Whether from feminine modesty or from a desire to placate the professional jealousy of friends and lovers, George Sand never seemed to recognize her own genius. She spoke slightingly of her writing and her gifts. But she regarded herself as a pioneer in experience. No woman ever made so bold a claim to recognition as a human being. It was this assertion of inclusively human, rather than exclusively feminine qualities which created the legend of George Sand as a masculine woman. Her biographer, Elme Caro, criticized her unwomanly character saying, "The one thing needful to this soul is resignation." Unfortunately for her reputation, most of her biographers have been old-fashioned men who regarded her from a viewpoint of established feminine traditions. To the modern mind, it is evident that George Sand's real fault lay not in her lack of submissiveness, not in her insistent spirit of revolt, but in the fact that these qualities were embodied in a woman where they did not belong, rather than in a man where they would have been deemed admirable and even distinguished.

George Sand was so far in advance of the women of her day that she was driven to associate almost exclusively with men. As a consequence she adopted their standards.

She regarded laws and customs as ephemeral, saw clearly how they would be changed and lived as though they were already altered. In this projection of her mind beyond her times she was a futurist, trying to live in a non-existing society which had not yet evolved.

The woman who came to be known as George Sand was born July first, 1804, at 15 rue Meslay, Paris. She was baptized Amandine-Aurore-Lucie Dupin. Her married name was Aurore Dudevant. Because women were unwelcome in the realm of letters, her own name could not well appear upon her writings, and she adopted the masculine name which she made famous.

MARIE JENNEY HOWE

October 4, 1927
Harmon-on-Hudson, New York

The
SEARCH FOR LOVE

I

AURORE

SHE was born to the sound of the violin. Her mother was Sophie Dupin, Sophie of the dark eyes, dazzling smile and careless laughter.

That evening the neighbors had gathered at the humble Dupin home to celebrate the betrothal of Sophie's sister. It was a gay betrothal. Everyone drank a toast to the bride-to-be and then a toast to the mother-to-be. Sophie, amazing person, had led the merrymaking. She had even been dancing. Reckless, radiant Sophie! How lovely she was in her gown the color of roses!

As a new quadrille was formed, Sophie stole away to her room so quietly that no one noticed her departure. The dancing continued, the violin sobbed and sang. As the long-drawn-out quadrille followed the course of its various figures, a new-created being entered a world filled with music. Her human wail was drowned in the cry of the violin.

It was her father, Maurice Dupin, who was the musician. When they announced the birth of a daughter he came running to see the marvel. They showed him an insignificant object, small, brown and solemn. It was hard to believe that she belonged to his beautiful Sophie. "The shape of her head is like the Dupins!" they exclaimed. "She is like your side of the family." So he named her Aurore because of Madame Dupin, his mother, who was born Marie-Aurore de Saxe, and because of the far-away first Aurore of his family, his great-grandmother, Countess Aurore Koenigsmark.

As soon as he decided to name the child Aurore, she seemed brought into line with his own family tradition. Maurice himself had been named for his grandfather, Count Maurice de Saxe,

3

France's great military hero. Maurice de Saxe was the natural son of the king of Poland, Frederic-Augustus II, and of the Countess Aurore Koenigsmark. When he thought of his own ancestors, Maurice Dupin was tempted to regret that his child was not a boy. How splendid for a boy's inheritance would be the temperament of a Koenigsmark, the imagination of a Saxe, or at least the artist nature that belonged to the Dupins. But when the proud father paused to consider Sophie's parentage, he was forced to change his point of view.

Sophie was true plebeian. She was born of the Paris pavements. Her father had sold birds in little cages along the quays of the Seine. Indeed, Sophie was very close to those who had believed in the guillotine for aristocrats.

In Sophie's child, then, there were mingled the blood of royalty and the blood of the common people. These two strains meeting in the French nation had resulted in revolution. This inflammable mixture in the nature of a man might result in fanaticism, melancholia, or even in the sufferings of genius. In a woman's nature, however, there was no danger of explosion, catastrophe or genius. The destiny of a girl-child, protected, kept at home and married, was commonplace, but it was safe.

It was just as well, then, that the child had been born a girl.

Aurore the third, knowing nothing of past grandeurs or present poverty, had for a cradle a plain wicker basket. She lay in her cradle and stared at the ceiling or slept. The days, the months, went by. Instead of the cradle there was a little bed; instead of the cradle dreaminess, a gradual awareness. Hour after hour she would lie in absorbed contemplation of some fold of the window curtain, or some gay flower in the wall paper. One day the candle, which had always given a single light, seemed to give two lights, side by side. She watched, she was enchanted, she tried and tried to make the twin lights come again. Sometimes she succeeded. She loved the illusion without knowing why she loved it, or what it was she loved. Illusion was her first interest in life.

For a long time people were vague shadows, and all her environment was a blur. As she grew older she learned that certain outside things came through to her, to the place where she lived in peace and quietness.

Her mother's voice came singing; the voice was music; it sang of a white hen who was laying a silver egg for Sophie's little child. The egg of silver seemed to Aurore a perfect gift, representing beauty, mystery, attainment. The promise, renewed every evening, kept alive her faith in its fulfillment. The gift must not be demanded to-day, it must be expected to-morrow, always to-morrow.

One day, when she was still older, silver tones from close at hand came through the void. They told of vague pleasurable things that had to do with blue sky, white clouds, flowers, birds, trees. Then from the outer blur a voice spoke: "That horrid man upstairs is practicing his flute again. I shall complain to the landlord. Let us rap on the walls and make him stop." After that the silver tones had nothing more to tell her; something beautiful had been destroyed.

The little girl from below stairs was going to her first communion, dressed in snowy white, over her shoulders a veil of misty softness. Aurore gazed and felt a little thrill of pleasure. Here was something remote from ugliness, remote from earth. A voice broke in: "Why don't they dress that child better? How badly the skirt hangs. I know that dress has never seen a tub; it is dirty, and her veil has yellow blotches!" The thrill of pleasure gave way to a quiver of pain. Then the veil was not really lovely? Dirty yellow blotches—how the words hurt!

So it was with all her pleasures; the grown-ups talked and talked, and in their talking the lovely things of life disappeared. Whenever she was feeling especially happy, someone was sure to exclaim: "What is the matter with the child? Is she sick?"—"No, no," Sophie would answer, "that's just her way of sitting still and dreaming. She has always been like that."

Aunt Lucy could not help observing that her own child Clotilde was much brighter than Aurore. Not but that Aurore was good; she was almost too good. Sophie had told her that when a child was disobedient the angels of heaven and even the Holy Virgin wept with sorrow. Aurore could not bear to make these heavenly beings suffer. If her conscience troubled her she would look apprehensively at the sky, where among the clouds she saw plainly row upon row of dear little angels with woebegone faces. Behind them, clad in flowing white and wearing blue sleeves, stood the Holy Virgin. What was that slight motion of blue sleeve against white robe? Was the Virgin wringing her hands? Was she beating her breast? "Oh, dear Virgin, don't take it so hard! I'll try to be good!" Who, indeed, could be naughty with such a picture before her eyes?

Clotilde had received the same admonition about the angels and the Virgin, but Clotilde was not impressed and her imagination was not excited, which effectively proved to Aunt Lucy the superiority of Clotilde.

There were other differences between the two cousins. One day a group of children joined hands in a circle, playing a game which began with a song. The words were set to a haunting refrain in minor key—

"No more, no more shall we go to the forest,
    The laurel trees are all cut down."

Suddenly a far-away look came over Aurore's face. She withdrew from the circle, and sat alone under the spell of words and music. Something in the two lines stirred her profoundly. Never yet had she seen so much as a grove of trees, much less a forest. Nevertheless, as she fixed her eyes on space, the brick court, the pavement, the city street faded away, and in their place was a mysterious forest, rich with the verdure of laurel trees. Woodchoppers came with cruel axes. They cut down the laurels. Oh, lovely laurels, cut down, broken, dead!

"No more, no more shall we go to the forest."

Aurore could not have expressed the sense she felt of beauty devastated, of illusion lost. But the hurt went so deep that as long as she lived she would never hear children singing those two lines without a recurrent sense of sadness. Aunt Lucy looked at the gnome-like figure, bent as if under the weight of some childish grief. "What is the matter, Aurore? Have you hurt yourself?" No answer. There were times when the child seemed deaf. Casting a glance toward the circle, Aunt Lucy noticed Clotilde, dancing gaily and singing prettily about laurel trees. No, decidedly Aurore was not bright like Clotilde.

2

Maurice Dupin came home from the war on a short furlough. He wrote to his mother: "Aurore does not say much, but she is not thinking any less on that account. I adore this child of mine." Since Maurice was satisfied, Sophie saw nothing to complain about. No one scolded Aurore for her dreaminess. She would sit for hours at a time gazing vacantly at nothing at all, her mouth half open. "Seeing fairies!" Sophie would exclaim. And indeed it was Sophie's own fault if her child were fanciful, for as fast as Aurore demanded fairy tales Sophie delighted to tell them to her, and the nine-year-old sister Caroline did her best to supplement her mother. Because Sophie felt responsible also for a certain amount of religious instruction, she related in simple fashion all the Bible stories she knew. As though this were not enough, Aurore discovered a popular abridged mythology, and before she could read asked for the legends that explained the pictures. Thus in her little brain were jumbled angels and cupids, magicians and saints, the Holy Virgin and the old witch, in strange poetic hodge-podge.

Sophie could not always be telling stories, for there were beds to make and sweeping and scrubbing and cooking to do. Aurore was at her heels like a devoted puppy. What could she do to get the child from under her feet? "I shall have to tie you up," Sophie threatened good naturedly. "Where can I put you? The chairs are too high. I wish I could afford a cushion or a foot-stool for my baby to sit on. Here is the warming-pan. Don't be afraid, it isn't heated."

The foot-warmer was placed in the centre of the room, and the child was seated upon it. Then she was barricaded by a circle of four chairs with their straw-bottomed seats turned toward her. The three-year-old was so tiny that in order to lean her elbows on the chair seats she had to stand on the warming-pan. This accomplished, she tried to remove the straw. Her hands thus occupied, something in her that longed for expression found release. She began to talk out loud.

A story was being told, and Aurore listened. Of course at the beginning she knew it was only her own voice talking, but soon she forgot that and became wholly the listener. Sophie too, from the kitchen near by, had to listen in spite of herself. The background of Aurore's story was a great mysterious forest, the hero a prince who had lost his way. The prince was obliged to meet all the fanciful characters that lived in Aurore's imagination: the good fairy, the beautiful princess, the kind giant, the three graces, the angel Gabriel, the nine muses, and the wise virgins. In this forest of Aurore's everyone was good and kind, and everyone was happy. The prince never met the devil or had a misfortune. Sophie thought it the most tiresome story she had ever heard.

The evening meal being on the table, Sophie picked up the romancer and seated her in her high chair. Aurore was stunned; she looked at the candles and the food, and wondered how she had been brought back. A moment ago she was far away in the forest. Could the supper table be real? "Eat your bread and soup and drink your wine and water." Obediently Aurore ate and drank and soon after fell asleep.

The next day the child was again seated on the warming-pan and given the chair seats to strip. As soon as her hands were busy, her memory picked up the thread of the story at the point where it had been broken. Each day Aurore added a chapter. Sophie was not impressed but she was amused. "It's a regular novel she is telling us. It continues from day to day."

Aunt Lucy, passing in and out, heard several chapters. After the prince had been wandering for many days Aunt Lucy grew impatient. "Come, come, Aurore," she interrupted, "isn't it time you were getting the prince out of the forest?" Aurore looked at her with unseeing eyes. "She doesn't hear a word I say!" exclaimed Aunt Lucy. "And she looks at me so stupidly."

"Oh, let her alone," called Sophie from the kitchen. "The only time I can do my work in peace is when she is composing her novel between those four chairs."

Aunt Lucy was dubious. "Do you think she is quite—well— bright?" she asked.

"I don't want her to be bright," said Sophie complacently. "She is a good girl and affectionate; that's enough."

"I don't agree with you," Aunt Lucy persisted. "The child's father—and his mother—and her father—were they all very different from us?"

At this Sophie bridled, her anger mounted into rage, and she began on the history of her wrongs. She wanted Lucy to know that she was just as good as those Dupins! Yet how they looked down upon her! Madame Dupin had tried to annul her son's marriage. Madame Dupin was rich and yet she let her son live in poverty. Madame Dupin could never forgive the existence of Caroline, Sophie's illegitimate daughter, yet Madame Dupin had adopted Hippolyte, Maurice's illegitimate son. And where was the difference? Was she, Sophie, any worse than the men? Nobody blamed men!

Aurore could no longer go on with her story. She felt herself, her prince and princess, and her good fairy flooded by her mother's outpourings. Without understanding what was said, she realized that someone had been unkind to her mother, and that she, Sophie's child, was wholly on Sophie's side.

3

Somewhere in the back of her head Aurore knew that dolls were only things to pretend with, but she distinguished between those that seemed real and those that were obviously mere toys. The seemingly real doll was adopted as a child. If it broke at the first fall, or leaked sawdust, or lost an arm, she cast it aside with entire lack of feeling,—cloth and sawdust must be treated as such. While it remained intact, she nursed it, fed it, put it to bed and made her friends treat it with respect. She was all tenderness for the doll that gave the illusion of reality. But if the creature could not help her create an illusion, if it fooled her after she had thought to find it real, she threw it away and in so doing felt she was protesting against a lie.

"My faith!" cried Aunt Lucy. "The child is first so soft, and then so hard. When she grows up I hope she will never treat people the way she treats her dolls."

Sophie had decided to take a long journey to the distant city of Madrid, where Maurice Dupin was fighting for Napoleon. With the four-year-old girl for companion, and with a defiant purpose in her heart, she left the humble Paris apartment and set forth for Spain. They traveled in a slow carriage along the lines of the French army. It was dangerous and difficult, but wild, reckless Sophie insisted on joining her soldier husband.

Long days in the jolting carriage. Restless nights in dirty, noisy hotels. Bad food, hunger, French soldiers all about, weary horses, weary Sophie, weary Aurore!

Why did the other lady traveler keep saying, "Sophie, in your condition you ought never to have made this journey." Why did Sophie reply, "My husband forbade me to join him and that's why I have to go to him."—"You are a jealous woman."—"Yes, I am jealous."—And Sophie's face was distorted by anger and pain. What was it to be jealous? wondered Aurore. She would never be jealous. It must me a terrible feeling, for it made her mother's lovely face look ugly.

At Madrid, Aurore found herself in a magnificent palace. Napoleon's general, Prince Murat, occupied the first floor. Maurice Dupin, the general's aide-de-camp, was given the third story for his family. Since Murat disapproved of families for his soldiers, he had to be reconciled to the presence of Sophie and Aurore. Sophie had received no education, but she well knew the art of pleasing men, and set herself to win the approval of General Murat. As she was clever with her needle she clothed Aurore in a little uniform exactly like that of Maurice the soldier. The trousers were amaranthine blue, braided with gold, the coat white and gold, the cape white bordered with black fur. A cap, a tiny sabre and gold spurs completed the costume. The child was trained to carry herself as her father did, throw the cape back over her shoulder, draw her sabre, and salute.

So dressed and so trained, Aurore was introduced to General Murat, and addressed him as "my Prince." He believed, or pretended to believe, that she was a boy, and treated her as one of his officers. Whenever he entertained a caller she was sent for and presented. "Here," he would say to his visitor, "is my new aide-de-camp." Then he would throw back his head and laugh delightedly at his guest's surprise.

These military duties, repeated, grew onerous. Aurore was more comfortable, though less important, when she could exchange her heavy uniform for the light Spanish dress which her mother had made of black silk, with a fringe to the ankles, and a mantilla. She had watched the peasants dance the bolero, and she soon could imitate their steps and dance like a Spaniard.

Day after day Sophie and Maurice went sight-seeing, leaving Aurore with a Spanish nurse who abandoned the child to her own devices. For the first time in her life Aurore was alone.

But she was alone in an enchanted palace. It was all her fairy tales come true. The furniture was of gold, the curtains of crimson damask. At the end of the salon was a full-length mirror called a psyche. In this mirror appeared the first companion to keep her company, sometimes in the guise of a small boy in uniform, sometimes as a little girl in Spanish dress. At the beginning, Aurore always knew she saw her own reflection; but as she danced and the other danced with her she forgot the mirror and the fancy, and her playfellow seemed real. When she acted the soldier in her uniform, he acted with her; when she built an altar and brought her white rabbit and offered it to the gods, he offered his rabbit also; when she danced the bolero he danced too. The illusion captured her imagination so completely that when she stopped dancing she was surprised that he did not continue. He would not make a gesture that she had not made. Again and again she would pass from pleasure to disappointment in her playfellow.

She found another companion, more fascinating because more mysterious. It was a voice that spoke on the great balcony outside; when she called, it answered; when she said, "Come here!" it demanded of her also, "Come here!" But when she went she found no one. She felt vaguely that she had another self, another me, and that it was hiding behind the wall or up in the air.

Her enchanted palace, her true fairy tales, her psyche, her echo, her rabbit—the whole experience of solitude was so delightful that there were days when she hated to see her parents returning.

One day at Madrid she was not allowed to see her mother. By strange coincidence a baby brother was sent to them that very night. The next day she saw Sophie, but, oh! how changed! Instead of the robust, red-cheeked woman, energetic with household duties, there lay a pale suffering being, too weak to hold out her arms to her own little daughter. At the sight of her mother's suffering Aurore felt her heart contract with tenderness. There was a choking in her throat, a rushing in her ears. She burst into noisy sobs and tried to fling herself on her mother's breast. "Take her away," said Sophie weakly, and Aurore was carried from the room. Four years old, and she had made her first emotional discovery! Her happiness depended upon another.

After that she was swayed by Sophie's moods. If Sophie caressed her, she was content; if Sophie pushed her away, her heart ached. She could not play or be at peace until she was restored to favor. She could no longer be happy alone.

4

As soon as Sophie was able to travel, another journey was undertaken, this time to the village of Nohant, the home of Maurice's mother, Madame Dupin. After long, proud resistance to the mortification caused by Maurice's lowly marriage, the great lady had condescended to receive her son's wife. Maurice was all expectation. His family was for the first time to be united. For eight years he had been trying to reconcile his mother to his love for Sophie, and at last he had succeeded. Sophie was frightened and excited. Aurore did not know what it was all about.

They left Madrid early in July and followed the route of the retreating soldiers of Napoleon. During the long journey Aurore was too exhausted to be conscious of anything but hunger, thirst, fever, and the numbness of fatigue. After six weeks of misery they arrived at Nohant late in August.

The child who was introduced to her grandmother was anything but attractive; her sallow face was covered with the effects of a skin disease caught from an epidemic among the soldiers. Her clothes were travel-stained, her dark hair was gritty with dust, her shoes were dirty. Her sense of humiliation completed her infantile woe. Abashed by her own appearance, the little girl looked up at her grandmother and saw a lovely and imposing person, dressed in silk and lace and smelling of roses and violets. She felt herself kissed and carried to a large room at the right of the big entrance hall. In one end of the room stood a magnificent bed, which, like its owner, was covered with silk and lace and smelled delicious. In this room there was no appropriate spot for a disheveled child. Aurore felt herself gently dropped on the luxurious bed in the midst of softness and fragrance. Her dirty shoes were on the dainty coverlet, yet grandmother did not seem to mind.

After she was rested, a boy of nine appeared bearing an enormous bouquet of flowers. "This is Hippolyte," said grandmother, and bade them kiss one another.

"What a fine boy!" Sophie exclaimed. Then, congratulating her husband upon his splendid son, she added, "He is mine also, as Caroline is yours."

When Aurore was able to explore the garden, Hippolyte insisted on holding her hand, as though he were afraid she would fall. Aurore was humiliated that he thought her a weak little girl, and quickly proved herself as strong as a boy and as able as a boy to compete with her rough playfellow. As soon as Hippolyte dropped his company manners he became a cruel tease. He hung her dolls from the trees head downward, undressed them, buried them alive and put crosses on their graves. Aurore took their sufferings seriously and hated their tormentor. But always after a day or two she forgave him and played with him again.

When the excitement of the homecoming was over, Aurore was more or less disregarded by the family. With passive satisfaction she withdrew into herself and continued the reveries that were so necessary to her strange being. For hours at a time she sat on her little foot-stool beside her mother, her arms hanging listlessly, her eyes fixed upon space, never speaking a word or hearing what others said. Grandma Dupin was disturbed by the child's long meditations. "She's dreaming!" Sophie explained. "When she was a little thing she used to tell her dreams out loud, until Aunt Lucy teased her. Now she never says a word. But, as her father always explains, she doesn't think less for not speaking."

"Yes," agreed Madame Dupin, "her father was like that when he was a child. He used to fall into reveries and dreamy ecstasies; they left him languid. It is not good for children to dream too much."

To counteract Aurore's habit of reverie, a playmate was provided; Ursule, the niece of Julie the chambermaid, was brought to live in the house. Sometimes the two little girls played active games, but a great part of the time Aurore persuaded Ursule to sit quietly beside her and meditate in silence.

5

At the beginning of their relationship the two Dupin women were brought into outward harmony by their common adoration for Maurice. Whatever Maurice said was delightful, whatever he did was wonderful. Each felt that the sun rose and set in him, each felt that she loved him best, each wanted him for herself alone.

"My son," Madame Dupin was fond of saying, "has been my whole life." The statement was no exaggeration. From the moment of his birth Maurice had been her sole preoccupation, her hope and her pride. Long ago, when she had discovered his love for Sophie, she had wept bitter tears and had cried accusingly, "You love another woman better than you love me!" It had been hard for her to receive the woman who had caused her so much suffering, and Madame Dupin had opened her house to her undesirable daughter-in-law for no other reason than that she could no longer bear to be separated from her son.

Sophie's attitude toward Maurice was no less jealous and possessive. It was left to Maurice, gay, charming, debonair, to maintain a spirit of friendliness. He pacified Sophie and tried to make his mother see his wife in the best light.

As if the two women did not supply enough adoration, Maurice had a third adorer in Deschartres, his former tutor and at present manager of the Nohant estate. Deschartres had once been a priest, but now prided himself upon his skill as a doctor. He was always wanting to prescribe for Aurore. But she was already the special patient of her mother. Deschartres was secretly opposed to Sophie and all her works. His hold upon his beloved pupil was lessened by the influence of this exacting woman. Jealous, too, of her pretensions as a doctor, he set up his skill against hers.

The victim of the conflict was the unfortunate Aurore. She had a strong constitution or she could not have survived this competitive medical tenderness. For every ailment or suspicion of an ailment Deschartres gave her a strong emetic. It took several days for her to recover from the effects. Sophie had a superstitious belief that all children suffered from worms—this was indeed one of the medical fads of the day—so Sophie kept on hand a stock of vermifuges of every variety, black, nauseous and evil-smelling. If Deschartres gave an emetic, Sophie would insist upon a vermifuge. Then, since both remedies were so sickening that the child could not eat, rhubarb was administered to create an appetite. Aurore's way of handling the situation was stoic. She learned to conceal her aches. Sometimes in the midst of play she would be taken with a violent cramp, but no pain was so hard to endure as the remedies, so she went on playing, with a control which few grown-ups could emulate.

The more she evaded her doctors and played outdoors, the stronger she became. But the baby brother grew weaker day by day. He could not throw off the fever he had caught on the journey from Spain. In spite of the healthful surroundings of Nohant he languished and died.

The death of the baby softened all hearts toward Sophie. Nobody felt like blaming her for the reckless journey to Spain which had doubtless cost the child's life. Maurice, always tender and indulgent of her vagaries, became, if possible, even more devoted. For some time he denied himself his usual pleasure of long rides on his spirited Andalusian horse. One evening, however, he went to the neighboring town of La Châtre to visit some friends, and rode home after dark. The horse shied abruptly, Maurice fell and was killed.

Aurore was scarcely aware of her father's death. Sophie wore black clothes and cried constantly, grandmother wore black clothes and never smiled; but Aurore could still climb to her mother's lap and fall asleep there, so she did not feel that anything terrible had happened. Every morning, as they put on her black dress and drew on the terrible black stockings, she would ask, "Is father dead again to-day?" So far, her world remained the same.

Soon, however, she became vaguely aware that the two women in black did not love each other, disliked each other, sometimes even hated each other. And this seemed to have something to do with their love for her.

6

After the months of formal mourning, the household slowly recognized that jealousy and possessiveness were still alive in the two women. They had been torn like vines fallen to the ground. Now they had begun to cling again and to compete again. They had found a slip of a girl to twine their affections about. Each felt that she loved Aurore best, each wanted her, but this time the object of their common affection was swayed by no divided loyalty. Aurore displayed for her mother a passionate partiality. Sophie was victor over Madame Dupin, or so it seemed.

Madame Dupin bided her time and invited Sophie to prolong her visit. Sophie consented, for she was uncertain about her future, and felt helpless without Maurice.

Aurore was deeply moved by her mother's sorrow. As she watched Sophie suffer she loved her more and more, until her little being was completely subjugated. But while Aurore was wholly occupied with her mother, Madame Dupin centred her attention on her grandchild, until she came to regard Aurore as her rightful possession. She even confused her with Maurice. Indeed the child was a replica of Maurice; her voice, her features, her gestures, her tastes and temperament, everything in the little girl reminded Madame Dupin of the little boy she had lost. In calling out to Aurore she would unconsciously say, "Maurice, come here." In answering a question she would say, "No, my son,"— "Yes, my son." Devoting herself to Aurore, she re-lived her own young motherhood, and in so doing renewed her youth. Aurore, precocious, understood all that her grandmother told her and taught her. She could remember and sing any music she had once heard, and showed great aptitude in learning to play the piano. Madame Dupin expected to make of Aurore the musician Maurice might have been—this girl-child could not go away to war. The old lady's happiness was bound up in the child; it was easy for her to convince herself that Aurore would be ruined if left to Sophie's capricious care.

A silent warfare began between the two women. They had a natural antipathy for each other. Madame Dupin was, in appearance and in temperament, the typical blond Saxon, grave and dignified, with the manner and reserve of a great lady. Sophie had the appearance and the nature of a Spaniard; she was jealous, passionate and weak, liable to anger and capable of great generosity. Madame Dupin could not understand strong passion and violent impulses. When Sophie burst into one of her rages, her mother-in-law would look on curiously, asking herself, "Why did he fall in love with her?" Sophie, equally amazed at Madame Dupin's calm and self-control, would exclaim contemptuously, "That old countess! What did he find in her to love?"

Madame Dupin was a lady of the old school. To her, leisure was a part of elegance; she spent the morning in bed. She had her personal maid, and she was physically helpless. The hands which she never used were gradually becoming paralyzed.

Sophie arose at dawn and was never idle for a moment. Somewhere in Sophie there was a little volcano, liable to eruption at any time, but suppressed by her innumerable activities. She made the clothes and the hats for the entire household. She tuned the clavichord and mended the ivory keys. She embroidered tapestry and fashioned with her own hands everything that anyone could need or desire. Her energy was terrifying but constructive. She scorned accomplishments, considering them the amusements of the idle rich. Everything that Sophie made or did was useful.

Madame Dupin despised usefulness; she was accomplished. She played the piano and sang. A charming hostess, she often entertained the country aristocracy. Sophie, seeing the high-born ladies come and go, spoke of them with scorn as "those old countesses." Madame Dupin read and studied and talked philosophy, while Sophie laundered, ironed, mended and embroidered. Watching these activities with curiosity and amazement, Madame Dupin sometimes called Sophie a "good fairy," but at other times, seeing her rages, she called her a "madwoman."

In truth Sophie did behave at times like a crazy person, but in other moods she was an adorable mother. She would scold and spank Aurore, then, realizing the wrong she had done, would burst into tears, draw the child to her breast, and overwhelm her with caresses. Aurore did not question her mother's justice. She was so happy to be restored to favor that she went so far as to ask forgiveness for the blows she had received.

Aurore was tender where her mother was passionate, controlled where her mother was violent, forgiving and incapable of rancor where her mother was bitter, critical, full of resentment and hatred. Madame Dupin decided that Aurore was a Dupin and a Saxe, and that she, the last of the Saxes, should be charged with the child's education. She saw that Aurore's life with her mother was an emotional orgy which devastated the child's nervous system. But she failed to realize Aurore's need of demonstrative affection. What if her mother did slap her and scold her for almost nothing! One impulse gave way to another. Aurore waited loyally and lovingly until the scolding was over, and then two soft warm arms would be held out to her. She would climb into her mother's lap and be rocked. At such moments she was satisfied and happy. In Aurore's mind, love meant mother, and slaps as much as kisses came to be identified with love.

7

During the three years that Sophie spent at Nohant, Madame Dupin gently insisted from time to time that she must be allowed to adopt Aurore. But poor distracted Sophie could not be persuaded to surrender her child.

When Aurore was seven years old, Sophie was still undecided. Madame Dupin felt it necessary to bring matters to a head. She announced her definite purpose. If she were allowed to take charge of her granddaughter's education she would make Aurore her heiress. The two women argued and re-argued this important project, while the child listened.

Alone with her mother, Aurore covered Sophie with caresses, and begged her not to give her to her grandmother "for money." Money became associated in her mind with separation from the being she loved best. She began to hate riches and to feel a strong prejudice against the rich. By fears and apprehensions her childish affection was intensified. She developed a morbid sensibility unusual in one of her age.

Though Sophie professed that she wished to do what was best for Aurore, she had also to think of herself. She did not like Nohant, she did not belong to the Dupin family, no one at Nohant admired her really, and she did not feel at ease there. She would rather have two rooms and a little stove of her own than to live in state, waited on by servants. She longed for her friends, her sister Lucy, and the others of her group. She hated the country. Paris was never too noisy and hot, never too rainy and cold, for Sophie Dupin. The noise of the Paris streets was her idea of music, the boulevard her heaven. But how could she support Maurice's child and her other daughter, Caroline?

In this crisis Madame Dupin offered Sophie a pension, limited

Aurore Dupin, seven years old

by a single condition. Sophie must sign an agreement giving
Madame Dupin complete charge of Aurore's education, and Aurore must be left at Nohant. There was nothing drastic about this.
Sophie could visit Nohant, and Aurore would be taken to Paris at
frequent intervals; it was merely a matter of the child's education.

Money and rank gave the older woman the advantage in the
argument. Sophie signed the agreement, and told herself that she
was being sacrificed for the future of her child.

But she was very glad to go back to Paris.

8

After Sophie's departure Aurore moved restlessly about the
house. Vaguely, unreasonably, she was seeking her mother. She
went into Sophie's bedroom, where the maids were stripping the
bed, putting everything to rights, closing the shutters. At sight
of the altered room Aurore was frightened. She went into the
garden, but fear followed her and took possession of her heart.
What was she afraid of? Not of her kind grandmother, not of the
pleasant life of Nohant. No; it was fear of loneliness, fear of life
without love.

Madame Dupin lived in her great bedroom on the ground floor;
she was afraid of a draft or of the sunlight, and could not bear
either extreme of heat or cold. In the morning when she kept
Aurore with her, the room, which had always seemed so beautiful,
became a prison. When grandmother said, "Amuse yourself
quietly," Aurore felt as though she were a butterfly shut up in a
tight box, against which she was beating her frail wings. In the
afternoon Madame Dupin walked around the garden once or
twice, and taught Aurore to walk beside her correctly, holding
herself straight and trying to be graceful. During these walks
Aurore was trained to pick up the handkerchief or the snuff-box
which the old lady continually dropped.

Instead of enjoying the daily tête-à-tête with her grandmother,
Aurore was unresponsive. Whenever Madame Dupin kissed her

formally she wept silently, because she was reminded of the passionate caresses of her mother. She hardly behaved like a child any more. She acted old and cold and sick.

As soon as Madame Dupin took charge of her education, Aurore was not allowed to address the servants with familiarity; she must not say "thee" and "thou" to anyone; she was instructed to write to her mother as "you." She was told to address her grandmother in the third person: "Will grandmother permit me to go outdoors and play?" She was taught to wear gloves, sit straight, curtsey to callers, play quietly, speak softly. She was not scolded, but she heard constantly: "My child, you are sitting like a hunchback." —"My child, you walk like a peasant."—"My child, you have lost your gloves again."—"My child, you are too big to behave like that."

After she had endured this régime for a few days she became subject to convulsive shiverings which even Deschartres could not diagnose. No, she was never scolded, but the sweet severity of her grandmother frightened her more than all Sophie's punishments. She wanted her mother, she wanted mother love, the love that had made her alternately a tyrant and a slave.

Madame Dupin, equally lonely, equally longing for love, would shut herself into her bedroom and weep in secret, saying to herself, "The ungrateful, obstinate child!"

9

It was Madame Dupin's custom to visit Paris every winter. She made the journey in an enormous blue family coach. This berlin, as it was called, was a veritable house on wheels. Inside it was lined with deep pockets containing everything that could possibly be needed by a person of refinement. Travel in the berlin was limited to the daytime. They stopped at hotels over night, and reached Paris on the fourth day. They made from fifty to sixty miles a day. The old lady was always exhausted by so much speed.

Madame Dupin maintained a charming apartment on rue

des Mathurins. It had been furnished in the days of Louis XVI, and everything remained as it had been before the revolution. To Aurore, who had never lived in a beautiful apartment, it seemed luxurious. There were carpets everywhere, and a fire in every room. Especially she admired her grandmother's room of blue damask.

Sophie was invited to dine at rue des Mathurins, and took the child for a walk every day. Aurore was delighted with everything they saw together on these walks. The toy booths, the bird sellers, the stamp collectors, the flower stands, the trained dogs dancing on the boulevard, all excited her enthusiasm; and Sophie, herself a child, shared every thrill.

Aurore was also allowed to visit her mother and see her half-sister, but, to Aurore's surprise, Caroline was forbidden to enter the Dupin home. Caroline's existence was an affront to the Dupin pride. Madame Dupin had some justification for her pride of family, for her connections on the left were distinguished. She was related by blood to the Emperor of Germany, and was also, by blood, first cousin of the former Dauphine of France. Since the Dauphine was the mother of Louis XVI, of Louis XVIII, and of the Duke who was to become Charles X, Madame Dupin was the natural aunt, so to speak, of three kings of France.

This was not explained to the children. All that Aurore knew was that her grandmother hated Caroline. One day Caroline called and was denied admittance. There were whisperings behind the door and a stifled sob. Aurore threw herself on the floor, crying, "I want to go back to my mother! I don't want to stay here!" They put her to bed, but all night in her sleep she cried out for her mother and her sister.

Madame Dupin's injustice to Caroline made Aurore more fiercely loyal. She loved her mother's poor apartment. The barrenness of Sophie's sleeping alcove suited her better than Madame Dupin's blue damask. She found pleasure in the smell of the soup that was always on the open fire in the sitting-room. The hard bread and the cheap red wine tasted better than the dainties of Madame Dupin's table. The free and easy life of Sophie's neighbors, the absence of servants, the ease with which the soup was taken from the fire and poured into earthenware plates, all these advantages of her mother's home seemed to her fascinating.

At rue des Mathurins Aurore was taught to respect the manners and opinions of aristocrats. The next day Sophie would teach her to despise them. Aurore found herself studying the men and women of her grandmother's circle. Already her strong predilections asserted themselves. She liked whatever was simple and natural and felt an instinctive shrinking from affectation and pretentiousness.

In the midst of the comings and goings of "those old countesses" and their friends, a silent, melancholy little girl observed everything. Unconsciously she was collecting impressions which were one day to be used. She perceived that the guests of her grandmother's salon seemed to lack strength to push forward an armchair or put a bit of fuel on the fire. They did not seem able to open or shut a door. Servants took the place of arms, hands and legs.

Aurore felt that she would rather be a dishwasher than an old marquise like those she saw every day in this atmosphere of musk and snuff. She admired her mother's friends because they waited on themselves and worked for a living. Between the aristocracy and the workers she chose the workers. And the choice was made for life.

10

When Aurore was nine years old, Madame Dupin announced that the yearly visits to Paris would be discontinued and that for the present she would spend her winters at Nohant. Sophie, who had just completed her summer visit at Nohant, told her child that she did not know whether she would return. These two statements coming together were overwhelming.

When Sophie brought out her traveling bags and began to fill them, Aurore watched in despair. As she saw the ribbons and laces put into boxes and the dear familiar dresses folded and laid in place, the child was gripped by fear. She began to beg speechlessly, as a dog might, to be taken along. She threw herself at her mother's feet, leaped into her arms and rolled on the ground with inarticulate cries.

Disturbed by her daughter's grief and terror, Sophie took the child in her lap and tried to use reason.

"If I take you with me," she explained, "your grandmother could reduce my income to fifteen hundred francs."

"Fifteen hundred francs!" exclaimed Aurore. "But that's a lot of money, that's enough for the three of us!"

"No, no," Sophie argued, "we would be so poor that you could not endure it."

"We would be poor, but we would be together, so we would be happy! We could live in a garret and eat beans."

"But in time you would reproach me for depriving you of your château and your wealth."

"Never, never! I don't want her château and her money. Let her give them to Hippolyte, or to Ursule, or to her maid Julie. I want to be poor with you."

"But if you do not have a fortune you cannot make a grand marriage."

"I would rather die than make a grand marriage," replied the nine-year-old child. "I would rather work for my living."

"Yes," agreed Sophie, "you would not be happy married to a marquis or a count. They would never forgive you for being my daughter and for having a grandfather who sold birds. Very well, then, I will go back into the millinery business. I will save a little money and I can borrow more. You can learn to trim hats much more easily than you learn that silly Latin and Greek. Caroline will help us, we shall economize, and in a few years I shall manage to save a dot for your marriage with a workingman. Now that's settled and you must keep our secret. When all is ready I will come and get you. Your grandmother will take away my pension, but I will snap my fingers in her face. We shall settle down in our little shop, and when she passes by in her fine carriage she will see in letters as long as your arm a sign that reads:

THE WIDOW DUPIN, MILLINER

Sophie was to leave at dawn, but at nine in the evening Aurore was ordered to go to bed and stay there until after her mother's departure.

Obediently she went to her room, but only to write a farewell letter to her mother. She added a postscript: "Put your answer behind the portrait of old Dupin. I will find it to-morrow after you have gone."

There was a crayon sketch of grandfather Dupin near the door of her mother's room. She hid the letter behind the portrait, and to let her mother know it was there, pinned to Sophie's night-cap a penciled note which read: "Wiggle the portrait." Then to bed again, but far too excited to sleep.

At dawn she heard them carry down the bags. Disobeying orders, she ran in bare feet after her mother, crying wildly, "Take me with you! Take me with you!"

Rose came and held her while Sophie rushed downstairs. At the last sound of the carriage wheels, the child gave way to cries of despair; she felt herself forsaken by the being she had believed in as she believed in God. She ran to her mother's room, threw herself upon the bed and kissed the pillows. One small consolation remained—the answer to her letter. As soon as she was alone she went to the portrait, her heart quick with hope. She felt against the wall. She turned the picture around.

Nothing was there.

The beating of her heart grew slower, it seemed almost to cease. She began to suffer from a grief that was worse than separation. She said to herself, "My mother does not love me as I love her."

From this day on there were very few letters from Sophie. Aurore would write three times before she received an answer. And in all Sophie's letters there was never a reference to their secret. Sophie had forgotten her promise about the shop.

"Your mother," said grandma Dupin, "loves her children as a bird loves its young; once out of the nest they are forgotten."

II

One, two, three years were passed at Nohant. Nothing more was said about the yearly visit to Paris. Hippolyte was away in training for his regiment. Ursule had been taken back into her own family. As grandmother grew older and more helpless, Aurore was left to the care of the maids, Rose and Julie. No one suspected her consuming loneliness. She fell back upon herself, and found a deep reservoir to draw upon. That limitless resource was her own capacity to create dreams. This capacity never failed her. It was not capricious like her mother, it was always there.

From the time of the story told between four chairs, Aurore had never ceased to live in a world of fantasy. She had, indeed, never finished or discontinued the endless story she was composing. In her walks, in her silences, in bed before going to sleep and again upon awakening, she carried in her brain a romance in the making, and added a chapter or two whenever she was alone. Among the people in her limited environment no one suggested poetry or idealism, but her temperament demanded both.

One night as she lay awake longing for an object of worship, a face appeared before her mental vision and a name came to her mind. The name was Corambé, the face was godlike, and the god talked to her, telling a marvelous tale. The communion was so perfect that Aurore was not sure whether she was telling the story to Corambé or whether he was telling it to her. It unfolded before her, transformed her playfellows, took possession of her play and touched it with magic. Corambé, as a figure in a dream, changed his own character and appearance. He had the attributes of

ancient kings and pagan gods, together with the virtues of the
Christian religion. On days when Aurore was heartsick for
mother-love, Corambé answered her need and became a goddess,
a glorified Sophie, with the tenderness of a mother.

In the thick woods she found a circular spot, surrounded by
shrubs and carpeted by moss. It looked like a chapel. Here she
decided to build an altar to Corambé. She searched the woods for
colored stones and flowers, and on the banks of the river Indre
found delicate shells. After a month of collecting and building
and weaving, she succeeded in achieving a thing of beauty. The
loveliness of it went to her head like wine.

It now seemed appropriate to offer some kind of sacrifice, but
Corambé would not allow her to kill even the smallest insect in his
honor; he was a god of liberation. If, therefore, Aurore could find
a butterfly caught in Hippolyte's net, or a bird that had fallen,
or an animal that had strayed, she would carry the little living
thing in a box, place the box on her altar, lift the lid and set the
creature free. Sometimes a liberated bird rested for a moment in
the branches of the maple and sang his gratitude. Then the heart
of Aurore filled to bursting, life was beautiful, the god was well
pleased. But it was difficult to find a lost or strayed animal to free
every day. Sometimes she picked up a frog or a lizard who might
not really have strayed, but whom she hoped had strayed, that
she might feel the joy of giving life and liberty. After a time,
lizards, frogs, beetles and butterflies did not seem important offer-
ings; birds were the loveliest things to free, because they were so
grateful.

In her passion to free them, she was obliged to set traps to catch
them. Each morning she examined her traps, tenderly handled the
little victim, placed him on the altar and felt her heart expand
as she cut the thongs.

For a month this delicious experience continued. Then one of
the peasant children interrupted her at her devotions. She pulled
down her altar, feeling that it had been desecrated. Part of Co-

rambé's charm had been that he belonged to her alone. An illusion cannot be shared by those who do not understand.

12

Madame Dupin, beautiful in brown silk and white lace, sat in her high-backed chair reading her favorite author, Voltaire. As she read she paused from time to time and jotted down her reflections in a notebook. Often the crippled hands fumbled helplessly and the gold pencil fell to the floor. Aurore, who was sitting in a low chair, would jump to pick up the pencil.

"Are you writing a book, grandmother dear?" asked Aurore, as she watched the keen old lady record her impressions.

"A book! No, indeed. I would not be so conceited. But all those notebooks on the library shelf are filled with my writings. I have always analyzed and classified my thoughts. That is a mental habit I inherit from my father."

Madame Dupin lifted her eyes to the proud compelling gaze of Maurice de Saxe, whose portrait faced his daughter and his great-granddaughter.

"But my history says," interrupted Aurore, "that Maurice de Saxe was a military hero, and that means a fighter."

"He was also a thinker and a writer," said Madame Dupin. "His capacities were tremendous. When he was in action he lived in a fever of fighting and dissipation. When he was resting in his tent his thoughts and dreams were exalted. He composed those *Reveries* which you will read some day, my child. They are the expression of a remarkable mind. It was he who first conceived the idea of compulsory military training. It was he who suggested trial marriage. According to his idea, marriage should last five years. The man and woman who had lived together for five years without children should then be forbidden by law to re-marry. All other couples should choose whether to separate or to marry again at the end of the five-year period. He loved to plan utopias for the welfare of mankind. He also wrote many valuable treatises on war.

"My father," Madame Dupin continued, "was a mysterious, magnificent figure. I will tell you his history. You are old enough now to understand."

Aurore listened. She did not notice the words, and afterwards she could not remember them. But as Madame Dupin talked, Aurore's imagination caught a series of pictures that revealed the life story of her illustrious ancestor.

The first picture was that of a boy so strikingly handsome that he was noticed and admired by everyone. His name was Maurice de Saxe. His father was the King of Poland: his mother was that great lady, Aurore Koenigsmark. Maurice was educated with his half-brother, the young prince of Poland. This brother was some day to be seated on a throne, while Maurice would remain a nameless nobody. The boy revolted against his position of semi-royalty. The bitterness of a bastard entered his heart.

As Madame Dupin continued, Aurore seemed to see the boy Maurice and his mother, Aurore Koenigsmark. She was dressed in nun's uniform; her hair cut, her head covered, her glorious beauty hidden from the world. Maurice well knew why the Countess Aurore had become an abbess; she was expiating the sin of being his mother.

From this mother and this father the boy of twelve ran away to war. There was a sort of fever in him which nothing but fighting could assuage. Sustained by an ambition to make a name for himself, he crossed Germany on foot and enlisted in the allied army that was fighting against France. At the age of twelve the plucky youngster took part in active battle. He fought with so much daring that he was reprimanded for recklessness. What wonder that he risked his life!—he was known as the bastard of Saxe.

As Madame Dupin went on with her story, scene after scene from the life of Maurice de Saxe passed before Aurore's eyes.

She saw him at sixteen, in command of his own regiment of cavalry. His horse was killed under him. His cap was shot with bullets. He exposed himself to danger as though he longed for death. At seventeen he married, ran through his wife's fortune and then divorced her. Thenceforth the battlefield was the only home he knew.

Still a young man, Maurice, soldier of fortune, hired himself to France as field-marshal. For many years he was flattered, adored, feared and envied as the chief military genius of France. In appearance he was godlike; half the women of France were said to be in love with him. He was called the Homeric Ajax of his age. But all this did not satisfy his ambition. He felt that fate owed him the royalty he deserved, nothing less than a throne would satisfy his sense of his own destiny.

Now, as Aurore listened, a new picture grew before her eyes. The scene was a certain duchy called Courland, bordering on Russia. The people were about to choose a duke. Maurice de Saxe rode into Courland on a magnificent charger and showed himself to the people. His power, his beauty, and his arrogance made their appeal, not only to the people but also to the Duchess of Courland, the Russian Anna Iwanowna. Anna straightway fell in love with him and encouraged him to aspire to her hand. He was elected Duke of Courland. A throne seemed within his reach. But hearing that the Grand Duchess Elizabeth of Russia was also in love with him, he began an intrigue with her. At the same time he carried on love affairs with various ladies-in-waiting, until the infatuated Anna discovered his infidelities and refused to marry him. Four years later she became Czarina of Russia. But for his inconstancy Maurice de Saxe might have been Emperor of Russia.

The great warrior, the unfaithful lover, had fallen. Without money or soldiers he could not defend his principality. Two months after his election the new Duke was banished and left the country with a price on his head.

But it was not in his nature to feel humility or remorse.

Instead of hiding from sight he went back to Paris carrying himself like a king. His picturesque adventures had made him conspicuous. Wherever he went he was pointed out and admired, and his prestige was greater than ever. His callous indifference to the women who loved him increased his fascination. He was faithless, remorseless, and adored.

The next picture was the battle of Fontenoy. By this time Maurice de Saxe was commander-in-chief of France's army. The great man lay ill, unable to move, but he had himself carried to the battlefield on a litter. From this rough bed he led the fighting, and wrested from the English a hard-fought victory for France. It was thus he succeeded in his ambition to make his own fame in an unjust world. Not as Count de Saxe nor as bastard of Saxe has his name gone down in history; it is as the hero of Fontenoy that every school-child in France knows him to-day.

Aurore, brought back from the battlefield, heard her grandmother say: "If he had been born after the monarchy and after the Revolution his personal ambition might have found means of fulfillment. Maurice de Saxe was the precursor of Napoleon, a man of destiny, born out of his time."

As though she could not leave this fascinating subject, Madame Dupin added, "After all, how did he differ from Napoleon, except in being born fifty years too soon!" Then she concluded, "My father carried with him to the grave all that France possessed of the science of war. In dying he said: 'Life is a dream. Mine has been short but it has been good.'"

And now Madame Dupin passed from her father's history to her own.

"It was late in life," she continued, "that Maurice de Saxe fell in love with my mother, an actress of the royal theatre, Marie de Verrières. Of this union I was born. I was known as Marie-Aurore de Saxe. It has often been said of me that I inherited the virtues of both my parents, without their faults. Like you, I was not brought up by my own mother. I was separated from her completely and was not allowed to see her. It was my cousin by blood, the Dauphine of France, who took charge of my education and my marriage. She was Princess of Poland and niece of Maurice de Saxe. He was said to have arranged her marriage with the son of Louis XV."

Madame Dupin next spoke of Madame de Maintenon's fashionable school, Saint-Cyr, where she had been educated. She told of her marriage at fifteen to the Count de Horn, the illegitimate son of Louis XV. The little Countess, so appropriately married, was introduced at court and enjoyed a taste of the gay life surrounding royalty. Her future as a member of the nobility was promising, but three weeks after her marriage the Count de Horn was killed in a duel, and the Dauphine placed her young charge in a convent.

In the course of time the Dauphine died, and her protégée, forgotten and ignored by the royal family, was obliged to return to her mother. For several years mother and daughter devoted their time to what was then called the cultivation of the Muses. They studied music, attended the theatre, read poetry and philosophy, discussed Voltaire and Rousseau. At the age of thirty Marie-Aurore of Saxe, Countess of Horn, married a man thirty-two years her senior, and became plain Marie Dupin. The sixty-two-year-old husband gave his bride a palatial château and a train of servants, and for ten years she lived in the greatest luxury. At the death of her too generous husband, part of his fortune went to pay his debts. The remainder disappeared in the Revolution. All that was left of Monsieur Dupin's wealth was a moderate income and a sum sufficient to buy the domain at Nohant.

"So now you understand," Madame Dupin concluded, "why I who was once a Countess, received at court, am now comparatively poor and obscure. Nevertheless I am an aristocrat by birth, and you also, if you remain under my protection, may marry an aristocrat."

Aurore was silent. She stared hard at the portraits that lined the walls of the salon. Then suddenly, noticing that her grandmother was waiting, she made an effort to speak politely.

"Thank you, grandmother," she began. "What you have told me is very, very interesting. But I've been wondering—where are the portraits of my mother's ancestors?"

Madame Dupin regarded her grandchild in shocked amazement.

"Your mother had no ancestors," she answered coldly.

"Oh, yes, she had," Aurore said eagerly. "She has often told me about her father. He taught my mother how to talk to the birds, and my mother taught me. That's why the birds are such friends of mine. That's why they come at my call and hop into my bedroom. I love my grandfather Delaborde. Where is his portrait?"

"Bird-peddlers do not have their portraits painted." Madame Dupin, trembling with anger, rose to her feet and asked fiercely: "And who was his father and his father and his father? Can you tell me that?"

"No, grandmother. I've never heard about them. But we could have a picture made of grandfather Delaborde with his birds around him—you know, like Saint Francis—and we could hang it alongside of grandfather Dupin."

"Either you are stupid or you are wilfully obstinate!" There was a long pause, in which Madame Dupin struggled for self-control. Then, taking her cane in her wavering hands, she refused Aurore's assistance and moved in stately fashion from the room.

Aurore gazed after her sadly. As the door closed she spoke more boldly than she dared speak in the great lady's presence.

"I shall never be an aristocrat!" she cried defiantly to the empty room. "I shall never marry an aristocrat! I'd rather be a milliner, like my mother! I'd rather sell birds!"

13

Ever since Sophie had explained that education belonged to aristocrats, Aurore had disdained education. Now that Madame Dupin had declared her own plan for her grandchild's future,

Aurore's aversion for books was more pronounced. She neglected her lessons and Deschartres scolded in vain.

It seemed strange to Aurore that no one understood her point of view. Couldn't they see that she had chosen to live with her mother and earn her own living? She was thirteen years old now. She intended to run away to Paris very soon.

One morning when she was feeling audacious she threw her books on the floor, exclaiming, "I will not study. I have my own reasons—you will know why some day."

Julie, passing through the room, heard this explosion and remarked tactlessly, "You deserve to be sent back to your mother."

"Back to my mother! But that is what I want most—to go to her, to live with her, and to obey no one else!"

Julie carried these words of ingratitude to Madame Dupin, and came back with the message that Aurore was to keep to her room and to eat her meals alone.

The whole household withdrew from her as though she were a criminal. She had no one to talk to but Corambé. She told him all her troubles and he upheld her and consoled her. She was doing exactly right, he said, in refusing the education that would separate her from her mother. But in spite of Corambé's sympathy, she grew tired of ostracism and decided to talk frankly with her grandmother. She rehearsed her speech: "I love you, dear grandmother, but I love mother best. I am grateful to you for wishing to make me rich, but I prefer poverty with my mother. The truth is, I cannot get along without my mother." Surely after such an explanation grandmother would let her go back to Paris and mother and Caroline.

She gained admission to the formidable room where Madame Dupin, bolstered by pillows, reclined on her luxurious bed. There was the usual silk, lace and perfume. The atmosphere was oppressive. Madame was dressed, as always, with utmost care, as though she had made ready for a reception.

Aurore, standing awkwardly in the doorway, forgot her speech.

She fell on her knees beside the bed, touched the bejeweled hands and was about to kiss them, when a voice hardly to be recognized as her grandmother's interrupted.

"Stay where you are, on your knees, and give me your attention. I have things to say that you have never heard, and that you never again will hear from my lips. I wish you to know the history of your father and your mother." Her voice vibrated with the strain she was feeling.

"My Maurice was twenty when he entered the army. He fought against the Germans, was wounded, was taken prisoner by the Austrians, held in captivity for several months, and then exchanged. At the age of twenty-two he followed the fortunes of Napoleon in Italy; he was known everywhere as the grandson of Maurice de Saxe; great things were expected of him. He was hardening under the soldier's life and was hoping for promotion. But he was ill from his wound, heart-hungry and homesick in a strange land. Poor boy, he needed his mother! It was inevitable that he should fall in love with the first attractive woman who could speak his language. This woman happened to be Sophie Victoire Delaborde. She had been a milliner. You admire her for that? Very well. But she did not long remain a workingwoman." Aurore tried to interrupt but she could not produce a sound, and the terrible voice went on.

"At the time I speak of she had already had a child, Caroline, by an unknown lover, and when my son met her she was the mistress of one of Napoleon's generals."

These bare statements, given without extenuating circumstances, without sympathy, without any consideration for the sensitive nature of the listener, affected Aurore as though she were in a nightmare. Her throat closed, her frozen hands pushed away her grandmother's warm fingers. The voice swept on like a wind in a storm.

"The general was old. He doted on his mistress, surrounded her with luxury, even let her pass as his wife. But Sophie was indifferent to everything but her new lover. The two young people were not content with furtive interviews. They eloped from the general, and when Maurice returned to France, Sophie followed him.

"My son Maurice was a romantic dreamer. In allowing his life to be ruined by a woman, he precipitated an army scandal. The aged general was loud in his complaints. He even sent word to me that my son's conduct was lacking in delicacy. I summoned the aid of my half-brother, Abbé Beaumont. The reverend abbé used all the persuasions of religion to save the name of the family. But Sophie, ignorant of social ethics and army etiquette, refused to go back to the general; she preferred poverty with her lover.

"The liaison was regarded as open disrespect to a superior officer. Maurice saw his cousins and his friends receiving rank and honor while he remained lieutenant in a country garrison.

"I did not imagine, no one imagined for a moment, that he would marry such a woman. Sophie had already given birth to a child by Maurice, a son who died. She was expecting another baby.

"About a month before the baby was born, Maurice Dupin married Sophie Victoire Delaborde. To his certain knowledge, she had already had two lovers. The wedding was secret. He did not dare to confess to his mother that he had committed social suicide.

"The child, their second child, was named Aurore."

As her own name fell upon Aurore's ears, she felt the sweat gather on her forehead. She wanted to get up and go away. She could not rise. Her knees seemed nailed to the floor.

"I tried to annul the marriage, but I could not free him from the woman who caused his misfortunes. Then I tried to free you. How I have waited for you to be old enough to understand.

"I have saved you, but you are ungrateful. You want to go to her. You want her to ruin you as she ruined my son.

"Your mother does not love you as you fondly believe. Now that you are almost a young lady you have outgrown her. Her hatred for me has turned her against you. She resents your superior education, your manners, your tastes.

"If you lived with her you would be unhappy. Her common friends, her cheap pleasures, her whole way of life would make you miserable. Besides, there is another influence in her life to which you would be sacrificed. I am not speaking of Caroline, but of a more dominating influence, one which would cause you to feel shame."

"Shame!" The word was like a sentence of death. Aurore pulled herself to her feet. Without a word or a caress, without any interest in being forgiven, she ran to hide herself in her room, where she rolled on the floor, given over to convulsions of grief.

For some time past she had been hiding her illusions about her mother, hugging them to herself for fear that someone would destroy them. Now they were dead.

She told herself that if her mother were despicable and hateful, she, Aurore, was equally to be hated and despised. But that did not remain in her thoughts as the thing of supreme importance. What stayed with her was the belief that her mother had ceased to love her. If that were true she no longer cared about herself.

As time went on she fell into a state of benumbed indifference, incapable of enthusiasm or resentment. It seemed as though she had ceased to think or to live. She told herself over and over that she loved her mother more than ever. But she had lost all capacity for day dreams; there were no more reveries, there was no more romance in her life. She turned to Corambé for comfort. Corambé was dumb.

14

The effect of shock upon Aurore's nervous organization resulted in conduct which her grandmother could not understand. Day after day Madame Dupin, watching from her window, saw the elusive form of her grandchild escape from the house, chase through the garden, and disappear among the trees.

The heiress of Nohant was running wild in the woods and fields. She was playing rough games with peasant gamins, wearing sabots, tearing her clothes, cooking her food over bonfires. Had she reverted to barbarism? Madame Dupin asked in dismay—My son Maurice was never like this, and certainly I was never like this. Where did she get this recklessness, this boisterous mirth, this frenzy to live outdoors? Is it possible for characteristics to skip two generations and crop out again? For this child is as like Maurice de Saxe as a carefully brought up little girl can be. She needs a threat of punishment.

After a fortnight of patient waiting, Madame Dupin pronounced her threat.

"My child, if you can't stop being such a tomboy, I shall take you to Paris and put you in a convent. You will be allowed to see your mother, then you will be shut away from her, and from me, until your education has been accomplished."

"I don't mind being shut away," was the unexpected reply. And all the while Aurore was thinking, "Anything to forget, anything to escape, anything to run away from myself! I shall be free some day. I shall choose my own life; not as grandmother has it all mapped out for me; not marriage; I shall never get married. I shall travel around the world, and see Mount Etna and India. I shall go to America. They say it is far away and difficult to reach. So much the better. They say one might die there. No matter, I am dying here."

At the English convent in Paris, among the eighty scholars there was no one who was not longing to go home; no one, that is, except the new pupil, Aurore Dupin. She never complained of imprisonment as did the other girls. The convent was cold and gloomy; the windows were barred; she was not to put her head outside of the door for a year. But she was at rest, in retreat, almost in hiding. The convent protected her from the torment of belonging to two jealous mothers.

The Convent of St. Augustine was, in 1817, the fashionable

Paris boarding-school for young French aristocrats. The curriculum included all the feminine accomplishments. Aurore acquired a smattering of Italian, music and drawing, but the study that awakened her keenest interest was English. She wanted to talk to the nuns in their own language; it was painful to hear them speak French. Then, too, if one could speak English one was invited to share their queer custom of afternoon tea. Aurore applied herself so well to the study of English that she learned to speak it fluently and read it easily; and before she left the convent she had formed the foreign-tea-drinking habit for life.

She saw very little of her mother. Sophie called sometimes, but mother and daughter found they had little to talk about. It seemed to Aurore that her mother had changed completely. Ignoring the fact that she had taught Aurore to despise riches and education, Sophie now stressed these advantages. After a bit of motherly advice, her conversation would lapse into reproaches. The unhappy woman knew that she was better fitted to be a child's nurse than a young lady's companion. It was this secret self-knowledge that had turned her against Madame Dupin, against Aurore, and against herself. Listening to Sophie's recriminations, Aurore began to fear the hatred that blazed in the fierce black eyes.

15

The love of her childhood being lost, Aurore's heart was aching with loneliness. She needed an object of worship that would call upon all her powers of loving. She withdrew into herself as though to find some deeper source of happiness. She shrank from gayety and play and human friendship. Her hours of recreation were spent in the empty chapel, where the altar, the stained glass and the painting of Christ crucified inspired the ardor of devotion. One day, long after the others had left the chapel, she remained on her knees until, in exhaustion, she sank on the hard tiled floor, where she moaned and wept in an agony of rapture. She had found a new love. She had found God.

Once converted, the intensity and idealism of her nature sought satisfying expression in religion. She was more religious than the novices, the nuns or the mother superior. She watched the nuns padding their slow way along the corridors. How could they be so heavy-footed, those nuns who walked with God! Aurore also walked with God. She did not seem to touch her feet to the floor. She had wings, she soared, she was no longer a body. She was not aware whether she ate or slept or breathed.

At chapel services the nuns recited paternosters. They said words, the same words over and over. Aurore made her own prayers, without words, without thoughts. The prayer of her soul was a dreaminess, a feeling, a yielding of will that became exaltation, a merging of self with the infinite soul. Her life with God was a torturing ecstasy. She spent all her energy in capturing and holding the mystic communion, which satisfied her need to give and receive love.

She would become a nun. She would sign away her life with a sacred promise to love no one but God. She would take a religious name, perhaps that of Marie-Augustine, and shut herself away in the cold damp convent with the stolid British sisters who drank tea.

She went to her favorite nun and declared her intention. But Sister Alicia discouraged her. "How can you know that you have the true vocation? You must be tested. So much intensity exhausts itself. Permanent religious experience is more tranquil."

Tranquil! How is it possible to be tranquil when one has found God?

She was willing to be tested. For several months the trance-like existence continued, and Aurore felt a triumphant conviction that she was proving a true vocation.

Then, alas, the fifteen-year-old nervous system could no longer sustain the unnatural strain. Instead of ecstasy in her soul she had cramps in her stomach. Her throat closed when she tried to eat. Her feet dragged when she tried to soar.

She stayed on her knees for hours, but no prayers came. Had God ceased to love her? What fault had she committed?

She took her tragedy to her father confessor. Abbé Prémord was a Jesuit, wise, kind, subtle, understanding all hearts, even the heart of a child. He told her that her sin was spiritual pride, and that her punishment must be the return to a normal human life.

She had, said the abbé, set a bad example to her schoolmates. She was a convert, but what a convert! Her friends had been turned away from religion by the sight of her pale sick face. She must win them to God by giving an example of happiness. She must play and be gay.

Aurore was horrified. Be gay? Play? She had lost all taste for such things. The punishment was severe, but obedience is the first duty of a Christian. She went into the sunshine of the garden, and, since it was a necessity of religion, she skipped rope, tossed balls, and played prisoner's base.

In a week Saint Aurore, as they now called her, was well again. Her prayers, morning and night, no longer left her exhausted. Still the abbé would not allow her to spend her hours of recreation in the chapel.

"Make them love you, make everyone love you," he commanded, "so that through you they will love the religion you profess."

As a duty to God she thought of games to entertain the children. She organized charades and little plays which relieved the monotony of convent life. Whoever offered was allowed to act. The group of actors grew larger, the plays more popular. The homesick little girls were amused and happy, the nuns were pleased, the mother superior approved.

Sunday was considered the most appropriate day for play-acting, so every Sunday evening was set aside for theatricals. The convent was never so harmonious; petty jealousies and personal grievances were forgotten; everyone was occupied. Those who could not act made paper feathers and gold crowns.

The mother superior, enthusiastic, ordered a special performance to which all the inmates were invited. Aurore was given the task of preparing and directing the play. Certain rules were laid down: there must be no love interest, and no one was allowed to wear trousers; girls who took the parts of men were obliged to tuck their skirts into their stockings below the knee. Fortunately for the playwright, swords and fighting were permitted and buffoonery was approved.

For the little missionary of religion this public play was a serious undertaking. She must hold the interest of nuns and pupils and make them laugh, but all this was to be accomplished without love interest. Aurore racked her brain for a suitable subject. She decided to borrow the theme of Molière's *Le Malade Imaginaire,* and make fun of stupid doctors; no religious person would object to that. Because Molière's works were prohibited in the convent, she was forced to rely upon memory. She composed the dialogue, rehearsed the actors, and had a huge success.

The nuns laughed and so did the mother superior. The fat nuns rocked in their chairs, the thin ones shrieked. Once started, they could not stop. The mere appearance of an actor was greeted with boisterous mirth. The comedy ended in noisy applause.

Aurore had been given an outlet for intensity. She had been told to win all hearts. And now no one in the convent was so popular as the stage director and leading actress of the sacred theatrical group.

To be loved, petted, praised and trusted was to feel that the English convent was a paradise on earth. She had found a new love, a group love, diffused, fraternal, human and deeply satisfying. Aurore was happy, thoroughly, completely happy for the first time in her life.

Then suddenly came the word that banished her from paradise. Madame Dupin, who was in Paris, had decided to remove her from the convent. Having heard of Aurore's piety, she was displeased. She had no intention of allowing her granddaughter to become a nun. Her plan and purpose for Aurore was marriage.

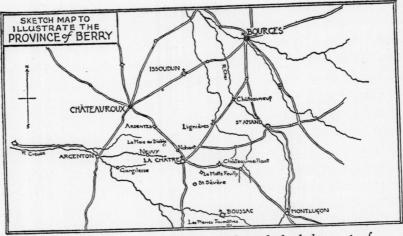

Paris is about 165 miles north and slightly east of Châteauroux

II

MADEMOISELLE DUPIN

MARRIAGE! The menace! It threatened her in her grandmother's gaze as that great lady complacently regarded
her. It frightened her in the smiles of grandmother's friends as
they cast appraising glances at her fresh young face and delicately
slender figure. It showed through the solicitude of cousin Villeneuve and uncle Beaumont. Their eyes held portentous interest,
as though they were saying, "Childhood is over, the time for
marriage draws near."

Aurore had always known that this dreadful fate lay somewhere ahead of her. From the time she was seven years old she
had heard conjectures, hints, suggestions, but never before had
the menace seemed imminent. Now it loomed large and sinister,
like the exaggerated shadow of a man in hiding.

Who was this man, this master, this enemy of her future and
her freedom? Had the family decided? Had they chosen him?
Was he waiting, ready to take her?

Mademoiselle Dupin was introduced into the coterie of Madame
Dupin's distinguished Paris friends. Calls were made and received,
young men were brought forward and introduced. But the brilliant actress who had held an audience of schoolmates and nuns
enthralled by her wit and cleverness had little to say to young
men. She was a poet in a dream. She was a child half asleep. She
was a nun saying her prayers.

Grandmother felt that a convent graduate should be modest
and yet coquettish. No one had such beautiful eyes as her grandchild, if only she could be taught to use them. But Aurore was
maddening in her lack of coquetry; she did not know enough to
drop her eyelashes or glance sidewise. She looked out of her eyes

frankly, or, worse still, in the presence of men, even of attractive young men, her gaze would seem fixed on some object far away in space.

There were family conclaves. It was evident to all that in spite of Aurore's attitude, nothing was easier than arranging a marriage for a girl with a dot. Sophie created the only difficulty. Obviously it was impossible to approach any eligible man with such a mother-in-law. If Aurore could be persuaded to sever all connection with her mother, a brilliant match could be arranged.

But the child seemed blind to her own best interests. She had told her grandmother and had promised Sophie that she would never marry a man who was ashamed of her mother.

"There is no use trying to force her," admitted Madame Dupin, who knew her best. "Her childish passion for her mother has given place to a sense of duty. Nevertheless she will always be loyal, as was her father before her. She will follow his example. She will let that woman ruin her life. What will become of her after my death?"

Cousin Villeneuve, who had important family connections, made a solemn promise to save Aurore from Sophie. In case of Madame Dupin's death he would take Aurore into his family and insure her future. Sophie could not be received in his home. He had no prejudices, but of course his wife must be considered.

It was left to Madame Dupin to win Aurore's consent to the arrangement. For this a few months' time would be required. After all, she decided, though Aurore looks like a young lady she is nothing but a child. It would be better to return to No-hant and postpone all thought of marriage for six months or even for a year.

As soon as she saw the trunks being packed for the journey home, Aurore emerged from her state of panic and ran to bid her mother good-by. Would Sophie go with her to Nohant?

"No," said Sophie, bitterly, "I'll never go back to Nohant until my mother-in-law is dead." And she added accusingly, "You belong to her now, body and soul."

Sophie's jealousy was for the first time not without foundation. Aurore did in fact at last love her grandmother. Her mind had awakened and found her grandmother more congenial and more understanding than her mother.

2

Her welcome home after three years' absence from the village was strangely disappointing to Aurore. She tried to renew old contacts with the playmates of her childhood, but their conversation was limited to "Yes, mademoiselle.—No, mademoiselle." Already they saw in her the future châtelaine of Nohant. She had become Mademoiselle Dupin.

At this discovery she burst into tears. She had acquired the habit of loving many people and being loved by them. Lonely fear closed about her heart.

But surely among the people of La Châtre she could find friends who would take the place of those she had lost? In the town of La Châtre, four miles from the hamlet of Nohant, were several families that had always been closely associated with the Dupins. As Aurore met the young people she greeted them as seemed to her natural, by shaking hands. Directly afterwards she heard that her behavior was considered eccentric. Hand-shaking was unladylike and unfeminine, a form of greeting intended for men. She ought to have kissed the young women, she ought to have presented the back of her hand for the young men to kiss.

Eccentric!

It was the first time she had ever heard the word applied to herself. But as the summer passed the word came back to her again and again.

She did not, she could not, behave like other girls. She did not betray a proper consciousness of the other sex. She did not blush and hang her head and act confused, as a young girl should in the presence of men. In vain did grandmother caution her against sunburn and against spreading her feet by wearing heavy shoes. In vain did they try to make her wear a corset and cultivate a small waist. She was as indifferent to her appearance as though she had been a boy.

Hippolyte, now an officer, came home for a brief vacation and taught her to ride. The young mare Colette was given to her for her very own. Grandmother made no objection to these lessons, but there were others who looked askance at this new feminine accomplishment. Ladies of the provinces did not ride horseback. If they had to travel without a carriage they mounted on postilion behind a groom. Aurore Dupin, riding side-saddle in a long skirt, was therefore eccentric.

Worse was yet to come. One day in the town of La Châtre the good people on the street saw coming toward them a girl on horseback, riding astride and *dressed like a man!* They gathered on the street corners to talk it over. They carried the news from house to house: "Aurore Dupin is wild, a wild woman!" From that day forth she was the "Wild Woman of Nohant."

The more ignorant villagers were the ones who felt most strongly about her conduct. "What if all our girls should take to riding horseback and wearing trousers! There would be no more marriages and no more babies. What then?"

And yet the dreadful costume was no more extreme than a long, loose blouse, with trousers tucked into leggings at the knee, and a boy's cap.

3

After Hippolyte's departure Aurore was alone with the two old people, Deschartres and Madame Dupin. She devoted herself to them both. She spent her afternoons with Madame Dupin, playing the harp or piano and reading aloud. Each day when Madame asked her to read the newspapers, Aurore consented, although it was with difficulty that she concealed from her grandmother the painfulness of the task. Nothing was so repugnant to Aurore as reading newspapers. After she had finished she was plunged into profound depression. This daily chronicle of the real world did violence to her inner life of dreams and idealism. Instinctively she wanted to protect herself against the outside world, in which she could not live and be herself.

The evenings were always enjoyable, because after dinner Madame Dupin and her granddaughter read Chateaubriand. Aurore found her grandmother delightful in discussion. She enjoyed the old lady's comments and responded to the keenness of her mind. Impressed by Madame Dupin's knowledge, Aurore was secretly ashamed of her own ignorance. Why had she wasted her opportunities? During her childhood she had despised education because it was aristocratic, and at the convent she had disdained it because it was worldly. As a result of this long indifference, Aurore told herself, her ignorance was abysmal. She could not remember history and she was not widely read in literature. Her knowledge was full of gaps.

Her education at the hands of others being finished, she now undertook to educate herself. But since she intended to be a nun, ought she to read profane literature? She wrote to Abbé Prémord to ask his permission. He gave it willingly.

"Do not fear the philosophers," he answered; "they are powerless against faith. Read the poets, all poets are religious."

She began with the philosophers: Locke, Mably, Montesquieu, Bacon, Bossuet, Aristotle, Liebnitz, Pascal, Montaigne—she read them all.

Chateaubriand's *Genius of Christianity* destroyed her former belief in the self-effacing religion of *The Imitation of Christ*. No longer did she believe it was religious to annihilate the mind, no longer did she desire to make of herself a nothingness, a grain of dust. She agreed with Chateaubriand: "Cultivate the mind, develop all your powers, for science, art and beauty are manifestations of God."

Her knowledge of English opened a new world. She read Shakespeare, Pope and Milton. She discovered Benjamin Franklin, committed to memory whole pages of his wisdom, and said his thoughts over to herself along with her prayers before she fell asleep.

But in all her reading the mind that had the strongest affinity for her own was that of Jean Jacques Rousseau. His principles matched her own instinctive opinions; his belief in simplicity and naturalness as opposed to the artificialities of society was in accord with her own. His faith in the inherent goodness of human nature was her faith. His emphasis on personal liberty and spiritual independence expressed her own sense of values. She became and always remained a disciple of Rousseau.

Abbé Prémord was right; the philosophers had not destroyed her faith, but they had changed its form of expression. She believed in God and continued to be deeply religious, but at the end of a year and a half of study, philosophy had crowded out orthodoxy, and the poets had replaced the church fathers and the saints.

Gradually she relinquished her desire to be a nun.

Cousin Villeneuve was invited to visit Nohant. Since he was to be Aurore's guardian, Madame Dupin wanted him to know and understand the strange, obstinate, adorable child.

René Villeneuve, Aurore's nearest relative on her father's side, was connected with several of the great families of France. His wife was a Segur and his daughter was to marry a Roche-Aymon. Count Villeneuve was distinguished by unusual culture and was so exceedingly well-read that nothing surprised him. Having no prejudices, he was tolerant of the most extreme convictions. He found Aurore delightful. Her conversation revealed to him an original and gifted mind. Her simplicity and independence seemed to him proof of a great personality. He read her poems and essays, was impressed by them and advised her to write.

Thus inspired, she began a novel, her second attempt to create romance. At the convent she had composed a brief novel to please her friends. In that earlier effort she had sketched a wonderful background for a love scene, but when the time came for the hero to talk of love he had turned coward and run away. Rather than return and kiss the heroine he had become a priest, and the heroine, breathing a sigh of relief, had become a nun. Aurore, older now, had thought more and read more and could write better. Still she found her characters awkward and tonguetied when they approached the subject of love.

She gave it up as hopeless. Dreams are best, she assured herself. Anything put into words is sterile and frozen.

4

In the January following Aurore's return from the convent Madame Dupin was stricken with paralysis. She fell into a childish state that left Aurore without guidance or authority. No French girl of good family had ever been given so much independence. Sophie was sent for but she refused to come.

Deschartres was a poor chaperon. He scarcely realized what was proper conduct for a young lady. Under his influence Aurore was drawn into his enthusiasm, the practice of medicine. As physician for the village, giving his services free, he was much in demand. He was growing old, and needed an assistant and a successor. Under his instruction Aurore studied medicine and surgery, and, since his training was somewhat out of date, he engaged a young medical student, Stéphane Ajasson, to teach her the modern ideas. Stéphane supplied an occasional skull or arm to enrich their studies, and gave Aurore a small skeleton which she kept on her dressing-table. The young girl found it nerve-racking to sleep with a skeleton by her side. At first she put it in the hall at night. Finally one day she gave it a gentle shaking and told it that she refused to be frightened by a bundle of bones. After that it stopped grinning at her and settled down as a quiet companionable creature who welcomed her back to her room with silent friendliness.

She had some difficulty also in overcoming nervousness at the sight of blood. Deschartres took her with him on his visits, and many were the broken bones and cracked heads she helped to mend. If she turned pale he was stern with her and made her ashamed to faint. He treated her as though she were a man.

Aurore enjoyed spending herself liberally for the sick and helpless. She alternated with Julie in nursing her grandmother. Usually she cared for her invalid at night. Then, after a ride on Colette, she devoted her time to the peasants. She had always loved them and now believed she was winning their love in return. But the villagers, instead of being grateful, were talking about her behind her back.

The trouble was that she was not a man. Her interest in medicine was considered unnatural in a woman. It required explanation. So her neighbors explained it by saying that she took a fiendish pleasure in the sight of blood. One of the servants had told her friends about the skeleton, so the rumor spread that the queer young lady liked to consort with the dead. As her light was seen at night they said she was given to occult practices, and no longer needed sleep: she had not slept for a year.

Aurore did not know she was being condemned. Strong in the consciousness of doing good she went cheerfully from hut to cottage nursing the sick. Then by way of varying her pastimes she practised target shooting with Stéphane and his brothers, and soon she could handle her pistol as well as any young man.

The disapprobation of the ignorant villagers, slowly gathering for months, at last developed into noisy rumors which reached her ears. She was told that someone had seen her ride her horse through the church door. They said she had been galloping around the high altar until an indignant priest had chased her out of the church. She had been noticed attending communion service—but for what purpose? They said she had stolen the sacred host, hidden it in her handkerchief and carried it home. Witnesses had seen her shooting at a target. They claimed that the target she had used was the stolen sacred host.

At first it had been said merely that she studied "the bones of the dead." In time this horror grew until they accused her of going to the cemetery at night to dig the corpses from their graves. Furthermore, André, her groom, was said to be her lover, and he was supposed to share her ferocious taste for blood.

Listening to these legends Aurore was able to laugh at them. She felt detached from the girl who had been calumniated. When she questioned, "Do they really say such things about me?" it was as though she asked, "Do they really say such things about her?" Deschartres, however, was angry and excited and advised her to conform.

"Conform to what?" she asked scornfully. "To ignorance and prejudice?"

"Or at least be prudent," urged Deschartres.

"No; once and for all I have decided; I shall never live for what people think or for what people say. I shall live according to my own conscience and take the consequences."

"That is not so easy as you think."

"But I shall arrange my life so as to make it easy. From this moment I am determined to break with what is called the world. I shall live in seclusion, either in the convent or here at Nohant, without asking approval of anyone. I care for God, a few friends, and myself. That is all."

Thus calmly did the seventeen-year-old girl dedicate herself to solitude and independence.

5

The next phase of her inner experience was profound depression. She fell into a melancholy that grew blacker day by day. She was haunted by the thought of suicide, tempted by the sight of her pistols and by the laudanum she measured for her grandmother. When she touched the pistols, when she gave the drug, she would say to herself, "Yes or no?" One day, riding with Deschartres, she was following behind him along the river's edge.

"Look out!" he called, "this spot is dangerous. The water is twenty feet deep and the current is swift."

Suddenly, as though an outside power had taken possession of her will, she seemed to hear a voice say, "Yes, yes!" She forced Colette to jump with her into the river.

The cold bath brought her to her senses and she clung to the brave little mare who swam against the current but could not find a place to land. Deschartres screamed with terror. They were carried downstream for some distance until finally, with Deschartres' assistance, Colette scrambled to safety.

Immediately after this adventure Aurore took to writing letters. For hours at a time she wrote to Hippolyte, to Sister Alicia, to the mother superior, to her convent friends, to anyone, to everyone, as though desperately reaching for the thing she needed. As letters came in answer to her own she felt less lonely, less a stranger to the world outside. Gradually her mood changed. Her heart, no longer wholly empty, told her that life was worth living, and she lost the longing for death.

She had come back to Nohant, hoping for new friends to take the place of those she had lost. During eighteen months she had been seeking love without finding it. She had expressed natural goodness only to be misunderstood. She had thought her way out of orthodoxy, she had risen above public opinion and the prejudice of the crowd. And in one black mood of despair she had invited death.

All of her future self was there in embryo.

Mademoiselle Dupin was now seventeen years old.

6

Madame Dupin died in December, 1821.

Aurore had lost her best friend. Ever since she had reached

the age of reason Aurore had loved her grandmother. During the years when she had needed instinctive maternal affection, fate had deprived her of a mother. Now that she needed wise counsel and intelligent companionship, the same perverse fate had taken away her counsellor and companion and had put in her place the mother whom Aurore had outgrown.

Sophie came to the funeral. The will was read. Everything was left to Aurore, a fortune amounting to a half million of francs. It included the château at Nohant, and a house in Paris on the rue de la Harpe. In a clause of the will Madame Dupin had stated her wish that Aurore should live with her father's people, the Villeneuves.

Although Sophie had known all along that this was in the will she pretended to be surprised. It was her cue to make a scene. She scolded and raged and threatened. Now that her daughter had become an heiress, was she, the mother, to remain unrecognized? She would have the law on her side, she would show them that she knew her rights.

Aurore, grief-stricken at the loss of her grandmother, shrank within her black clothes. Listening to this outburst of temper, she felt that she would willingly do anything for her mother except live with her.

Sophie was persuaded to depart without her daughter. Aurore remained at Nohant, alone with Deschartres; she needed time to reach her decision. Should she go to Sophie or stay with cousin Villeneuve?

It was the first turning-point of her life. If she could summon motives of worldiness or ambition, life would smile upon her. She would have the surroundings she needed and would live with people who recognized her true self. Furthermore she would become an important person. Introduced from the home of the Countess who was born a Segur, an attractive girl with a striking personality and a generous dot would make a brilliant marriage.

Aurore understood the importance of her choice. Count

Villeneuve was probably the most congenial man she had ever met, and Sophie was without doubt the least congenial woman she knew. Her love for her mother had become compassion. She now saw Sophie as she was—common, vulgar, uncontrolled.

And so she chose Sophie. The reason she gave seemed to her sufficient. Sophie was her mother.

After Aurore and Sophie were settled in Paris, in grandmother's apartment which was now Aurore's apartment, Count Villeneuve called and explained again, as he had already explained, that Aurore must choose one family or the other. A few days later cousin Auguste Villeneuve appeared. Less delicate than his brother, he told Aurore bluntly that unless she left Sophie the Villeneuve family could do nothing for her. He told her further that if she were seen in public with Sophie and her friends, she would lose her reputation, and no eligible man would ever marry her.

After several weeks of Sophie's outrageous treatment, Aurore's eyes were wider open than ever and her heart was by way of being broken. It was her last chance. She did not hesitate. Sophie was ignorant and unreasonable, but again she chose Sophie. She would not abandon her mother.

So the Villeneuves, finding Aurore obstinate and ungrateful, left her to her fate. She felt that they were cruel. She wanted to live with them and accept their protection, but she refused to be protected against her mother.

Aurore had demanded the impossible. She imagined a world free from class prejudice, and she insisted on living in her non-existent world. If she could not make others live in it with her she would live in it alone. She could not objectify her ideal. Sophie herself refused to accept it. Full of class hatred, she was worse, much worse, than the Villeneuves. They ignored her, while she hated them.

When Aurore begged permission to live at the convent, Sophie refused. When she begged to go back to Nohant, Sophie refused. In using her maternal power Sophie was wholly within her legal rights. Aurore was a minor and subject to parental authority until she reached the age of twenty-one. There were three more years to wait, three more years of Sophie's dominance. As she heard Sophie boast that she would marry her daughter according to her own choice, Aurore was afraid of the future. It had never occurred to Aurore to disobey her grandmother, and now it did not occur to her to disobey her mother. Religion, duty, the ties of blood, all made their claims on her. French children were brought up to respect and obey their parents, no matter what the parents were or how the parents behaved.

There were days when Aurore felt disdainful and indifferent; at other times she felt tenderly compassionate. There were moments of warm impulse left from her childish love, followed by intense sadness, as she recognized the gulf between herself and her mother.

She could not cope with Sophie. In vain aunt Lucy told her how to handle her mother. "It is perfectly simple," said aunt Lucy. "When Sophie begins to get angry, you must get angrier. When she shouts, you must answer back. Be violent, walk up and down, break something, scream. Then she subsides and you have the best of her."

Aurore recognized the soundness of her advice, but she could not follow it. She could only wait for Sophie's rage to exhaust itself. The finer nature was helpless, the coarser nature prevailed.

Sometimes Sophie regarded her child as a secret enemy. If she had indigestion she thought she was poisoned and suspected Aurore. She was a woman given to strange caprices. She was still handsome; her flashing eyes and abundant black hair gave her a striking appearance, but she was dissatisfied with herself, wanted to be different. One day she astonished Aurore by appearing in a blond wig. The next morning she changed to a red wig; then she chose others of ash-blond, of brown, of gray, of white. Aurore grew accustomed to the sight of her mother in hair of a different color for each day of the week.

Sophie was equally restless in altering her hats and clothes. She had innumerable dresses which required constant attention. Aurore continued to wear the one black dress she had brought from Nohant. She disliked shopping and hated to fuss over clothes.

Sophie was irritated by her daughter's lack of vanity, and jealous of her interest in study. If she caught Aurore reading she snatched the book from her hand and refused to give it back to her.

A day came when Aurore found her book shelves empty. "Where are my books?" she asked her mother.

"I threw them away," said Sophie contemptuously. "I tried to read them and I couldn't understand a word. I know they are immoral."

"But, mother, you promised to let me keep my books and my maid and my dog! You let me bring them from Nohant, you gave your consent. When you sent away my maid the other day I never said a word. Now of all that I brought from Nohant there is nothing left but my dog."

"You will never see that dog again. I chased him away too. And don't talk to me of promises! I know things about your conduct that prove how you should be treated." Sophie produced a bunch of letters which she had received from Nohant. She held them out at arm's length so that Aurore could read them without seizing them. There, set down in black and white, were all the stupid scandals and superstitions that had been circulated about Aurore before Madame Dupin's death.

"But you don't, you can't, believe that nonsense!" cried Aurore.

Yes, Sophie believed it. Without a word of protest she had accepted the peasant legends as truth.

"So much for the fine education for which you were taken away from your mother!" And Sophie, carried away by excitement, took Aurore by the shoulders and shook her and slapped her as though her daughter were still five years old. Then suddenly, looking into her child's despairing eyes, Sophie came to herself and was ashamed. She fell on her knees, kissed Aurore's hands, and begged for forgiveness.

It was exactly like her behavior of ten years before, only more excessive. But if she remained the same Sophie, it was a different Aurore who received these excesses of love and hatred; it was a thoughtful, serious-minded young girl who regarded the middle-aged woman in silence.

After Sophie had left the room Aurore was unable to move. She sat in her chair until daylight, stupefied, as though her body and her soul were dying. She felt herself alone in the world.

7

Living in the country near Paris was a certain Monsieur Duplessis, who had been in the army with Maurice Dupin. He knew Hippolyte, and through him was familiar with Aurore's history. Monsieur Duplessis invited Aurore and Sophie to spend a week-end at his country home, and Madame Angèle, his wife, took a fancy to Aurore. Sophie felt it her duty to inform these friends that her daughter was a perverse, pedantic highbrow. In no wise intimidated by this motherly recommendation, Madame Duplessis invited Aurore to extend her visit, while Sophie, who hated the country, returned to Paris.

Madame Angèle had five daughters, and her sister Agnes had three more. There was always a horde of children running in and out of the house. They adored Aurore, and she invented games for them as she had done for the children in the convent.

As the weeks became months and Sophie did not reappear to claim her daughter, Aurore was adopted into the large, harmonious family. She was made to feel that her presence was indispensable, and she responded to this kindness and affection by becoming as happy and carefree as one of the children. Prisoner's base, blind-man's-buff, and hide-and-seek were played among the trees of the park. No one understood why Sophie had called her daughter pedantic, for she never looked at a book. She lived out-doors, and seemed to everyone a gay laughing child.

Seeing the dilapidated state of the girl's wardrobe, Madame Angèle fitted her out with new clothes. Since their home was near the city, father and mother Duplessis took Aurore with them on a trip to Paris. One day after the matinée they were sitting at a table at Tortoni's eating ices when Aurore heard Madame Angèle exclaim: "Look, here is Casimir!"

A good-looking young man joined them. Seating himself be-side Madame Angèle, he asked in a low voice, "Who is the young lady?"

Madame smiled and answered aloud, "She is my daughter."

"In that case she is my future wife," said Casimir, and Madame Angèle laughed as he explained promptly: "Haven't you always said I was to marry your oldest daughter? I supposed you meant Wilfred. Now I see you have a daughter more appropriate for my own age."

"And how old are you, Casimir?"

"Twenty-seven."

"You must come with us to the country and see the children."

So it was arranged. Casimir Dudevant, like all the friends of Monsieur Duplessis, had been in the army. He was a clean, well set up young fellow with a military bearing. Aurore felt at ease with him, he was so like Hippolyte, simple and friendly and good-natured. She wrote to Hippolyte, "I have found a companion with whom I laugh and play as I do with you." There was no nonsense about Casimir. He never made love to Aurore, he merely joined her and the children in their games. For his part Casimir felt at ease with Mademoiselle Dupin. She seemed sensible and gentle, as a woman should be. Obviously she was domestic and fond of children. Best of all, she was gay, and he liked gayety.

Already Aurore was being pursued for her fortune. Her mother had received several offers from young men whom she had never seen. The young girl had a horror of these fortune-hunting strangers, and although her French training forbade her to think of love in connection with marriage, she wanted to find a husband who would be to her a friend.

Casimir became her friend, her adviser, and then her confidant. She told him she would never marry a man who was ashamed of her mother, and when he met Sophie he was sympathetic. So when he suggested marriage Aurore listened willingly.

Of course it was unusual for a Frenchman to approach a young girl on the subject of marriage, but the circumstances were unusual. He wanted to know her feelings before he proffered his suit to so peculiar a mother as Sophie. He told Aurore frankly that he did not consider her beautiful, and that he had no use for sentiment, but that he felt as though he had known her for a long time. That pleased Aurore; it was nice to be liked in such a sensible way. She had suffered so much from Sophie's excesses that this calm attracted her. Aurore was longing to live at Nohant; a husband was her only means of accomplishing this wish.

She accepted his proposal without a moment's hesitation. Sophie accepted it also, though she changed her mind every few days. When she gave her consent it was because Casimir would make an ideal son-in-law. When she turned against him it was because she did not like his nose.

After several months of this uncertainty, Baroness Dudevant called on Sophie and was most gracious in urging the suit of her step-son. Sophie's self-love was flattered to such an extent that she signed the contract. In handing over Aurore's fortune she was clever enough to insist on the dotal régime, which allowed Casimir to administer his wife's fortune but prevented him from spending her capital or selling her land. She also stipulated that her daughter should retain for her own use a personal allowance of three thousand francs a year. This agreement was written into the marriage contract.

III

MADAME DUDEVANT

IN September, 1822, Aurore Dudevant returned to Nohant with the husband who was so like Hippolyte and who would help her to make a home.

She was grateful to him because through his protection she had achieved her wish to live at Nohant. She congratulated herself also that she had escaped the threatened fate of being married to a stranger.

But there was one drawback to her new status. Before the ceremony she had been an heiress. After a few words had been said over her by a priest she became dependent on the bounty of a dashing military man about whom no one seemed to know very much.

Young Casimir Dudevant was the natural son of Colonel Dudevant, a Baron of the Empire. As soon as he was acknowledged by his father he inherited the title. His income was not sufficient to support a wife. He wanted a home, he fancied himself as a gentleman farmer, and he liked the idea of authority over a sweet, obedient woman. His mind, not different from that of the average young soldier, was empty and commonplace. A typical Gascon, he had never had a deep feeling or a serious thought in his life. He was exceedingly anxious to better himself and acquire possessions. This ambition, carefully hidden, was his dominant characteristic, but no one yet suspected it, least of all his confiding little eighteen-year-old wife. Although she was wise in philosophy and poetry and religion, in worldly matters she was a child. She had lately been trying to write a novel, but once again she had been discouraged, for she could not write about

Aurore Dupin, at eighteen, the year of her marriage

love. Her senses were unawakened, and her imagination was occupied with her reading and her dreams.

And now her friends looked in vain for any expression of a free, untrammeled personality in Madame Dudevant. Marriage did to Aurore Dupin what all other influences had failed to accomplish: it made her conform. There were no more eccentricities. The wild girl had given place to the child-wife. She adjusted herself to Casimir, and yielded to his authority. Immediately Casimir began to talk economy, and his wife economized. He seemed so worried about finances that she voluntarily gave up her personal allowance, and the three thousand francs reverted to him.

Toward spring a baby was expected. Madame Dudevant, who had never used a needle, speedily learned to sew. A pile of little dresses, coats and bonnets quickly accumulated. The neighbors said she had fairy fingers.

When the baby was born Madame Dudevant became the most devoted of mothers. She nursed her own baby, a thing almost unheard of. She tended him herself, and was anxious if she left him for an hour. Her letters were full of her child's perfections; he was "an angel, a cupid, a love, a beauty."

For the first year Deschartres lived with them. Then his term as manager expired and after his departure Casimir took charge of Nohant. He was happy to rule over so large an estate, and to prove his authority he changed everything. Aurore tried her best to appreciate these changes. The old horse that she was keeping in reward for past services was sold; the dog who for years had had his place beside the fire was killed; the peacocks who had eaten out of Madame Dupin's hand were disposed of as a nuisance. Her favorite trees were chopped down. The furniture in the house was moved back and forth. Aurore told herself that her husband was within his rights. No doubt he was bringing in a reign of law and order, but somehow with each change she felt heartsick. She was not possessive except as sentiment and association made her so. But the associations of a lifetime were being broken.

2

At the end of the second year Aurore tried to resume her former interests, but Casimir could find no occupation. He had played with his authority until the novelty had worn off, and now he was bored by his duties as manager. Boredom made him restless. It horrified him to see his wife reading; he could not read a paragraph without falling asleep. He hated music, and when she played the piano or the harp he asked her not to make "such a noise."

Casimir had nothing to offer by way of conversation. His mind was not open to impressions or ideas. He ate heartily, drank heavily and was usually sleepy. He never left her presence to take a nap in solitude; he liked to sleep in his chair wherever his wife happened to be reading. Sometimes the sight of his dull, heavy face and closed eyes disturbed her studies, while his gentle snoring took the edge off her mental keenness.

Negatively he was a good husband, and negatively she was a good wife. There were no open quarrels. They were quite polite to each other. And yet Aurore fell into a profound melancholy.

It was hard on Casimir to see his little wife droop and pine in the happy home he had made for her. Her chief attraction had been her gayety, and now that was gone. He began to feel abused, and naturally he grew irritable. Afterwards he was always ashamed of being cross and tried to make amends.

One day as they were seated at table Aurore watched her husband, hunched over his plate, feeding himself in heavy silence. Why didn't he say something? She looked through the window and saw the clipped hedges and the clean new paths he had made; the picturesque beauty of the garden was gone. Suddenly it came over her that the horror she had combated for years had overtaken her. This man sitting opposite her was a stranger. She began to weep.

Casimir regarded her with consternation. What was the matter with the woman? Wasn't he a good husband? Didn't he stay at home, around the house and on the place all day? Wasn't he there every evening, sleeping by the fireside while she read? What more could a woman desire?

"I don't like Nohant," Aurore explained. "I want to go away."

Casimir was dumbfounded. "You don't like Nohant? But I thought you said your one desire was to live here."

"That was when I was young."

"When you were young? That's good, that is. Why, you're young now, you're under age. If ever anybody needed a guardian, you do!"

"Well, when I was younger, then," Aurore amended meekly. "I think now I would like to live where there are more people about—and children. I would like to spend the summer with the Duplessis."

"But I thought you got married because you didn't want to live with them. You said you didn't belong there, you wanted a home of your own."

Alas, that was just the point. Nohant was no longer her home, it was his home. He had taken possession and she felt crowded out. Her personality was crushed.

"Yes," assented Aurore. "I don't know what is the matter with me. Perhaps I need a change."

Casimir responded with simple manly directness. "You needn't think that I like Nohant," he admitted. "I hate it. I would like a change myself. Very well, then; we will spend the summer with our friends."

We, we—there it was; no matter where they went, they went together. They would always go away together, come back together, stay together, tied together for the rest of their lives.

When Casimir took his wife to stay with her adopted parents she was a sick, listless woman, whose mouth drooped at the corners and whose gaze was fixed on space. After a few days he found her transformed; the flush of health was on her cheeks, her eye were shining with vitality, her mouth was curved with smiles She was exactly as she had been before he married her, gay, happy healthy, a radiant child.

This sudden change hurt his self-love. It seemed ungrateful During all the time that he had given her his exclusive presence she had been sorrowful. Now that she was surrounded by friends how dare she show herself so glad? It was as though she had hit at him. As he watched her laughing light-heartedly with the children the streak of brutality hidden in his nature came to the surface. He wanted to hit back.

One evening after dinner the family group were taking coffee on the veranda that bordered on the terrace. The two older children, with Aurore, began to chase up and down on the terrace. Somebody threw a handful of sand, and a few grains fell into the coffee cup of father Duplessis.

Casimir shouted to his wife to stop her nonsense. But Aurore was excited and paid no attention. It was the first time she had refused to obey her husband. Casimir lost control of himself; rushing to where she stood he struck her in the face.

Aurore hesitated a moment as she looked at the brave soldier who was her husband, then she ran across the park and hid in the woods. After several hours she came back again and joined him in their room. She told herself that whatever love she had felt for him died that night.

But it did not die; the tie of marriage is not loosed so easily. It was merely that something had gone out of her love for him. Their lives were interwoven, their home, their purse, their personal affairs were shared in common, a child was theirs. They had to make the best of the mistake they had made.

From this time on Casimir lost all respect for her. He reached a decision which he retained for the rest of his life: she was an idiot, he had married an idiot, he pitied himself.

Aurore accepted her husband's contempt in passive silence. She was more obedient, as he wished her to be. She made greater efforts to suit him, to see through his eyes, to think and behave as he wished. But as soon as she was in accord with his ideas she was no longer in harmony with her own instincts; she fell into depression and was ill. Then when she was ill and depressed he was irritated and bored. She seemed to him stupid, half alive, drawn into herself; he wanted a lively wife.

Casimir was as anxious as she was to escape a prolonged tête-à-tête. In the autumn they rented a small house outside Paris, where they could spend the evenings with friends. Casimir went to Paris every day and so relieved the strain of too much intimacy. Later they took an apartment in Paris. They both hated the city and loved the country, each would have been happier at Nohant alone; but since they had to be together, they preferred the city with its distractions.

What did Casimir do with his time in Paris? Nothing in particular. He had married a fortune and he did not need to work; but somehow, although he had no work to do, he was restless. He became more irritable. His face grew ruddier, his body heavier, he was losing his slim waist. The dashing military man was becoming a heavy country gentleman.

3

During the winter in Paris the young wife proved herself a charming hostess; she was popular, she made friends. But her popularity was for her gay, superficial self; her friends did not know her. No one went with her into her own inner life.

Often she became a child again. It was, in part, a release for her repressed instinct for happiness. It was also her way of meeting all sorts and kinds of people. In becoming a child she reached out to the universal that is in men and women of all ages. No matter what differences existed in the people around her, they could all play games together. So she played games.

When they returned to Nohant and these diversions ceased, she often felt a vague desire to write, but the scene or character she tried to describe eluded her. Restlessly she turned from writing to music, from music to painting, and lost interest in them all. So long as her heart was unsatisfied, the way ahead seemed blocked.

The young woman of twenty was no longer unaware of men, and her awareness increased her despair. She judged all men by her limited experience. They were merely so many more Hippolytes and Casimirs, incurious, complacent, satisfied with the commonplace.

It would have been a rare man indeed who could have answered the devouring need of Aurore Dudevant. Her need grew out of years of loneliness. She had been loved because she was somebody's child, wife or sister, but she had never been loved because she was herself. Unconsciously she was waiting to be discovered.

While she waited, her health grew steadily worse. She coughed and strangled. She had palpitations of the heart. The doctor diagnosed these symptoms as consumption and recommended change of air. They decided to take a trip to the home of Casimir's father, Colonel Dudevant, at Guillery in the Pyrenees. Aurore left Nohant feeling that probably she would not live to return. Her journal, written at this time, reveals her state of mind.

"July 5, 1825.
Journey to the Pyrenees

"In ten minutes I shall have left Nohant. I leave behind me nothing that I truly regret, except my brother. But how cold our old friendship has grown! Now that I am on the point of leaving, he is laughing, he is gay! Good-by, Nohant, perhaps I shall never see you again. . . .

Chalus

"In the carriage I have been reading several pages of Ossian. I have decided to reflect a bit, and that is not a small matter for me, because I want to live without ever thinking of anything. I have made some good resolutions for the trip: try not to worry every time Maurice cries, try not to get impatient at the length of the journey, try not to mind when *my friend* is in bad humor.

Périgueux

"I have passed through charming country; I have seen some splendid horses. This town has seemed to me delightful, but I am sad unto death. I have wept a great deal on this journey; but what is the use of weeping? Death in the soul and a smiling face, I must get used to it.

Cauterets

"Marriage is good for lovers and useful for saints.

"But apart from lovers and saints there are a lot of people with average intelligence and peaceful hearts who do not understand love and who cannot attain to sanctity.

"The supreme object of love is marriage. When marriage exists without love there is nothing left but sacrifice—that is all very well for those who understand sacrifice. It is a quality which presupposes an amount of heart and a degree of intelligence which are not always to be found.

"Sacrifice offers certain compensations to the vulgar-minded: the approbation of society, the pleasant routine of habit, a tranquil, sensible little affection that doesn't care to become exalted. Or there are the things that money brings, such as playthings, clothes, luxuries: a thousand trifles that make one forget that one has missed happiness.

"Apparently, then, the present arrangement is right, since the majority are vulgar-minded; not to be content with the pleasures of the crowd proves inferior judgment and a lack of common sense.

"Perhaps there is no middle ground between the power of great souls who achieve sanctity, and the convenient apathy of small minds who enjoy insensibility.

"—Yes, there is a middle ground; it is despair. . . .

"But there is also childishness, some of which is good and sweet

to keep, in spite of what they say! To run, ride horseback, laugh
at nothing, feel careless about health and about life! Aimée scolds
me a great deal. She cannot understand why one should try to
lose oneself and why one needs to forget. 'Forget what?' she says.
—How should I know! Forget everything; forget, above all, that
one exists."

Cauterets, where they stayed for a time, was a fashionable
watering place. They fell in with several congenial people, among
whom were Aimée and Jane Bezouin, old convent friends. Aurore
formed a new and strong friendship with Zoé Leroy. Zoé was independent and intelligent. The two young women had long talks
on love, marriage, literature, religion. They compared their terrible melancholy and their intellectual superiority. "We have a
little more capacity for intelligence and reflection than most people," said Zoé. "So much the worse for us."

How young they were, how girlish! If there had been such
things as colleges for women, they would have been sophomores;
yet Madame Dudevant had a child two years old, and Zoé was
engaged. Zoé's fiancé, M. Rayet, accompanied them on all their
expeditions, and soon a friend and neighbor of Zoé's joined them
also. This friend from Bordeaux was Aurélian de Sèze, a young
lawyer of distinguished family, very different from the country
gentlemen to whom Aurore was accustomed. He was intellectual,
sensitive and high-minded.

Aurore, having revealed herself to Zoé, continued to reveal her
true self to young Sèze. That was dangerous, for when Aurore
Dudevant was animated and interested, her intensity made other
women colorless. When she was happy, her mysterious, magnetic
eyes could glow with feeling and deepen with thought. A man's
gaze, and finally his soul, could easily be lost in them.

The play of ideas between Aurore and Aurélian was stimulating. Their minds and natures met, then merged, then could not
pull apart.

4

Madame Dudevant had been too weak and ill for music; but now, when she played the harp or sang to the piano, Aurélian listened with pleasure, and she could play and sing for hours. She had been too tired to ride horseback; but now, when she went on expeditions with Zoé and M. Rayel and Aurélian, she could ride without fatigue. Because Aurélian found her interesting, she was interested in herself.

But Aurore was a good woman. When the young lawyer, no longer able to restrain himself, confessed his love, Aurore "repulsed him" with severity and coldness. He was hurt, and an estrangement followed. For three days they did not speak to each other.

She had been good and she was miserable. The joy went out of her walks and rides. There was no beauty in the scenery, no pleasure in life. Even Zoé's friendship failed to console her. After all, she was not first in her friend's heart; Zoé had a lover, and Aurore was alone.

All this time Casimir had neglected her. People noticed the situation and commented on it. His neglect followed naturally from his opinion of women. In Casimir's opinion women were either good or bad. He had classified his wife as good, therefore he could safely neglect her. Since his property was self-protecting, he was freed from responsibility, he could go where he pleased and leave her to loneliness.

Aurore did not live up to Casimir's classification. True, she was terribly good, but she was even more terribly lonely. She could not see happiness in the person of Aurélian de Sèze go out of her life. And so she did a shameless thing; she gave him an opportunity to explain. Given this opportunity, Aurélian assured her that he did not ask to be her lover in the ordinary sense of the word; he did not ask anything. He wanted to give, not take.

At last she had found someone who could love as she herself

was capable of loving. At last he had found someone to whom he could devote his life. In the joy of this first mutual understanding Aurélian forgot for the moment to be wholly consistent. He pressed her to his heart and touched his lips to her cheek. And Aurore, equally inconsistent, in the violence of her emotion did not this time repulse him. She "accorded him a kiss."

They could have forgiven each other, for they understood that the caress was innocent and exceptional, and could never occur again. But how can an onlooker understand two lovers who forget even for an instant the "rights of a husband"? And if that onlooker happens to be the injured husband? Yes, it was Casimir who caught them. He had followed them when they withdrew from the crowd, he had come upon them at the supreme moment, and he was horrified.

There were violent scenes between husband and wife. Aurore confessed her guilt, begged forgiveness, and promised never to accord another kiss. But the conflagration had been started. Two souls were on fire. Aurélian and Aurore understood each other, that was all they asked, all they needed. They had sacrificed earthly passion, they had sublimated love.

"You know me, you know me," she wrote in ecstasy.

And his answer was, "I would rather love you without hope, even without return, than to have the affection of all the women in the world."

She had found love.

All her life she had been seeking this one man, Aurélian. For him she was born, for him she would live. Never were two young people so infatuated, and so determined to be good.

Aurélian being a lawyer, his point of view was legal; a husband owns his wife, a wife should therefore conduct herself as a sacred piece of personal property. The man who touches another man's wife commits a penal offense. Alas, his lips had touched the cheek that belonged to Casimir Dudevant! It had been criminal—a criminal caress!

Aurore was as moral as Aurélian was legal; unfaithfulness was a sin of which she was incapable. Her grandmother's teachings, her convent religion, and her own ideals of purity would have protected her against the boldest lover. And Aurélian was neither bold nor bad; he was a second Sir Galahad.

"If I forget the respect that is due you, resist me," he entreated. She held herself in readiness to resist him. Indeed it was easy, since the more she resisted him the more he respected her, and the more he respected the more he loved her. Love-making was not indispensable to Aurore's happiness; what she wanted was love.

Aurore had never objectified any of the dream worlds she had created, because no one had ever believed in her creations. But Aurélian believed with her, created with her, lived with her in their world of two-in-one. It was all she needed for happiness, she was no longer alone in the world.

5

Aurélian went back to Bordeaux, sustained by the thought of his beloved who was always close to his heart. Aurore at Guillery lived in an exaltation of spirit that was like her religious experience. She had found an object of worship. Wherever she moved, whatever she did, Aurélian was by her side. To be together, although separated, did not seem strange to them. They knew and felt the truth of their mystic union, therefore it was true.

Casimir did not rightly know what a mystic union was. He didn't want it himself and wouldn't have known what to do with it, but he didn't propose to allow his wife to give it to another man. And he could not prevent it. He could prevent meetings, he could prevent letters, he could positively and legally prevent any physical contact. But this thing that his wife gave to another man evaded him. She gave it over his head, into the air, up to the moon and the stars, and somehow—that was the strange irritating part of it—the other man received it. Even though Casimir should place his wife under lock and key, the other man could still take what she gave, and by so doing deprive a legal husband of his rights. That's what happens to a man who marries an idiot.

And the idiot wife became idiotically happy. The color came back in her cheeks, the light in her eyes. She kept well, recovered her appetite, derived more health and happiness out of a spooky relation with a man who was absent than from the presence of her normal husband. Of course, Casimir continued to assure himself, there is nothing in it, and yet there *is* something in it, a maddening something that makes a red-blooded man feel like laying down the law. But here is where the law doesn't help a man. There are things, mean, tricky, mysterious things, that evade the law.

Casimir was therefore unable to rejoice in his wife's improved health. He could not take pleasure in her happiness, he felt wronged and dispossessed. He begged her to surrender her source of health and happiness for his sake.

She took long walks to think it over. Must she sacrifice her mystic love? She was torn between her desires and her ideals. If she goes on writing to Aurélian she hurts Casimir; if her letters cease she will break Aurélian's heart. She must choose between them. Aurélian means more to her than anyone on earth. But Casimir is her husband, so Aurélian must be sacrificed. She is a good woman. Her ideals are stronger than her desires.

6

The Dudevants had long planned a trip from Guillery to Bordeaux. A business trip for Casimir, it was something quite different for Aurore. A terrible ordeal was before her; she must tell Aurélian that all is over. She must explain.

A meeting was arranged between the lovers. Aurore explained Casimir's suffering. The excellent Aurélian recognized the superior claim of a husband's pain. He had already surrendered his desires. With equal nobility of spirit he renounced his dream. Then, burying his face in his hands, he exclaimed, "Now let me die!" Aurore almost fainted with emotion. And of course Casimir had carefully followed at a distance and witnessed this scene. He carried Aurore away with him and talked to her all night. She was terribly ill, and he cared for her tenderly while between her attacks of pain he continued to plead his own cause.

The day after this painful scene Casimir, Aurélian and Aurore were driving to La Brède, the home of Zoé. In the carriage Casimir took the seat beside his wife. Aurélian was opposite, with his back to the horses. Aurore could study them both, choose between them if she would.

Aurélian was distinguished by a sensitive, expressive face. He was dark like Aurore. His black eyes flashed intelligence and spirit; in moods of tenderness they spoke his love. But in the presence of a husband, since breeding imposes restraint, his eyes now seemed attracted to the landscape; he leaned back, looked at the scenery, and talked generalities.

Casimir was a florid blond. According to a description by the poet Heine, he had "porcelain eyes and a Philistine physiognomy that expressed nothing." Also there must have been something four-square, set, monotonous and repetitive about Casimir, since Heine says that he was like a Chinese pagoda.

On the drive Casimir was all solicitude. Would his darling like a lap-robe? Would his dearest have a pillow? His attentions were as officious as they were unnecessary. There was someone sitting opposite who longed to care for her.

Aurélian's hands, long-fingered and slim, were clasped, carefully restrained, close to Aurore's magnetic fingers, yet Aurélian dared not touch her. A husband has a right to caress his own wife before a lover's eyes. Casimir took his wife's hand and held it.

What was passing in the mind of Madame Dudevant? Was she smiling to herself at Casimir's possessiveness? Was she comparing his present devotion with his past neglect? The simple creature was incapable of suspicion or rancor. She was grateful that Casimir had suddenly become a perfect husband, and responded to his kindness, feeling that she had never understood him, never appre-

ciated him before. Her face lighted, her eyes held a deep contentment. She was with the two beings who were dearest to her in the
world. The two seemed friendly and her heart was full of peace.

Casimir looked at her and saw in her a weak inferior. Soft,
helpless, feminine thing! She was unable to cope with him, he
would always have his way with her, that he knew.

Aurélian raised his eyes discreetly to study the delicate face,
pale from sleeplessness. Had Casimir argued with her half the
night? Aurélian found her infinitely touching. To know her was
a privilege, to love her was a sacrament. She would always have
her way with him, that he knew.

But of the two men who loved her weakness, neither realized
that the frail body was merely the outward envelope for a tremendous force that carried her, compelled her, and made her do
its bidding, so that even now, as the two of them were trying to
amuse her, she was thinking to herself: if only there were some
kind of world in which we three could live together and be happy,
some world apart from laws and social sanctions where each could
be free without hurting the other. Why couldn't we three make
a world of our own, above human passion and prejudice?

Only last night she had surrendered her dream of love. Now
she began to weave a new dream, less ecstatic, less perfect, farther
from heaven, nearer to earth, a dream made to include Casimir,
since he so wanted to come along and enter in. If he entered he
would have to act in the only capacity he understood, that of
master. She would allow him to be master if he would only let her
keep Aurélian, in some way that did not hurt his masculine self-
love. If he could trust her, if he could trust them both, oh, then
how she could love Casimir and keep faith with him!

She dreamed on and forgot the painful illness from which she
had suffered. She was weak from loss of sleep, but she felt so
happy, so full of love for all mankind, that she was no longer ill.
The new dream had made her well again.

7

The next day Aurélian and Aurore walked in the garden together in plain sight. This was their idea of a pure rendezvous,
and it gave them a chance to finish their interrupted talk. If the
first explanation of two months ago had led them away from
duty, this one was to bring them back to the right path.

"Forgive my momentary weakness," said Aurélian, "I am calm
now. I have collected my ideas, I have conceived a hope. May I
ask you to share it, and will you promise me to agree to it?"

As Aurore looked at him her eyes were full of trust. "I think
I can promise you that, because you would not suggest anything
that I ought to refuse."

Encouraged by this confidence, Aurélian explained his cherished hope. Was he so close to her that he had read her thoughts
on the drive the day before? Or was he so like her that they
thought together and shared the same ideals?

Aurélian, like Aurore, had decided that Casimir must be master.
They would take nothing that Casimir could not authorize, they
would ask for no happiness he could not share. According to Aurélian's plan, Casimir, who had no interest in love, marriage, literature and religion, was to listen to all their conversations. Casimir,
who could not understand books, philosophy, poetry and ideas,
was to read their letters. He was even to read Zoé's letters, so as to
assure himself she would not act as an intermediary. He was to
treat them as abject beings completely in his power. He was to
shut his wife away from Aurélian and keep her under observa-
tion. If at the end of a year she had proved her wifely virtue he
might then trust her to see Aurélian occasionally, perhaps once
or twice a year, but then only in his presence. They would humbly
request a friendship of three, with Casimir as the always welcome
third. They would begin a new life.

But they did not agree to begin immediately. They needed to
wait a week—or two—or three. Their souls had merged, and

needed time to pull apart. Is it quite safe for people to drop suddenly from the mountain-tops? No, they should descend step by step. They must descend slowly, roped together. Not until the bottom is reached can the rope be cut.

The correspondence between the lovers continued after Aurore left Bordeaux. Then Casimir made a trip to Nohant, and Aurore found herself writing letters of love to Aurélian and letters of wifely affection to Casimir. A sense of guilt began to overwhelm her. She knew she was immoral. She had been kissed, she had been pressed to a heart that was not her husband's, she had leaned on Aurélian's shoulder, and both had written letters in secret. Both were sinners, therefore, and deserved punishment. They decided that confession and the cessation of all love letters would be sufficient punishment. It would be the equivalent of sending themselves to prison.

On the appointed day, the day of Casimir's return from the trip to Nohant, Aurore could almost hear an iron door clang behind her as she sat down to write for Casimir a full confession. It comprised eighteen pages of fine handwriting, in which everything was laid bare. But in writing her confession and in stating Aurélian's legal brief on their case, she added a wife's entreaty: would Casimir take Aurélian's place in her life and interest himself in her tastes? Would he read aloud in the evenings while she sketched or sewed? Would he be her true companion, her best friend? She would be Casimir's wife to the very spirit of the law, if he would be her companion and relieve the loneliness of her life.

Casimir agreed to the compact; he would gladly be her true companion. But since they were spending the winter at Guillery he felt that the matter of intimate comradeship, reading together and all that, might better be postponed until their return home. Then in the spring, when they reached Nohant, he found that business called him away. He spent the entire summer in Paris and Bordeaux. The close companionship never began.

Casimir's business affairs at Bordeaux were vague. He talked importantly of ship-building interests. The truth was that a man named Desgranges had persuaded him to invest money in a ship. Casimir gave notes to Desgranges to the amount of 25,000 francs which it took two years to pay off. When the debt was settled he discovered that the ship had never existed. He could not understand this catastrophe, because Desgranges had shown him a picture of the ship. Casimir's chief affair at Bordeaux, it developed later, was with Desgranges's mistress. Casimir had, in fact, run away from his wife's companionship to find a woman who suited his own taste.

When news of this scandal came to Aurore's ears she felt a sick horror. Was it for this she had sacrificed a true and beautiful love? She tried to express her misery in words: "If you wish to know what suffering is, tear your flesh with your nails, cut it with a sharp instrument, and pour on your wounds melted lead and boiling oil, or hold in your hand burning coals, or hit your head against the wall of a prison. Even then you will not know what suffering is."

When Casimir went to Bordeaux, Aurore could not ask to go with him because Bordeaux was Aurélian's home. She kept faith with her husband, and as soon as she was alone she used her freedom as she had used it once before, to nurse and doctor her friends, the peasants. Casimir had given his wife charge of the estate during his absence, had told her exactly how much money she could spend. When, upon his return, he looked over her accounts, there was a terrible scene. He found that she had bought medicines for the peasants, and had even on certain occasions handed out hard cash. This was to Casimir the height of frivolity. If there was one thing about his wife that annoyed him more than disobedience, it was generosity. Her giving nature had always affronted his sense of justice, except in the one case where she had given him her personal allowance. That seemed to him just—was he not her husband?

Aurore was crestfallen by her failure as a manager. She had

tried in vain to cultivate what Casimir called thrift. The accounts she kept during the year of her management had been a daily torture. The mere sight of ledgers gave her a headache. Even as a child the study of arithmetic had always made her sick. She hated figures, they were symbols of money, and she had no money sense. But although she was humbled by constant quarrels about money, she could not feel that she was an extravagant wife. When at the end of nine years of marriage she asked her husband to settle her personal debts, he discovered she had spent on clothes and personal expenses the sum total of five hundred francs (one hundred dollars).

8

During the five years from 1826 to 1831 Aurore's real life—what is called real life, that is, her outer life—was uneventful. She lived at Nohant, with occasional escape by trips to Paris or to La Châtre. Sometimes they lived at La Châtre all winter and entertained the country aristocracy.

Throughout this period Aurore was constantly thinking of ways to earn money. She could not spend a sou without Casimir's permission. Money had always meant to her merely something to give away, and now whenever she felt generous she was powerless to give. She determined to extricate herself from this humiliating dependence.

How could she develop an earning capacity? She was certainly intelligent, and she was accustomed to extravagant praise for her many talents. Which of these talents could she turn to some account? She embroidered beautifully, she played the piano and harp, and her painting was considered remarkable. Perhaps as a portrait painter she might achieve success. She made several portraits but was critical of the results. She saw that she would need to study under a master to perfect her technique. Music was her passion. She preferred it to all the other arts. But she did not feel qualified to teach. She had been badly taught, and her attainments did not enable her to compete with professionals. For a long time she continued her efforts to write, but they came to nothing. She decided that her talents were mere accomplishments. Having reached this decision, Aurore brooded over her uselessness. Life seemed futile and she was beginning to feel old.

All this while she kept up a correspondence with Aurélian. Casimir was allowed to read the letters, but found them hard to understand. They were about books, philosophy and morals. They seemed to him maudlin. It was easier to let them go without oversight.

And so, as time went on and the friendship endured, Aurore poured out her soul to her one friend. She told Aurélian everything, even told him of her soul's revolt from prejudice and authority. Against the revolt Aurélian preached submission, endurance and patience. But no matter how often he told her to calm herself, she could not remain calm.

From the beginning he had constituted himself her mental guide. He had told her what to read and what to think and whether her thoughts were wrong. At first she had yielded to all his opinions. Gradually she dissented from some of them. Then she discussed their differences of viewpoint, and finally dared think for herself. This was the beginning of the end.

There was some dissonance in the quality of their minds. Aurore was seeking for truth. This compelled her to discard any tradition or superstition that seemed rooted in error. She looked toward the future, while Aurélian faced the past, so that instead of standing side by side they found themselves back to back. He was reactionary and conventional, she was progressive and free. Her mind was growing, his was fixed. His ideals would never alter in any particular, while her ideals changed from year to year. Unfortunately for their friendship, the only contact they had was epistolary. They saw each other at long intervals, sometimes two or three times a year, more often once a year.

On one of his rare visits to Nohant Aurélian found Madame

Dudevant busily occupied. While she talked to him she did not put her work aside. "What are you doing?" he asked, as he watched her folding a formidable array of little garments.

"Don't you see?" she replied. "I am getting ready in haste for someone who may arrive sooner than I expected."

This unlooked-for news was disillusioning. Aurélian had always thought of Aurore as spiritual and ascetic. If the expected baby had been his own child, the mother might have seemed to him sacred. But there stood Casimir, who had come in from the farm wearing corduroys and heavy leggings. Casimir had never seemed to Aurélian so red-faced, heavy and coarse. Where was the appropriateness, the beauty, or the poetry, in such a woman bearing a child for such a man?

As Aurélian looked at his matronly friend she seemed to him very different from the fascinating young woman of five years ago. True, he had told her to do her whole duty, and doubtless her duty included motherhood. If he had married her they would have been happy, he felt sure. They were perfectly mated except for that mental quality of hers which disturbed him, that freedom of mind. If she had been his wife he could have dominated her mind, and their union would have been perfect. But as things were, the relation was too ethereal. He was tired of inhabiting a dream world, tired also of his rôle of celestial purity. He wanted a woman of his own, a wife, a home.

After this visit he wrote one friendly letter. Then came a gap in the correspondence. The six-year-old web of dreams had begun to break. There were no explanations and no reproaches. By the following summer they had arrived at what Aurore called a "tranquil divorce." They remained friends, but the letters were almost discontinued. During the summer of 1830 he wrote to her once. Three years later he married.

9

After the birth of the child Solange many changes took place in the life of Madame Dudevant. In order to leave her time free for the baby she engaged a tutor for Maurice. This tutor was Jules Boucoiran, a young man who possessed a chivalrous nature and a capacity for friendship. As soon as he realized the domestic situation of the Dudevants his sympathy went out to the young wife. She had hidden her unhappiness from other friends, but nothing could be hidden from a member of the family. Jules became her devoted ally. She found in him an understanding heart.

The family group was still further augmented by the inclusion of Aurore's half-brother, Hippolyte Châtiron, who came to live permanently with his sister. He brought his wife Emily and his child Léontine, who was about the age of Maurice. Hippolyte and Casimir were great cronies; they were, as Aurore had always felt, surprisingly alike. Each was the illegitimate son of a gentleman and a woman of the people. Each had married a fortune, each administered it badly, and each drowned his sorrows in drink. As a young man Hippolyte had possessed something of the charm of his father. By the time he reached thirty he had lost his looks, his refinement and his amiable character. This was equally true of Casimir, who began to deteriorate at the same age.

After the advent of Hippolyte, Aurore tried to arrange family evenings, games, conversation, reading, anything to create a semblance of companionship. But Casimir protested. How could a man make a companion of a woman? Why should he bore himself with feminine things like books? Casimir felt himself a real man and he sought manly pleasures, such as drinking and swapping masculine stories with other men. Besides Hippolyte, the constant companion of his drinking bouts was their neighbor, Aurore's former teacher of anatomy, Stéphane Ajasson. Often the family friend Dutheil, who lived at La Châtre, formed a fourth.

The joys and the noise of these parties were sometimes prolonged until six or seven o'clock in the morning.

Aurore escaped to the little room which had been her grandmother's boudoir. It had only one door, so that no one could use it as a passageway, and it adjoined the large bedroom where the children slept. While she read or wrote she listened to the children's breathing and watched over their sleep. The boudoir was small, and it was filled with books, herbs, butterflies, and the stones she had collected in her study of natural history. In the midst of this clutter of possessions there was no room for a bed. She therefore hung a hammock from wall to wall and slept there when she needed to be alone.

Since she felt herself an exile from Casimir's world and interests she was obliged to create a world and an interest for herself alone. What should she do with her evenings, those long evenings she had so often begged Casimir to share with her? She studied a great deal, but she was not satisfied with books. She felt a craving for blank paper, pen and ink. Five years of writing to Aurélian had formed a habit, and a five-year habit is not easy to break. Since her friend had lost his passionate eagerness for her letters, she would write for herself.

She began a novel—how many times she had begun a novel! This time she was capable of sustained effort. She carried it through to a finish, and christened it *Aimée*. Her beloved book *Aimée!* She put into it all of her ideals and none of her desires. The characters were virtuous, high-minded, devoted to duty. No character was any less perfect than she had been, or than Aurélian had been. Sacrifice and suffering was the philosophy of her book, as it was the religion of her life. After the book was finished she could not decide what to do with it. She tucked it away with a sense of waiting. Would someone come along, would something happen, to create an opportunity for her book? Nothing happened, no one came.

10

One day when Aurore was lying in bed beside her baby she heard Casimir making indecent overtures to the chambermaid in the next room. The young mother felt heartsick with disgust. The maid Pepita evidently did not react as did Aurore to these proposals, since Casimir had an affair with her which caused a village scandal. He had already had a notorious affair with a preceding maid named Claire, who sued him for the support of an illegitimate child.

Madame Dudevant, who had been so sensitive to the rights of a husband, was beginning to wonder what were the rights of a wife. Patience and forgiveness seemed the chief of them. She had forgiven the affair at Bordeaux, but felt that there were limits to forgiveness. Two months after the birth of Solange she wrote to a close friend that all intimacy between herself and her husband had ceased.

"Your honor," she had said to Casimir at Guillery, "is dearer to me than my life." For this honor of a husband she had sacrificed an ideal love. What of the honor of a wife? Did it not deserve protection? Apparently not. Her friends and neighbors, even the servants, knew how she had been deceived, but her humiliation excited no sympathy. These amiable weaknesses of Casimir's were regarded by the friends of the Dudevants with good-natured amusement. Casimir's scandals were the subject of gay jokes. No one was horrified by his looseness or his drunkenness, because such relaxations were considered the masculine pleasures of country life.

Often Jules Boucoiran was astonished at Madame Dudevant's "elasticity and force of character, which enabled her to rebound after the most violent scenes with her husband and laugh the next day as though nothing had happened." It seemed to him that "under the weight of her unhappiness her head was unbowed." In the autumn of 1830 this unbowed head, however, was stricken with cerebral congestion, and for forty-eight hours Aurore Dudevant lay unconscious.

During the period of convalescence she went to her husband's desk one day to look for something. As she opened the drawer, a bulky package caught her eye. It was addressed, "To my wife." She picked up the package and read, "To be opened after my death." Was it his will? Was it a letter? Would it tell her the things he would never say or explain? Under his meanness and drunkenness and infidelity, did Casimir reproach himself for his disloyalty? Would he at last speak from his soul?

She needed to know, but had she any right to open the letter? Right—what were rights in comparison with this compelling need to know? Her life depended on knowing. The inscription said, "After my death." Her own inner urge said: "Why not suppose him dead? Then I can open it now." So she supposed him dead; she supposed it so thoroughly that it seemed as though the funeral were over. She opened the letter.

It contained nothing but maledictions. She read on; nothing but accusations against herself. And curses. He cursed her for perversity, stupidity, coldness. He covered her with contumely. She was stunned.

He hated her; she knew now. There was no more need of patience and forgiveness. She was free. The question was settled as though by a court decision, as though a judge had announced, "Let the prisoner go free."

Free to leave him? No, she would never be free. Her life was bound to her children, and they were his to control. She could not, would not, leave her children. But the voice insisted, "Let the prisoner go free."

It was impossible. The law made no provision for divorce and the church forbade it. To defy church and state requires money. She had none, not so much as one sou. These facts beat like hammers on her brain, but throbbing in her head was another fact, a certainty. She knew she would leave him. The revelation gave her strength.

She could not wait to sleep on her resolution. That evening she sought him out.

Madame Dudevant's little figure seemed almost tall as she confronted her husband. The law was behind him, the church upheld him, public opinion was on his side. But she had lost her fear of him; he was not her master. For nine long years she had belonged to Casimir, now suddenly she belonged to herself. Her inner revolt was surging to her lips.

Her eyes were luminous. As they tried to look into his, she found no light or depth behind the glazed surface of Casimir's blue gaze. She noticed with surprise that his eyes were porcelain; he seemed to her a big doll stuffed with sawdust. And dolls stuffed with sawdust should be thrown away. She discarded him with the fewest possible words.

"I am going to Paris, but I cannot leave my children. I shall go back and forth, here half the year, in Paris half the year. As soon as possible I shall take Solange with me. I must have my allowance."

Casimir was staggered by this sudden announcement. He argued and scolded but she remained unmoved. He begged and entreated, she did not yield. He wept, but since he no longer gave an illusion of reality she watched him without concern, waiting for his acceptance of her plan.

Where was her feminine softness now? Where were her pity and mercy? She was as hard as a man, as unyielding as a master. Casimir summoned all his strength in opposition to her wishes, there was nothing left between them but the battle of two wills. He tried bullying. It had always worked before, but now her will was more powerful than his. As he looked at her set face and blazing eyes, he who had always had his way with her could no longer dominate. He found her proposal atrocious, but he was obliged to give or pretend to give a grudging consent.

He expected her to change her mind. During the next few days he got their friends to plead with her. Hippolyte took his side, as did Dutheil. The only person who sided with Aurore was Emily, Hippolyte's invalid wife. Emily saw reason where the others saw nothing but madness. Upheld by the invalid against their little world, Madame Dudevant stood firm. She was relying on Jules Boucoiran, who was away at the time, to take her place with the children. She wrote to him and explained the situation:

"Up to the present time he has treated me as though I were odious to him. Now that I am sure of it I am going away. To-day he weeps for me; so much the worse for him. I shall show him that I will not be supported like a burden, but sought out and asked for like a free companion, who will not live beside him unless he is worthy. Please do not think me impertinent, remember how I have been humiliated. It has lasted eight years."

Jules responded like the true friend he was, and pledged himself to guard and teach the children. If they were ill, if for any reason she were needed, he would summon her from Paris. The diligence service was remarkably quick. She could get back to Nohant in a day and a night.

It seemed to Aurore entirely natural to leave this young man as a mother to her children. He had lived in the family for two years, and she knew no woman whom she could trust as she trusted Jules. The children's welfare being settled, she made her preparations for departure, and on January 4th, 1831, just one month after her discovery of the momentous letter, Aurore Dudevant deserted the man who was regarded as a kind husband, and fled from what everyone but Hippolyte's wife considered a comfortable home.

II

In France in the year 1831 there was no divorce, there was only Christian fortitude. There were no girl bachelors, there were only old maids. The people of Madame Dudevant's world saw no reason why any wife should ever leave any husband. Desertion on the part of a woman was without precedent. It defied the canons of good taste.

On her journey to Paris Aurore Dudevant faced the awful fact that she intended to violate public opinion. She knew that as soon as her new way of life was established, her aristocratic friends, even her dear Aimée and Jane, would have nothing more to do with her. She realized that her beloved nuns would not approve of her life. It was not too late to change her mind, she could still return home. She considered her plan of independence, saw how shocking it was, and decided to carry it through. When she reached this decision she was no longer merely Madame Dudevant. She began to be herself.

It seemed to her that she could now pick up her life from the place where it had been broken off by marriage. She could return to the person she had been at seventeen.

There were in Paris three young men who had come from Aurore's own province of Berry—Berrichons, she called them. They were Jules Sandeau, Félix Pyat, and Alphonse Fleury. Jules and Félix met the diligence on her arrival and escorted her to Hippolyte's apartment at 15 rue de Seine, where she took up her temporary residence.

During the first few weeks at Paris she was too busy and excited to think about the future. She heard music. She devoured books at the National Library, and spent long hours at the Louvre standing in front of Titian, Tintoretto, Rubens, drinking in the color with intoxication. To her Berrichon friends who watched her enjoy her first taste of liberty she seemed drunk with enthusiasm.

The country girl in Paris was timid and apologetic about herself and greatly impressed by others, especially by others who did things, who painted pictures, made music, acted, or wrote plays. Each person who did any one of these things became to her a bright star. From each celebrity she expected a revelation. Not that she was able to meet celebrities as yet. She was nothing, she was nobody. A woman nine years married is old to make a beginning. How do people begin? How do they learn? How do they make a place?

Her painting seemed more immediately promising than her writing. She made a small portrait of her janitor and hung it in the café which occupied the ground floor of her building. This was her advertisement as an artist. She had a knack of catching a likeness. Everybody recognized the janitor, but nobody ordered a portrait.

Painting did not seem likely to prove lucrative. Summoning her courage she decided to apply for work on a newspaper. A letter had been given her to M. de Kératry, the book reviewer of the *Figaro*. She called, found him at home and confided to him her ambition. M. Kératry was a middle-aged gentleman with a pretty, young wife. He gave it as his opinion that women should be protected and that no woman could or should write.

"In that case," said Madame Dudevant, rising, "we have nothing to talk about."

Following her to the door he uttered this parting advice: "Don't create literature, create children."

"Apply the preaching to yourself if you like it so well," smiled Aurore as she closed the door.

Another more fortunate visit was made to the editor of the *Figaro*, Henri de Latouche. He also was a Berrichon. Perhaps it was because he wanted to help a young compatriot that he took an interest in Aurore. Then, too, he was amused at Kératry's opinion of women, and it pleased him to prove himself more broad-minded. It was almost impossible to find a place for a female in journalism, but Latouche had moral courage and liked to attempt the impossible, so he put Aurore on his staff, hoping to teach her to be useful. Aurore began by feeling prejudiced against him. He was brusque and rude, and his criticisms were never tempered by tactfulness. But after a time his fundamental kindness won her affection.

At last she had found a critic for her beloved *Aimée*. Aurore showed Latouche the novel. He read it and laughed. He told her it was all very charming but lacked common sense. It was too virtuous. No people in the world ever did such moral things in such a moral way. The public would never stand for such heaped-up goodness. He advised her to do it all over again from the very beginning.

In the meanwhile he set her to writing articles for the *Figaro*. Each morning he gave her a subject, told her to do her best and to bring him back the result. And each evening the result was a failure. Aurore could not stick to the subject. Her imagination went out on either side of it, soared above it, circled around it. She covered many sheets of paper and then threw them into the fire. Latouche had promised to pay her seven francs a column for all of her writing that he could use. At the end of a month she had earned fifteen francs.

12

She soon tired of the Louvre and the library as her only means of recreation. She wanted to meet the young literary group. That meant entering Bohemia. But Bohemia was limited to men, and to women of no reputation. Ladies in those days were not literary, and they could not afford to be seen in the Latin Quarter. Aurore hesitated to hurt the feelings of her family and friends by defying this convention. There was the haunting fear of gossip and the daily danger of meeting somebody from home.

Before leaving Nohant Aurore had discussed this difficulty with her friend Jules Boucoiran. He reminded her of the boy's clothes she used to wear as a young girl when riding or tramping with Deschartres.

"Why not dress as a student of the Latin Quarter?" he had suggested. "Then you will pass unnoticed."

Aurore had decided to think it over. And now as she tramped the streets of Paris she did think it over, from more angles than one. Women's skirts of the period were clumsy and voluminous, puffed out with crinoline until they looked like huge balloons. They swept the floor and hampered all free movement. They were appropriate only for those who possessed a carriage or who remained indoors. The rainy weather of Paris was destructive to her clothes. Day after day she came home drenched, dragging her heavy skirts soiled from the muddy streets. Her one good gown was in constant need of repair. Her thin shoes were broken, and the flapping soles tripped her feet. Shoes, clothes and little velvet hats were all going to ruin with frightful rapidity, and she had no money with which to buy anything new.

The three Berrichons were kind and neighborly. From time to time they showed her about Paris and taught her how to economize. She envied these young friends of hers. Their clothes cost so little. She envied especially their stout, comfortable boots. How easily they walked! And their coats, those long frock coats that reached to the knees, seemed to her appropriate for women, especially for a woman like herself, with a thin, undeveloped figure. People were always telling her that she looked like a boy in girl's clothes.

It really seemed ridiculous *not* to dress like Jules and Félix and Alphonse. All the masculine customs of dress made it easy for a woman to pass as a man. The literary youth of the day were wearing long hair, often to the shoulders. Effeminate young poets and writers were the vogue. What could be simpler than to wear the costume of the Latin Quarter? It would save the feelings of the family, it would save her strength, and it would save hundreds of francs.

The expense of being a woman in Paris was not merely a matter of clothes. Aurore could not afford to live in the style which her station demanded. At theatres and concerts the Baroness Dudevant should occupy a box or an orchestra seat. But no one knows

or notices a student. He may perch in the gallery or sit in the pit
—and save money.

As a result of these considerations Aurore ended by accepting
Boucoiran's advice. Privileged by her boy's attire, she occupied
cheap seats where Madame Dudevant could not properly be
seated. She ran about to republican clubs and students' meetings
where Madame Dudevant could not prudently be seen. She loafed
in cafés along the Boulevard Saint-Michel, where there was much
talk of books and art. She wandered about at night without attracting attention. By the simple expedient of a change of costume she was free, as no other woman in Paris or in all of France
was free.

But how was this freedom to be maintained? Even Bohemia
costs money. The frugal meals along the Boulevard, combined
with her trifling expenses, demanded more than her allowance,
and the allowance did not always arrive. Aurore was obliged to
earn money or go back home—she could take her choice. She
decided against going home. But as her work on the *Figaro* did not
improve, the situation grew daily more desperate.

13

Latouche was not satisfied with his lady editor. He began to regret his bold experiment of trying to train a female to work like
a man. He could not teach Aurore to be useful, because her imagination was beyond control. Seeing that she romanced all over
his articles, he suggested that after all she had better stick to
fiction.

Jules Sandeau also had been added to the staff of the *Figaro*.
The two literary apprentices had already begun to work together.
Aurore had persuaded Jules to help her write an article for the
Revue de Paris. She needed his help for two reasons. She felt she
could not write in "the sublime style of the *Revue*," and, more
important still, she was obliged to borrow a man's signature, since
the editor of the *Revue* detested women and refused to consider

their work. The would-be authors, having dashed off an article together, now decided to continue their collaboration with a more
ambitious attempt. They would follow Latouche's advice and try
a novel.

Jules was twenty years old, and looked up to Aurore's maturity.
Aurore felt great respect for Jules's manhood. Each of these com-
panions in inexperience needed the other to lean on, and each
needed money. They went to work in feverish haste.

Aurore conceived the idea of two contrasting heroines, an
actress and a nun. She called them Rose and Blanche, and put
them into a convent so that she could use the material of her own
experience. The two heroines talked in an exalted manner on religion and the consecrated life.

Jules, who thought all this a bit soft and school-girly, introduced a libertine hero named Horace. In an effort to offset the
convent atmosphere he wrote of orgies, dives and the lower world,
hoping, no doubt, that Horace's wickedness would help to sell
the book.

When Aurore showed Jules a deeply religious chapter, he would
want to discard it because it was so lofty. And when Jules showed
Aurore a scene of debauchery, Aurore would vote against it because it was so low. But both collaborators were in a hurry. The
pressure of their debts prevented argument. Wickedness and religion were run together and the book was finished in six weeks.

At the Café Pinson they had met a publisher. He was persuaded
to read the manuscript, which he accepted. He thought it might
please the people at each extreme. M. Dupuy was so uncritical
that he even accepted Aurore's title, *Rose et Blanche*.

Then arose the question of the signature. How could the two
young authors conceal their identity? Aurore realized that her
name signed to a book would mean certain scandal. Her mother-
in-law had already said to her, "I hope you will never put the
name I bear on the cover of a *printed* book." Aurore had answered

meekly, "No, Madame, certainly not." And she intended to keep her word.

Young Sandeau feared to displease his father by his scenes of debauchery. They took their problem to Latouche.

"Cut Sandeau in two," he suggested, "and drop the last half."

This seemed a clever way for the budding authors to escape detection. The book was signed Jules Sand.

Rose et Blanche was a second-rate novel, but it brought the authors what was to them a small fortune, 200 francs apiece (forty dollars).

Aurore had taken a tiny apartment at No. 5 Place Saint-Michel. Up five flights, it contained three rooms, and cost 600 francs a year. She wanted to make a home so that she could have Solange with her. From time to time she bought a cheap table, a second-hand chair, and a few dishes, until the place became habitable.

For the furniture and her frock coat she had gone into debt to the extent of 500 francs. This debt weighed on her mind and kept her awake nights. She would have to write another novel. But she needed encouragement. She longed above everything for someone who believed in her. Had she any talent? Or was she stupid and commonplace? Under the influence of Latouche she had lost faith in herself.

As a friend Latouche was generous and helpful, but as a literary critic he had been crushing. He was always telling her what not to do. He reproved Aurore for her dreamy detachment from life, and accused her of living within herself.

"You don't know the world nor the people in it," he would exclaim, "you haven't lived. You have no experience. You must wait a long time before you can write. Your mind is empty."

Aurore agreed with him. She decided that she could not write.

14

With the coming of spring, April, 1831, she went back to Nohant, taking up her life where it had been broken off in January. But now there was a difference in her position at the château. She had lost her place as mistress of the house. Even the servants regarded her as an outsider, and Casimir treated her as a visitor. She spent the days as well as the evenings in the little cell-like room beside the children. This was neutral ground reserved for her. The rest of the home belonged to her husband; she had forfeited all claims by going away. She made an effort to adjust herself to the new ways of the household. But as the days went on and she continued to feel herself a stranger, she withdrew from the life around her and sank back into the world of fantasy where she felt at home.

Living in dreams and reveries, she conceived the character of a poetic Creole whom she christened Indiana. The character became more real to her than herself, more real than any of the people around her. When Aurore went into the garden she saw Indiana walking among the trees. She seemed to read her thoughts and fathom her unhappiness. When Aurore sat alone in the evening she saw Indiana in a corner of the room and they communed together.

Aurore had no intention of describing Indiana as herself. They were indeed very different, because the Creole was surpassingly lovely and Aurore was not beautiful. Besides, Indiana was trusting and inexperienced, whereas Madame Dudevant had become quite worldly-wise. No, Indiana was merely another woman whose life seemed enacted before Aurore's eyes. The other woman suffered, and Aurore ached with sympathy. It soon became evident that the innocent, trusting creature was married to a husband who was far too old for her and who was violent and mean. Certainly the husband was not Casimir, because Casimir was comparatively young.

What would be the fate of the beautiful Creole? What would life do to this wistful soul?

Aurore drew toward her paper and pencil. Where could she sit and write? There was a little cupboard in her room. It had a folding door that let down to form a table. She drew her chair in front of it, placed her paper on the improvised desk, and began to write.

She began without any definite aim or hope, without any plan. She had no theory of the novel, and no intention of criticizing laws, institutions, or society. Shutting the door of her memory on all that had been taught her, she had a sense of yielding herself to an outward power, that took possession of herself and of her characters and did with them as it pleased. If she thought out a scene, the characters would behave unexpectedly and change everything. Aurore was as interested in each day's happenings as a reader who begins the next chapter of a new novel.

Who was writing the novel? It was not herself. She had written *Aimée,* she had written her share of *Rose et Blanche.* But this was different. Whoever had created her several-years-old serial dream, whoever had told her the childhood tale between four chairs, was telling her the story of Indiana.

The author was Corambé. It seemed to her that Corambé seized her as easily as she picked up a pen. He used her as his pen. She could feel him and yield to him until they two became one spirit. Then, without wholly knowing him, she waited and listened while he spoke to her, and wrote what he spoke.

While Corambé possessed her she was almost unaware of the life about her. Casimir, the servants, the friends who called, were shadows whose voices came to her faintly as from a great distance. When Casimir scolded it sounded rather soothing, like the patter of rain on a distant roof. No one hurt her, nothing annoyed her, because she was out of reach, like an indrawn turtle who scarcely knows whether or not someone is touching its shell.

For three months while she listened to Corambé she went about her own existence like a sleepwalker. Finally the fate of Indiana was determined, Corambé disappeared, Aurore stopped writing, and behold, the book was finished. She awoke from her obsession and the life about her became distinct.

15

When she returned to Paris she carried with her the precious manuscript. She intended to have Jules edit it, but Jules was lazy and delayed helping her. Then she forgot the story. She could hardly realize she had written it. She could remember the circumstances under which it was written, but not what the book contained.

If her Paris experience had altered her attitude toward Nohant, how much more had her stay at Nohant changed her point of view toward Paris! She was tired now of the carefree life of a student and more than ever bent on serious work. It was too late to go back and be a wife again. She was going forward into a life of her own.

She had made up her mind about the new world she wished to enter. It was man's world. How could a woman get into that wide, free, wonderful world of men? It was merely a matter of independence; the key to man's world was self-support; if you could pay your way you could enter. She would pay and she would enter. She would take what she wanted of their freedom, she did not want it all. If she assumed masculine responsibilities they would admit her to their privileges and immunities, and judge her as they judged themselves. She was sure they would, because that was fair and logical, and it was only women who were illogical and unfair.

It was this delicious mixture of knowledge and ignorance that impressed itself upon her young companion, Jules Sandeau. In his novel, *Marianna*, of which the heroine is Aurore, he says of her:

"She had been brought up in the country and now for the first time left it, and her manners showed a strange combination of boldness and timidity. Her proud chastity and her instinctively aristocratic air mingled the suggestions of a virgin and a duchess, contrasting strangely with her disdain for the proprieties and her ignorance of the world. Life—palpitating life—seemed to move among the curls of her beautiful black hair, and there burnt as it were a hidden fire beneath her delicate and transparent skin. The expression of her eyes spoke of terrible interior struggles, ceaseless but unconfessed."

Jules Sandeau had become acquainted with Aurore in the country at La Châtre, where he had been somewhat in awe of her, but when they became fellow workers in Bohemia and fraternized on terms of equality he lost his fear and began to make love to her. She was not sure whether she loved him or not. It took her several months to make up her mind.

One day suddenly she heard herself telling Jules that she loved him. She said naïvely that he knew of her love, therefore, as soon as she did. It seemed to her right and beautiful to love Jules.

Her ideas were free enough now to permit a lover. Why not, indeed? Was she not in everything but appearance a divorced woman? Was not Jules in everything but appearance her real husband? She was through with appearances. Their union was to be dignified by permanence. It was to continue as long as they lived. Jules understood that they were as good as married. She asked so little of him—just two things, love and faithfulness. These he promised and gave, and they were happy.

There was no concealment about it. A room in her apartment belonged to Jules, and she received him openly and with the knowledge of their half dozen friends. Irregular unions were usual in the Latin Quarter, and nobody noticed or cared.

Her letters to Emile Régnault, Jules's intimate friend, were full of dreams and plans of work and travel. She had one complaint against Jules—he was frightfully lazy. Otherwise he seemed to her ideal. In a letter to Régnault she wrote:

"To live! How sweet it is and how good, in spite of annoyances, husbands, boredom, debts, relatives, scandal-mongers, suffering and irritation! To live! It is intoxicating! To love and to be loved! It is happiness! It is heaven!"

16

In December, 1831, about a year after her first departure from Nohant, *Rose et Blanche* was given to the public. It was not noticed by the critics, but it sold fairly well; so well, indeed, that the publisher came demanding another novel by Jules Sand. The collaborators had no other novel. But the would-be author, Aurore Dudevant, had one ready, entitled *Indiana*. Would M. Dupuy accept it?

He would and did. He had been impressed by the fact that the best passages of the Jules Sand story had been written by Aurore. He was willing to risk her first novel, but he wanted to use the same signature, as it might help to sell the book. Aurore was willing to use it and give Jules half the credit, but Jules objected to the subterfuge. Would M. Dupuy permit Madame Dudevant to choose another signature? No, M. Dupuy for once was obstinate. He insisted on the pseudonym Jules Sand.

Once more the two authors took their problem to their faithful councillor Latouche. He settled the question with Solomon-like wisdom. Each collaborator deserved one-half of their common property. The Jules half was obviously Sandeau's own, therefore the Sand half must by rights belong to Aurore. Jules Sandeau could continue to use his own signature, and Aurore could select a first name to go with Sand. Any name would do, William, Jack, George. Aurore decided on George.

The new novel was signed George Sand.

Aurore was indifferent to her pen-name because she had no idea of becoming famous. She had written *Indiana* with an emotion that was sometimes ecstasy and sometimes pain, but she did not divine that the story was remarkable. She wrote to Boucoiran that her pen-name would not be discovered by the people at home because her fame would never travel as far as La Châtre.

Having sold *Indiana*, she returned to Nohant in January, and worked with increased self-confidence on a second novel, en-

titled *Valentine*. When she had finished *Valentine* she felt herself in a fair way to earn more money. That meant she could
afford to keep her child.

April, 1832, was a triumphant month for Aurore Dudevant.
When she returned to Paris she brought Solange back with her,
and soon after her arrival *Indiana* was given to the public.

It was too late now for Aurore Dudevant to choose a better
pseudonym. George Sand was an immediate celebrity. "His" book
was a sensational success. On the evening of the day on which it
appeared people talked of it with palpitating interest. Indiana
was a new type of heroine, a type that was to be imitated for
twenty years. She was the misunderstood woman, *la femme in-
comprise*.

"If you had seen her," Aurore had written, "so pale, so sad,
so fragile, beside her aged husband, sitting elbow on knee, half
hidden under the mantel of the vast fireplace, you would have
pitied her."

And the readers did pity her! They pitied her all over France,
in Germany, in Russia, wherever French was read. They pitied her
so hard that they made the author famous.

The fury of enthusiasm began in Paris. In the salons of the
aristocracy, at Madame Récamier's, in the foyer of the Comédie
Française, at the St. Simon Club, and in the offices and stores,
everyone was discussing *Indiana*. The book was not only read, it
was devoured.

Novels of adventure were the fashion of the day. Here was
a novel of the heart, written with an intensity of conviction that
gripped and held the most sceptical. People began to question,
"Who is this George Sand?" And no one was able to answer.
After a time rumors began to circulate. George Sand was said to
be a woman, a young woman, attractive but totally unknown.
After this first rumor, nothing—no further information to be
procured. A woman, it is true, but a woman of mystery, who

refused to be interviewed or advertised. She hides behind the name George Sand.

Her way of hiding was to remain in plain sight. In the after-noon she was in the Luxembourg Gardens with Solange. Towards evening she returned to Place Saint-Michel. She carried the child up five flights of stairs, prepared their simple meal and put So-lange to bed. Then she rested in the little balcony looking out on the Seine and Nôtre Dame.

As she sat in her balcony alone and dreaming, all literary Paris, gathered about their dinner tables, were discussing her. There were critics who insisted that George Sand was a man. There were others who concluded that, if a woman, she had a bold masculine personality. A few had heard shocking accusations. She had left her husband. She was a loose woman. Some claimed she was a beauty who dazzled and seduced.

They might all have looked in upon her in her hiding-place. They would not have recognized their celebrity, she was so unlike the pictures they had made.

The boy's costume had long since been laid aside. She wore a plain loose gown of nondescript appearance. Her brown hair fell in curls to her shoulders. Her elfin height, her slenderness, her pallor, gave her a seeming frailness that was appealingly feminine. There was nothing unusual about her face except its sadness, nothing noticeable about her features except the great dark eyes; "eyes that devoured the face,"—"once they rested on you they took possession of you,"—"the whole face is focused in the eyes," said her friends.

While the outside world discussed her she was being obsessed by a new set of characters, dreaming them into a new dream, weaving her dream into words. She had forgotten *Indiana*. If anyone had asked her opinion of the book she would have been obliged to reread it in order to have something to say. She had forgotten *Valentine*. She was absorbed now in a short story. It ought to take a month of work. She would do it in a week.

Every evening after Solange had been put to bed she lighted her lamp and covered page after page. When the oil was used and the lamp went out, she brought candles and went on writing until the daylight came through her window. Then, exhausted, she fell asleep.

The next morning she would awake heavy-eyed and silent. She always felt apologetic about her silence. She could not pretend to a keen wit or ready repartee. Her friends often spoke with surprise of the clever dialogues in her books, contrasting so strongly with her own lack of conversation, though they forgave her silence because she was such a good listener. It was a relief, after all, to find an author so detached from self. She never wanted them to listen to the last chapter. She never asked them to discuss her characters. She didn't solicit their advice on the best title or the best ending. "George," they said laughingly, "is the only man of letters who never talks about his work."

She had sold *Valentine*, but she had not spoken to anyone about this second book. No wonder, then, that friends as well as the public were amazed when in July, three months after *Indiana*, *Valentine* appeared.

Sainte-Beuve tells us that he opened *Valentine* with fear and foreboding. He had felt about *Indiana* that it was partly personal experience, and that probably the talent of the author, like that of so many women, was limited by the one situation she had actually lived. He believed that everyone who has lived a life of emotion and who dares write simply what he has lived is capable of one novel, but between that achievement and the creative gift there is a great distance. From the first pages of *Valentine* his foreboding gave way before the charm of the book. He lived and moved in the story, he was carried along by the current of events. "The author," he concluded, "is not merely endowed with a soul which has suffered. She has the key to human hearts. She has the creative gift. The name of George Sand conceals one of the masters, to whom the whole world is open."

Reading these words of praise, Aurore was elated and frightened. She had written two books, and the prince of critics had placed her name among the famous. This meant to her that by her work she could go on earning her freedom.

Would she be able to go on? She was almost rich. For *Valentine* she had received four times as much as for *Indiana*. She wanted to move into a better apartment. She wanted a governess for Solange, a servant for herself. She would educate the children. She would pay her husband's debts. Perhaps, who knows, some day she would be able to afford a home of her own for her children.

All these things were possible if she could continue to work as she had been working. But she was always upset emotionally about something or someone. Last winter it had been separation from her daughter, and now it was the fate of her son.

The eight-year-old Maurice had been placed by his father in a boys' military school at Paris. Maurice hated the school. Aurore wanted him with her, but Casimir insisted on keeping the sensitive, delicate child in a school where he suffered. There were scenes, the child crying to be taken away. Aurore had wept until her eyes were bloodshot.

Every family tie tortured her, yet she could not break these ties. Though a new personality had begun outside of herself, though a name had been projected and thrown out to the public, she was not the virile, successful author. She was still the mother, still the half-tied, half-free wife.

To George Sand the year 1832 was a year of triumph, but to Aurore Dudevant it was the saddest year of her life. She was fighting against odds to keep her freedom.

Must she always dispute with Casimir the control of the children? Was she to spend her entire existence traveling back and forth between Nohant and Paris, living one half the year with the man she no longer cared for, and one half the year with the man she loved? If only the law would permit her to keep the children, divorce Casimir, and marry Jules! The long absences twice a year were weakening the bond between herself and her lover.

17

Jules Sandeau as a pseudo-husband was not a great success. He had not as yet been sufficiently energetic to prove his earning capacity, whereas Aurore was rich enough to give her poor boy financial assistance. In one of her letters to Emile Régnault from Nohant she expresses regret because that month she had a big debt to pay and had not been able to send Jules any money. She fears he cannot afford to buy proper food.

In November Aurore moved to a larger apartment at 19 quai Malaquais. At last she had a servant to cook the meals and help take care of Solange. During the time that Solange was with her she wrote more of Solange and less of Jules in her letters to Emile Régnault. Nevertheless she was full of solicitude for her careless lover. A room was reserved for him in the new apartment.

Why did the gifted and fascinating Madame Dudevant give her heart to young Sandeau? He was to become a distinguished author, and no doubt he had budding possibilities. But during the period of her infatuation he was a rather crude youth, far from interesting and not even handsome.

There was nothing remarkable about Jules that made Aurore fall in love with him. But there was something remarkable about Aurore that made her fall in love. She was endowed with a thousandfold power of imagination. When she found an object on which to center and expend emotion, her powerful imagination began to function and that object was glorified. He became the golden lover of her dreams and she was hypnotized by the mirage she had made.

A hypnotic subject when brought to his senses by a clap of the hands will exclaim, "Where am I? Who are you? What have I said or done?" So Aurore, if awakened from her dream with a shock, looked at the abject creature who was no longer golden, no longer glorified by illusion, and said to him, "Who are you? I do not know you."

Poor little Jules, unconscious that he had mated with a magnificent imagination, took advantage of his sweetheart's absence to establish the laundress in her place. George came back from Nohant unexpectedly and found them together. The shock awakened her. Jules ceased to be her golden lover: she was dazed to find in his place a stranger. She wrote of her suffering to Emile Régnault, "I have been too deeply wounded by Jules's conduct to feel for him anything more than an affectionate compassion."

She suffered, but with her usual generosity she paid Jules's rent to the end of the year, and since they had talked of a trip to Italy and she did not want the boy to be disappointed, she paid his expenses for the trip they were to have taken together.

18

While Jules was enjoying sunny Italy, George, in rainy Paris, tried to rearrange her life. But she could not adjust herself to work or play or loneliness. In losing her illusion she had lost her mental poise.

In the crisis of her childish life, when her passionate love for Sophie had been ruthlessly destroyed, Aurore had reverted to the primitive. The woman of twenty-nine, with the identical nerves, temperament and inheritance of the child of thirteen, reacted to shock in the same way. She swung around the same circle of emotion: wildness, defiance, melancholy, despair.

But now there was no one to shut her in a convent and subject her to the influence of nuns. On the contrary, she was living in the midst of Romanticists and the core of their philosophy was the conviction that the artist is a law unto himself. George had heard this philosophy for two years. True, it was preached by men, for men, and they never intended it for women. The trouble with George was that she listened to men and then applied their teaching to herself. Had not Sophie, Madame Dupin and Deschartes always treated her as though she were Maurice? How often had she said to herself and others, "I have never been a young lady."

After this experience of man's infidelity, George not only suffered intensely, she was mentally confused. She had felt so safe in her conviction that a monogamous permanent free union was ideal. It had looked simple and logical when she had reasoned about it. Living with a husband whom she did not love was evidently immoral, therefore living with the man she did love seemed obviously moral. Yet her ideal love affair had ended as her marriage had done and left her wondering, "Is man's love always casual?"

She was seeking an ideal union. What mistake had she made? In thinking it over it seemed to her that if she had taken her love affair lightly, as men do, she could have recovered easily, as they do. But she had taken it seriously, as a marriage, and she suffered accordingly.

It was the woman in her that made her suffer, she reasoned. She had loved like a woman and a wife. What was the use of trying to live as men lived if she could not love as men love? She had not proved herself a citizen of the man's world which she had tried to enter, nor could she go back into the woman's world she had left behind. She stood between the two, alone. She did not belong anywhere. There was no one of her kind, no group with which she could identify herself. She had broken with convention and propriety and had put in their place her own innate sense of right and her self-respect. Was this enough? Was she seeing straight? She needed a friend like herself, one who faced the same problems—a woman. How could she find the sort of woman she was seeking? The women of Bohemia were light and loose, she disapproved of them. Her former women friends disapproved of her. Both groups of women lived in dependence and her integrity demanded independence.

For friends she was limited to men. They saved her from solitude, but they did not penetrate to her identity or understand her problems. The right to independence was granted them.

She had to prove hers and earn it by work. They could not see, not one of them ever saw, that her work was the price of her freedom.

Decidedly she needed a friend of her own sex. She knew a woman who was more like herself than others, one who had a career in the only profession open to women, that of the theatre. Marie Dorval was emancipated from prejudice. Aurore knew her slightly, for she had once, in a moment's enthusiasm over the great actress's art, written Dorval an admiring letter, and Dorval had answered impulsively by coming to call. This responsiveness had warmed Aurore's heart so that now in loneliness she remembered Dorval and turned to her for companionship and counsel. She wanted to listen to another free woman's philosophy of life.

Marie Dorval was delighted to befriend the fascinating and mysterious Madame Dudevant. She poured out her confidences and willingly gave advice. She was positive and convincing. Aurore was tending to believe that friendship with men gave more happiness than love, but Dorval contended that the cure for love was more love. "If your heart is broken, love again, recklessly," was her advice. She was sincere, charming, magnetic. She believed in yielding to every emotion without thought of consequences. Aurore said of her, "I had beside me a woman who knew no restraint and she seemed to me sublime. I seemed to myself hideous in my egotism and my isolation."

While under the influence of this friendship Aurore met a man for whom she felt great admiration. He was handsome, distinguished, and apparently very wise. In Prosper Mérimée it seemed that she had found the masculine intelligence suited to her own. His calm philosophy impressed her. She thought he knew the secret of happiness and believed he would teach it to her. She was fascinated, her imagination began to function, and Mérimée was glorified.

She lent herself to the new attraction in reckless haste. But instead of trying to understand and help her he ridiculed her ideals and laughed at her seriousness. His realism was materialism. His sympathy was sarcasm. A week of misery cured her. She left him in disgust.

Five months after the affair was over she tried to understand what she had done. Writing to a friend, she said:

"You have not asked my confidence, and in telling you this I am not being confidential, because I do not ask discretion. I would be ready to tell and publish all the facts of my life if I thought they would be helpful to anyone else. . . . In one of my moods of restlessness and despair I met a man who was free from all doubts and questionings. The force of his character completely fascinated me. I believed he had suffered as I had suffered and that he had mastered his sensibilities. Instead of an affection that could pity me and relieve my suffering I found only a bitter, mocking frivolity.—But why should I be ashamed of being ridiculous if I have not been guilty?

"After having believed that years of intimacy were required in order to unite my life with another's, I jumped to the conclusion that a fascination which had lasted only a few days could determine the course of my life. And in the end I did at the age of thirty what a girl of fifteen would have known better than to do. The experiment failed completely."

She did not know why she had failed. But she had learned from failure what she needed to know—love was not for her, she could not take it lightly.

And that incapacity to take love lightly was exactly the difference between herself and her men friends, the difference, too, between herself and her friend Marie Dorval.

There was, to Aurore's way of thinking, no moral question involved in her experience with Mérimée. She merely reproached herself for lack of intelligence. She had been stupid, she had made a mistake.

But her way of feeling was in conflict with her thought. The mistake she had made so violated her nature that for her it changed the face of the universe.

A third novel was slowly taking shape. In her writing she analyzed herself. Always she had needed an object of worship. When she had dreamed of Corambé she had felt her loneliness consoled. Her first love also, it seemed to her as she re-lived it, had been a dream love. Aurélian, like Corambé, had been a sort of god to her. The mere fact of his existence in another city had saved her from mortal loneliness.

But Jules and Mérimée had been real. And they had plunged her into despair. Dream love had satisfied her better than reality. What was she? Why was she completed so easily through imagination? She could identify herself with everything in nature. She could become one with the stone she touched, the flower she gazed upon, the river she bathed in, the cloud whose flight she followed through the sky. In moods of communion she felt herself one with God. Man alone, actual man, as she knew man, had failed to meet her spirit. He had been incapable of or indifferent to a need of completion, a merging of two beings into one.

Then why could she not resign herself to loneliness? Why could she not accept a scheme of life that left man outside of her unrealizable longing? Alas, she was only half alive unless she was in love. There was something lacking in her. Was it self-sufficiency? Wholeness? She was the half of someone who eluded her. She needed her male, her mate, her answer. She was woman, made for man.

And now, at less than thirty, she must renounce love, she must face growing old alone, she must continue to drag on half alive until she died. Her search for love, she told herself, was over. She would accept friendship, nothing but friendship, from this time forth.

As she brooded, remembered, analyzed, her soul went into her book. It was the expression of her own inner life. She called it *Lélia.*

"I have offered myself to God in every way," cried Lélia. "Ferociously I have sounded the depths of my own heart. I have snatched that heart from my breast to see what it was made of. I have torn it into a thousand pieces. I have pierced it with a thousand poignards so that I might know it! I have offered the shreds of it to the most high gods, as to the least significant. I have evoked spectres, struggled with demons. I have implored all the saints, all the angels, I have sacrificed to all passions. Truth, truth! Thou dost not reveal thyself. Ten thousand years I have sought thee and found thee not!"

IV

GEORGE AND ALFRED

L ELIA had been begun as a journal, a series of sad and cynical reveries not intended for the public. But the mood of melancholy was sustained from week to month, and the journal grew to book size. Slowly it took on some sort of story form, part fantasy, part allegory. It was anything but a novel. It became a prose poem.

A letter to George Sand from one of her friends expresses the amazement that greeted *Lélia.*

"What the devil is the matter? Why did you write this book? Where did it come from? It is not in the least like you who know how to be gay and appreciate a pun, you who sew so well and make such good jam."

Lélia came from the depths of Aurore Dudevant's despondency. The defeat and disgust of her own soul were repeated and reflected in the world outside her. Wherever she looked she saw suffering. She was oblivious to joy. The misery that Aurore could not, would not, talk about, Lélia wrote. Her lament was the cry of a lost soul.

In the midst of the admiration and criticism produced by *Lélia,* two book critics from two different magazines met and fought a duel to decide the value of the book. It seemed that George Sand could not write without causing commotion.

There was in her a many times multiplied capacity to feel. This capacity, suppressed, denied, and suffering, had turned to cynicism. Failing an object of worship, she had spent her emotion in cursing the world.

"She outdid Goethe. She outdid Byron. To the many masculine voices which had been lifted to blaspheme life," says René

Doumic, "a feminine voice was now added and it dominated them all."

During the time that she was writing this blasphemous book she identified herself with Lélia. Strangely enough, the lover of cynical Lélia was Stenio, a poet. Aurore had never known and had never wanted a poet lover. But Stenio seemed to belong with Lélia. Somewhere out of Aurore's imaginings he came and claimed her.

No two highly endowed human beings, it seemed to Aurore, can ever find happiness together. They try to approach and know and understand each other. But they do not meet each other, they meet whirlpools and frozen barriers and floating ice. They sing across impassable distances that widen between them. They wave and shout, but the two remain separate. They remain alone, Lélia and Stenio, woman and man, you and me, she seemed to be saying, you and me. And who was the you whom she seemed to be calling forth from the unknown? Who was the poet lover she had never wanted and had never known?

There was no one. She lived almost in solitude. Her most devoted friend was uncouth Gustave Planche, literary critic for the *Revue des Deux Mondes*. Planche was a caustic critic with a reputation for rough bitterness, but under the surface manner of this big intimidating man Aurore saw a sensitive little boy, lonely and in need of a home. She took him into her family group, and in gratitude he followed her about like a faithful dog; did her errands, helped look after Solange, took Maurice back and forth from school on his days of vacation, and in general played the part of dependable friend. If he was in love with her he was too timid to tell her so. He seemed content to make a cult of her and defend her against adverse criticism.

Jules Boucoiran, equally devoted and faithful, was also a frequent caller. These two men, with an occasional Berrichon friend, came sometimes to sit in front of her fire, drink her beer, and scold her for working so hard. Outside of this casual group she had no contacts. In the literary world of Paris she had no friends.

In the month of January, 1883, Aurore made the acquaintance of the master critic of the nineteenth century, Sainte-Beuve. He was brought to call by Gustave Planche at her request, as she wished to thank him for his sympathetic criticisms. The acquaintance rapidly developed into friendship. Sainte-Beuve read to her from his novel *Volupté,* and she let her new friend read from her own uncompleted book. Sainte-Beuve was deeply moved by the lyric quality of *Lélia.* In March he wrote Madame Dudevant a eulogistic letter expressing his admiration for her work and the pride he felt in her friendship. He protested against her hermit-like existence. He felt that he had discovered a wonderful personality, and he wanted to bring his friends to her— among others, Alfred de Musset.

The day after this suggestion had been made and accepted Aurore wrote to Sainte-Beuve:

"By the way, on second thought, I don't want you to bring Alfred de Musset to call on me. He is too much the dandy. We wouldn't get along together. I think I felt more curiosity than interest in agreeing to meet him."

There the matter might have rested had it not been for an editor, one of those editors who represent fate. The man was François Buloz, the great Buloz who had lately taken over the *Revue des Deux Mondes.* For two years now he had drawn about him the best writing talent of France, and he was not slow to notice the two dawning stars, Sand and Musset. These two appeared above the horizon at about the same time, so Buloz hitched them to his wagon with business contracts. Alfred was to contribute to the *Revue* all the poetry he felt inspired to write. George Sand, as a person more amenable to business, promised to provide the magazine with thirty-two columns every six weeks at a salary of 4000 francs a year.

In June, 1833, two months after Aurore's sagacious letter refusing to meet Musset, the great Buloz gave a dinner to his con-
tributors. It pleased him to seat the two young authors side by
side. So they found themselves together, the dandy and the blue-
stocking, each prejudiced against the other. Aurore was surprised to find the dandy so unaffected. Alfred was impressed by
the modesty of the blue-stocking. He regarded her with curiosity.
She was singularly unlike his preconceived idea of her. Was it
possible that this girlish creature had written two virile novels?
Would she ever produce another?

Alfred stole a glance at the slim olive-brown woman, the only
woman capable of competing with the Buloz group of distinguished men. He kept saying to himself, "How small she is!"

Quietly, without smiles or animation, she sat beside him. She
did not exert herself to please. He had never seen a woman so
lacking in coquetry. All the mystery of her being was in the great
dark eyes that looked at him candidly, as a man would look at a
man. He noticed her hands. Lovely, lovely hands, small, white,
with pointed fingers, the hands of an artist. They were deeply
satisfying to his sense of beauty.

He lifted his eyes, furitively noticing her attire. Her dress was
unusual, not Parisian, rather oriental. Instead of the fashionable
stiff large hat set on top of rolls of hair, she wore a sort of turban
that suited her small head and the short dark hair. Instead of the
big sleeves and small waist of the prevailing style, her brown
gown of dull silk had no modishness, no particular cut or line.
But the wren-like quality of vague brown was contradicted by
a gay short jacket of braided gold. That jacket and the turban
gave a Turkish effect not unpleasing to the eye of the poet.
Alfred felt confused. He wondered why her appearance pleased
him. He liked a woman to follow the dictates of fashion.

Aurore, who despised a dandy, observed that the poet was
dressed in the extreme of style. A green coat heightened the effect
of his blue eyes and blond coloring. His cheeks were pink like a

girl's. His hair revealed an almost infantile tendency to the kind of curl a woman likes to wave around her finger. He was undeniably handsome. He looked the aristocrat. His manner was almost too excessively polite and well-bred. Decidedly he was unlike her group of friends. The men she knew and liked were all Bohemians, careless of dress and of demeanor.

The conversation at the table was general. Aurore, the only woman present, talked little and listened much. From time to time her dark eyes were lifted to the poet. He exerted himself to be agreeable; he was agreeable, but, oh, so young! Too young, too precocious, to be writing poetry. And what about the rumors of his dissipated life? In his world, the aristocratic world, most young men were dissipated, but this one was notorious.

Aurore did not pretend to compliment the poet. The first words she spoke to him were serious and sincere. She confessed that his poetry was too frivolous to move her deeply. His *Tales of Italy and Spain* and his *Ballad to the Moon* were lightness and laughter mixed with naughtiness. They were charming, she admitted, but would he not lend himself to something more worthy of his gift?

As she talked to him she realized that she did not respond to youth any more. She felt old. She found life tragic. She was writing *Lélia.*

Alfred in turn was entirely flattering. He understood women too well to treat them with sincerity. He told the author of *Indiana* how much he had enjoyed her book. True, he had enjoyed it in his own facetious way. He had taken a blue pencil and had scratched out all the superfluous adjectives, much to the amusement of himself and his friends. Now he found himself praising the lacerated novel. Lies like these were to Alfred merely the necessary social amenities. Luckily for Madame Dudevant he was too much the gentleman to speak the truth to a lady. What would she think if he blurted out his thoughts: Madame, I have said to others, and I now confess to you, I cannot bear your

Alfred de Musset, by Roffaut

heroes. Why are all your men characters cowards and poltroons? Have you never in all your life known a decent man worth describing?

While these irritated comments, carefully repressed, were racing through the brain of young Musset, he continued his expression of polite phrases until the dinner was over.

The dinner was over, and no attraction was evident between the two new stars of the Buloz *Revue*. Nothing had happened. Aurore went home to curse the world in a few more pages before falling asleep. While she was thus occupied, Alfred lay awake and re-lived his impressions of the evening, remembering those eyes of hidden fire.

There was a subtle excitement to Musset in meeting this strange Madame Dudevant, so different from his mother, his sister, the women he knew in high society, the women he had known in the half world. Many women had made a sex appeal to him. But this one was sexless. Or was she sexless? Was she perhaps a new incarnation of sex! She was irritating, she was arrogant. She did not suit his ideal of helpless womanhood. A salaried worker on a men's magazine—horrors! He fell asleep reminding himself that he did not care to meet her again.

The next day Alfred found himself restless, touching the piano, pacing back and forth across the floor of his study.

The one thing he demanded in a woman was beauty. Madame Dudevant, he assured himself, was not beautiful. Yet she acted upon his nerves and imagination with all the force of rich feminine seductiveness. He kept seeing those deep glowing eyes of liquid amber. Why was she alone in Paris? Why did she write books? He tried to think of some excuse to call on her. He had no excuse.

Baffled, curious, he re-read *Indiana*. Strange, it was not so long ago that he had treated her book with ridicule. Now he was conscious of enthusiasm. Scarcely had he finished the second chapter when he felt inspired to write a poem. After the poem was fin-

ished he felt moved to send it to the author. The poem was
accompanied by a note:

"Madame, I take the liberty of sending you some verses which
I have just written in re-reading a chapter of *Indiana*. Their value
is so slight that I would hesitate to offer them, were it not that
they afford me an opportunity to express to you the sincere and
profound admiration by which they have been inspired."

This respectful note received a courteous response. The response was followed by a call, by several calls. The two new stars
wavered slightly in their orbits, as though drawn by a common
force.

The first conversations were literary. After pledging her to
secrecy, he showed her fragments of his new poem, *Rollo*. They
talked poetry. As she followed his flights of fancy, his thoughts
unfolded before her.

After knowing Madame Dudevant, Alfred lost his taste for the
talk of other women, that talk, half chatter and half flattery,
to which he was accustomed. He found that this one woman
listened with entire attention, understood without protestation,
and responded quietly without effort or strain. She had, he
thought, a mind that equalled his own, the mind of a man.

They discussed everything, books, plays, life, morals, and ended
inevitably by discussing themselves. Alfred learns that Madame
Dudevant is a disillusioned human being. She is through with
love, emotionally dead. She is capable of friendship alone. He
hears these statements and he believes them.

Not wishing to be outdone in world weariness, he assures
Madame Dudevant that he will never make himself ridiculous
by falling in love with her. He has possessed so many women that
possession has lost its attraction. A lofty companionship is all
he demands.

He enters upon this experience with all the elation of a new
adventure. He loves novelty. He is a chaser of sensation. Here
is something sensationally new, friendship with a woman, an un-

paralleled woman, one who has somehow, by a freak of nature, climbed to the level of men.

In an impulsive moment he writes another letter:

"I can be, if you consider me worthy, not exactly your friend —that is much too moral for me—but a sort of comrade without importance and without rights, consequently without jealousy and without embroilments. . . . If, in this capacity, you would like me for an hour or an evening when you have nothing better to do, I will go to see my dear Mr. George Sand, who is henceforth for me a man of genius."

On receiving this letter Aurore believed Alfred's self-analysis as entirely as he had trusted hers. Each was accepted by the other as possessing complete self-knowledge. Alfred was above jealousy, Aurore incapable of passion. They would meet as two liberated minds.

And so the Platonic friendship began. It was absolutely safe. They could never fall in love, because too many things stood between them.

They were separated by difference in age. Alfred was twenty-three years old, while Aurore was twenty-nine. She felt motherly toward the young man, and a motherly impulse is a safeguard against romance.

They were separated by difference in education. Alfred had been brought up to have his own way. His family had always existed to help him get his own way. He was born lazy and trained to self-indulgence. Aurore, subjected to the severe training of her grandmother and to the strict discipline of a convent, had acquired habits of self-denial and self-control.

They were separated by associations. Alfred went with a fast crowd in the great gay world. Aurore stayed at home and received a few friends, mostly men.

There was also the difference of temperament. Alfred lived on excitement and needed constant stimulus which he spent his life in seeking. The only recreations of a gentleman, he said, were wine, women and gambling. Aurore sought her satisfaction in the student life. She liked tranquillity. She was by nature and necessity a worker.

Love between two such different beings would be dangerous. On this they agreed. But friendship was appropriate and permissible.

On their long walks, they lingered on the bridges or bargained for books at the stalls along the quais. They sat at little tables on the sidewalk across from the Seine, where they drank their wine or coffee as they watched the world pass by. When the evenings were cool they gathered round the porcelain stove in Aurore's salon, with good old Boucoiran and devoted Gustave Planche and the artist Laurens. Sometimes Buloz dropped in, or Sainte-Beuve. There were a dozen others, painters, writers, critics, journalists, new friends of George Sand. To them she was not Aurore, but George, and from this time on she was to be called George more often than Aurore. At her table in the corner, she wrote while the others talked. She smoked cigarettes and half listened to the talk while she wrote. In the little apartment on quai Malaquais there was an atmosphere of home and family. Once a week Maurice spent his holiday with his mother, and Solange was always dancing in and out of the apartment. Alfred made a sketch of George with Maurice and Solange. He wrote jingles about the family group, making fun of them all and describing George as an abbess wrapt in dreams. During all this time George called Alfred her good child or her bad child, as the case might be. She tried to help him to keep straight. Strange to say, he did keep straight. He had lost his taste for dissipation. He found in this adventure all the new thrills that he needed.

Toward the end of July, after a long walk, George told Alfred that she was soon to leave Paris for Nohant. Alfred felt suffocated, but he said nothing. He was still somewhat timid in the presence of his idolized friend. On returning home he wrote to her:

"My dear George, I have something stupid and ridiculous to

tell you. I don't know why I am so foolish as to write it instead of having said it when we came back from our walk. You will make fun of me, you will think that in all our association up to the present I have been only a maker of phrases. You will shut your door to me and you will think that I lie. I am in love with you. I have been in love with you from the day I first called on you."

2

She did not shut the door on him, neither did she open her arms to him. She dared not take a lover. She was more afraid of suffering than she was in love with love.

Men had always made her suffer. Perhaps it was the fault of her own nature. She could not give a casual love, she gave wholly and ended by being broken. Whether or not it was her fault, she felt that she must protect herself. She must harden her heart.

His letter had ended on a plaintive note: "The truth is that I suffer." He suffered, and she was afraid of suffering. Which should be considered?

In the following days they debated the question. She argued for the emotional freedom of friendship. He argued for love. As fast as she set forth her fears he overcame them with promises. He swore by all that was holy that he would make her happy. He reproached her for classifying him as a man like other men, and assured her that he was different, exceptional, trustworthy. His love was eternal, incapable of change or faithlessness. She was his guardian angel, his guiding star, his savior, and he wanted to be guarded, guided and saved.

Their friendship had endured for a month. Their argument lasted half as long. At the end of two weeks she surrendered. "More out of friendship than love," she wrote to Sainte-Beuve. Later she added, "It was his tears that made me yield."

The poet's tears! From this time on they brought him whatever he begged for. Tears of self-pity, of entreaty, of repentance,

of sorrow, of anger. As child or man, he wept his way to what
he wanted. His tears ended by touching his own heart and making him weep again. Infantile tears, voluptuous, tyrannous tears
they were, but for some mysterious reason they endeared him
to George.

That he needed her and that his need appealed to her were
the essential facts of their mutual attraction. She had no egotism
as a writer and almost none as a woman. All her egotism was
maternal. She needed to be needed.

On August 25th she wrote Sainte-Beuve that they were lovers,
and that there was no reason to keep it secret; he was welcome
to tell anyone.

They lived in an intense mutual absorption. All former experiences fell away from them and were as nothing. Each gave
the other a first great passion. It was as though he had never
touched a woman, as though she had never known a man.

What had become of the barriers that once seemed dangerous?
They seem to have been disposed of, one by one. What if they
were of different temperaments? George gave up her serious ways
and lent herself to his gayety. What if they did belong to different worlds? Alfred left his world and came over into George's.
Not that he adjusted himself to her or her friends, he adjusted
them to himself. He insisted that George's Bohemian group should
imitate the elegancies to which he was accustomed. His sensibilities were outraged because Boucoiran and Gustave Planche
lounged in their chairs or sat on the floor. He criticized their
manners and opinions. One day he criticized George. He found
her too moral, too religious. He felt it too evident that she had
been brought up in a convent. When her friends defended her,
Alfred was annoyed. George was the only one who never reproved
him, the only one who understood. He wished the others would
stay away.

Alfred's first act of dominance was to get rid of Gustave
Planche. One had to give in to the poet's jealousy. It was ab-

normal, a sort of frenzy which ended in illness if it was opposed. But as soon as one yielded to his frenzy he fell asleep exhausted and woke up sweet-tempered and repentant.

Gustave Planche was banished, and George looked forward to a period of peace. Yet there was no peace. George's life became a series of excitements. Alfred the accepted lover was a different person from Alfred the respectful friend. He took possession of George's apartment. He ran it. He ran her. He did it all so charmingly that George could only look on and smile. When he was happy, when he had his own way, he was adorable. He organized parties which were but backgrounds for his ebullient exhibitiveness. The guests were their co-workers of the Buloz group or they were George's new friends. Debureau, the famous pantomimist, was sometimes invited. There were sleight-of-hand performances, costume parties, masquerades, charades. On one occasion George was persuaded to give a dinner to some literary folk. Alfred's place was vacant. The guests were served by a new servant dressed in peasant costume with short skirts and bare arms. The awkward waitress broke the plates, dropped the food and made everyone uncomfortable. Finally she emptied a carafe on a solemn gentleman's bald head. At this climax of hilarity the maid took off her wig, pulled down her sleeves and revealed herself as Alfred. Everyone except the bald man was delighted.

At these and other escapades George looked on and smiled. She smiled as a mother does, watching her clever boy, his tricks, his tears, his cunning ways of showing off. Alfred was like a child who keeps calling out, "Now look at me!"

During these weeks of close association George was learning many new things about her "sublime child." He must never be crossed, it destroyed his equilibrium. He passed in quick succession from tears to laughter, from anger to tenderness, from exaltation to gloom. And every mood was excessive. He could not be merely depressed or merely unhappy. If depressed he wanted to kill himself in utter despair. If happy he wanted to die from sheer ecstasy.

Calm bored him, agitation was his natural element, and a brainstorm was the height of his delight. He was a sentimental sadist. He deliberately precipitated his own mental crises, that he might feel himself tremble, hear himself cry out, and taste the delicious salt of his own tears. He enjoyed unhinging his mind from time to time. But he was haunted by the dread of a permanent unhinging. In the reaction after drinking or in the collapse that followed a mental crisis he sometimes spoke of this dread of insanity. In these moods one had to treat him as an invalid and nurse him back to mental health. Poetry, intoxication, madness, were the one-in-three and the three-in-one of his religion. He worshiped this holy trinity of his own temperament.

Alfred was at his best as a talker. His use of words was little less than inspired. There was never a lover who could vow such splendid vows. He told his beloved that he loved her as no man had ever loved woman. He swore their love would go down in history like the love of Romeo and Juliet, like that of Abélard and Héloïse. Her name and his would be linked together throughout the ages, to prove the reality of deathless passion.

If gradually he seemed less magnificent than the words he spoke, George excused him because he was a poet. When he was childish she excused him because of his youth. Whenever he failed her she forgave him. Was he not a genius?

She accustomed herself to his moods, and learned to take his words as little poems unrelated to life. No hurt, no disappointment really mattered. She loved him. He was as he was. He was jealous of everyone, of everything, of her work, of her past. But one could not blame him for these jealous rages, because they were uncontrollable. And always afterward he was so tender, so full of promises, so lovable and loving, one could almost forget the rages, almost believe they would not recur.

Their first slight disagreements were due to the difference in their social viewpoint. George sympathized with every democratic tendency and sided instinctively with the oppressed. This irritated Alfred in every nerve of his being. He considered such sympathy vulgar. It was a matter not of social ethics, but of good taste. He believed in a privileged upper class and sided with the monarchists. This was merely the correct attitude of a gentleman. As fast as she found out these dangerous topics of conversation George avoided them, until at last they could congratulate themselves that all barriers were removed.

The contemplated visit to Nohant had been postponed. George did not work any more. She did not think, she did not reason. She was like a ship loosed from its moorings, carried out to sea and caught in a whirlpool. The calm safe land lay miles away, lost and forgotten. Nothing was close or remembered or real but the daily maelstroms by which she was alternately drawn under or driven forth.

3

Alfred's desire for exclusive possession drove them at last to Fontainebleau, where they spent a belated honeymoon late in September. They lived outdoors all day, and their changed surroundings brought them into close accord.

Sometimes they rode horseback. Alfred had heard that George could ride astride but he had scarcely believed it. Now he saw this novel sight. His adored one, riding in knickerbockers and leggings, looked like a boy of sixteen. Sometimes they spent whole days tramping in the forest. For these walks George wore her student costume, with a loose blue blouse held by a black belt. Contact with nature lent her a mysterious vitality. She seemed to Alfred at the height of her attractiveness. He liked her best when she was gay and spontaneous, and to please him she sang the peasant songs of Berry and danced the steps she had learned as a child in Spain. The further they went into the forest the more at home she seemed. She ran after flowers, and called them all by their names. She knew the trees and the birds and was one with them. She belonged in wide green spaces with all that was wild and free. She was a wood nymph, a fairy, a creature who should never be caged.

What had become of the silent woman, the worker, the mother? She had been left behind in Paris. And now at last Alfred possessed an ideal mistress who devoted her days to delightful childish play.

He also was transformed. The outdoor life restored his balance, and he was at his charming best.

On September 21st George wrote to Sainte-Beuve:

"I am happy, very happy, my friend. Every day I grow more attached to him. Every day I can see the gradual disappearance of the little things which made me suffer, while the fine things I admire grow more plain."

One day at Fontainebleau they were sitting on a high rock that overlooked a dangerous abyss. As Alfred's spirits rose he soared into a mood of exaltation. He covered her face with tears and caresses. Putting his arms around his loved one, he dragged her to the edge of the rock. Then he demanded that they throw themselves over, declaring that they must die together. It was one of those moods in which he liked to feel his mind unhinge. George fought for her life and finally succeeded in pulling away from him, although she was obliged to kick at his hands. She did not want to die.

It was the first time she had ever refused him anything. He never forgave her. Several times he referred to the incident and reproached her for lack of sensibility because she could not understand a poet's love. On their way home after this experience he made a bed of moss and asked her to spend the night in the forest. Still frightened, she refused.

"Afraid of what?" he exclaimed. "Afraid of me who would die a thousand deaths to protect and guard you!"

There was another brief madness in the forest. Late one afternoon George had wandered away and Alfred was left alone. He saw coming toward him a man who was a stranger yet vaguely familiar. He was clothed in torn black garments. His face was pale, his hair was ruffled by the wind. On looking closer Alfred recognized in this ghostly being the image of his own future self. The man was Alfred as he would look at forty, sick, dissipated, worn with debauch. The revolting creature was drunk, horrifying: he cast looks of hatred and scorn at the young poet. Alfred sat paralyzed with terror until George came to his rescue. And then when she tried to lead him home he would not take the paths they knew. He dragged her through the thick woods where they wandered around until dawn. In this long tramp he restored his balance and rested his nerves, but George reached home in a state of collapse. The next day she was sick with exhaustion, but Alfred arose in the morning refreshed and strong.

He seemed to revel in this experience. Much to her surprise he treated it lightly. He made a sketch of their expedition and entitled it "Honeymoon in a Cemetery." Under the figure of George he wrote, "With heart as badly torn as her dress." Later on he made poetry out of the hallucination. The spectre of debauch appears in one of his most famous poems.

On their return to Paris Alfred made a book of drawings. There were sketches of George lying down, standing, sitting, smoking a long thin pipe, leaning on the balcony, dressed in oriental clothes. There were sketches of Mérimée, Sainte-Beuve, Buloz, of himself as Don Juan, imitating Byron, who was his ideal. "Musset must have been extremely gay," says Adolph Brisson, "when he was not suffering from sickness or debauch."

The parties began again. George was criticized for giving a literary dinner to which Planche, Boucoiran and Laurens were not invited. But regardless of her friends she continued to indulge the fantasies of her sublime child. It was not difficult to keep him amused. He loved the unexpected. Just before sitting down to dinner she would put on her hat and announce that they would dine instead at a restaurant. As they prepared for an evening at home she would suggest the theatre. These diversions satisfied his restlessness for a time. Then he demanded change, excitement, something new. They discussed a trip to Italy. George welcomed the idea as a solution to all her worries, because he promised that in Italy he would work and allow her to work.

Alfred had lived as a guest in Madame Dudevant's apartment from the first week in August to the second week in December. To the poet the apartment represented warmth, light and comfort. He knew there was a servant and he saw that there were meals. He took all this as a matter of course. Whenever he returned to his mother's home he found it running smoothly. It seemed reasonable that George's home would conduct itself in the same way. His mind saw no relation between the upkeep of a household and the need of earning money. His hostess never spoke of bills. She pored over her accounts when her guest was absent. She hid the accounts as well as her worries when he returned.

Whenever she spoke of working he reproached her: "You don't love me any more. You are a cold woman. You are too moral, too serious. You know nothing about love." When she tried to keep regular hours he jeered at her. "A creative artist should not work like a dressmaker or a laborer." George's habit of life had been to write for a certain number of hours every day. By so doing she had produced a book in four months and for this book she had been paid 4000 francs. During the four months of her intimacy with Alfred most of her time had been expended in entertaining Alfred. Her time was her capital and he was consuming it.

All this was invisible to the poet. His mind was on other things. He liked being seen abroad with Madame Dudevant on his arm. She was known and noticed. People would turn and look and whisper, "There goes the author of *Lélia*." Alfred and his world called her his mistress. Alfred was proud of his possession, his achievement. Not every young man of twenty-three could afford a mistress.

4

Lélia was daily becoming more celebrated. No book George ever wrote created such a stir or added so greatly to her fame. Many little Lélias sprang up in France and Germany. She had created a new vogue.

In *Lélia* George had advocated woman's independence, her equality, the need of changed laws and a single standard of morality. These ideas were a sensational novelty. They awakened a tempest of indignation. The author was called impious and immoral, a dangerous teacher of corruption. Young girls were forbidden to read the book, and married women read it in secret.

George was a precocious feminist. The slow, conservative woman movement would some day pave the way for feminism. But the woman movement had not yet begun. Her ideas were therefore not chronological. They antedated history. She confused the thinkers, angered the critics, and threw the times out of joint.

While the superficial woman question was thus agitating public opinion, the author of *Lélia* was facing the permanent woman problem, man. Whenever Alfred grew restless they talked of Italy. It was necessary to give him a change of surroundings and to find a place where he would let George write. Over and over he promised that when they reached Italy he would work and let her work.

But how could the trip be provided for? George had spent all her money. She persuaded Buloz to advance her some hundreds of francs for extra writing which she promised to forward from Italy. She borrowed more francs from her friend La Rochefoucauld. The question of money being settled, George was free to leave. Maurice was at school. Solange was spending her half year at Nohant in charge of a faithful maid. George was beholden to no one.

But Alfred was not entirely self-supporting. He could not

leave until his widowed mother gave her permission. She was a doting mother, she had not objected to his long stay in George's apartment, but she was afraid to let her boy go far away.

George wished she could talk to Alfred's other mother, but there were difficulties. George might feel herself an independent woman with a right to a free union, but Madame de Musset and all her friends looked upon George as Alfred's mistress. Nothing could change the point of view which held it improper for mother and mistress to meet. They were the two women most interested in Alfred's welfare, but they could not talk it over. The more George thought about it the more she resented these absurd proprieties. Finally she took a carriage to 59 rue de Grenelle and sent up word that a lady was waiting below. Madame de Musset, accompanied by a maid, went down to investigate. She appreciated the delicacy of Madame Sand's reception of her in a carriage. Of course the woman was wicked, but were not all dear Alfred's women wicked? It was rather a relief to see one of them.

Instead of a panted jade she found a simple sincere woman who talked devotedly of Alfred and his soul. The silent George could be very eloquent when under the sway of conviction, and she was certain that she had been chosen to save Alfred. She promised his mother to take good care of their genius. Madame de Musset was impressed by George's personality, she was certain of her sincerity. She wept, like Alfred, with emotion, and in weeping she gave her consent.

The lovers left Paris December 12th. They traveled by diligence to Lyons, by boat on the Rhône from Lyons to Avignon, by diligence again to Marseilles, and by boat to Genoa.

At Genoa they rested. One evening they received a call from two young Italians whom they had met on the boat. These two, with de Musset, talked, as young men will, on love and women. They spoke freely before Madame Dudevant, as one may before a married woman. Some remark was made about bad women.

Suddenly George took up the cudgels. She asserted that a free woman was often more moral than a conventional hypocrite. She contended that a woman might be unconventional, even irregular, in her love affairs and yet remain good. She quoted her mother as a glorified proof of her argument. Her own mother, she said, was a good woman, yet she had lived with Maurice Dupin before their marriage. She was not blaming her, she was defending her. She regarded her as a victim of social injustice. Once again George was eloquent with the force of conviction. They had hit at her, at her mother, at a hundred other women who did not deserve their contempt. George defended them all, herself, her mother and the others. She knew these men were sinners and self-righteous. She tried to make them see and understand.

Alfred was shocked. It was perfectly proper for him and his friends to discuss their liaisons with women, because they knew these women were bad and they called them bad, therefore the family and moral standards were not disturbed. But for George to talk about bad women as though they were good women was destructive to morality and the family. For the good name of France he felt compelled to assure the Italians that such ideas did not exist in Paris.

When the men left he told George just why she was wrong and just what she should and should not talk about. George was furious and for once did not yield. Alfred flew into a rage and for once his rage was not followed by repentance.

He was sure he was right. He was proud of his world and his birth. All his sex traditions were back of him. George was sure she was right. She was passionately loyal to women and her sex convictions were back of her.

This first serious quarrel frightened the two lovers. It pushed them asunder. In a passage of words they had felt their way back to their beginnings. Each was true to his roots. No one who wants to go on living can be expected to pull up his own roots. The subject was dropped but the estrangement remained. There was something like a garden wall between them. Alfred belonged in the garden and George flourished better in the field outside.

At Genoa George began to suffer from a fever. She visited Campo Santo in a state of apathy. She saw Pisa without caring whether the tower was crooked or straight.

Sixteen days after leaving Paris they reached Florence.

In Alfred's version of the Italian journey given by Louise Colet he says: "When we went to the opera the music awakened in us divergent impressions. The cries of passion to which I responded did not reach her. She was moved most by religious music and by the choruses expressing collective feeling. It required a merging of many souls to move her own. She has a wide universal sympathy which goes out to the infinite in charity, in love, in utopia, but the personal and passionate escapes her. Even in the hours of most complete happiness I never felt her entirely mine. She never was jealous and possessive, as I was. Her emotions were not concentrated on me.

"When we met a beggar we were equally ready to give money and I often felt my eyes fill with tears. She would express her emotion by condemning extremes of wealth and poverty and by saying that we ought to put an end to human inequality. I would listen with a lassitude which hurt her. I would often run away from her to get back my liberty to think as I pleased."

At Florence Alfred ran away often to think as he pleased and to do as he pleased. He began to seek his own amusements. And he found occasion for jealousy because George visited the galleries alone. When she went out without him he felt sure she must be meeting some other man.

For the first time since Alfred came into her life George had moods of loneliness and sadness. She was indifferent as to where they went. They flipped a coin to decide whether their destination should be Rome or Venice. The coin turned up Venice three times. They continued the journey in a kind of fatalism and reached Venice on January 19th. The trip had lasted twenty-three days.

Twenty-three days of exclusive possession. Twenty-three days of prolonged tête-à-tête. Days of riding side by side in stage coaches, and on boats where Alfred was seasick. The long journey was a severe test of companionship. Part of Alfred's mind was congenial to George, and part of George's mind was congenial to Alfred. But they could not talk poetry all day long and then begin on it again in the evening.

Twenty-three long dinners and longer evenings at strange hotels. George had found Alfred fascinating in Paris because he was different from her Bohemian friends. Now she sometimes longed for someone who would not be bored by social questions and impersonal conversation. One of de Musset's friends, Count d'Alton-Shee, says of him: "When he was with men he talked little and laughed good-naturedly at the wit of others. He reserved for women all the grace and charm of his coquetry; with them he was gay, amusing, eloquent, mocking, having, like them, a horror of politics and of serious subjects."

"George Sand," says Wladimir Karénine, "could not endure talking for the sake of talking. She frankly admitted that she preferred the conversation of men to that of women. Women wearied her by their silly gossip and their chit-chat."

Alfred had fallen in love with George because she was different from other women. Now he resented the difference. He had admired her seriousness, her calm detached mind. Now he wanted her to chat and laugh. The more she saw his irritation the sadder she grew, until he begged for brightness, even a little coquetry.

When the stage coach rattled out of Paris Alfred had said to George, "At last I have you all to myself!" When the gondola left them at their hotel in Venice he exclaimed, "George, you are the most tiresome woman I ever knew."

5

On the day of their arrival in Venice George fell ill, but in spite of fever and lassitude she struggled to begin writing. Her effort at work annoyed Alfred, and her illness seemed to him a personal injury. He saw her lying in bed, weak and in need of sympathy and attention. Had he not told her a hundred times that he would gladly die to save her a moment's unhappiness? Now was the moment to prove his Romeo devotion, his Abélard protestations of exalted, loyal love. One glance at his sick Juliet and the poet-lover felt extreme irritation. One long look at the patient Héloïse face, propped up by pillows, and Romeo Abélard Alfred ran away. All his vows could not withstand an attack of dysentery.

George was left alone at the hotel without nurse or doctor. She could work or she could sleep or weep or grieve. She was free to do as she pleased.

Alfred went forth into Venice like a schoolboy on a holiday. But the schoolboy began to regret that he had brought teacher along. He couldn't pull away from her. She was always there, if not in fact, at least in consciousness, spoiling his good times.

The French consul called and offered his services. Alfred wanted to see the dives and vulgar resorts of Venice. He had known this side of life in Paris since he was a collegian, and he was eager to compare the excitements of Paris with those of Venice. The consul was delighted to play host to the charming Frenchman. He took him behind the scenes of the theatres and introduced him to chorus girls and dancers. All this would have been wholly enjoyable to Alfred except for the disagreeable fact that he had to go back to Her, take dinner with Her, see her pleading eyes and listen to her counsels. She begged him not to gamble, not to drink to excess.

But according to Alfred it was her fault that he drank to excess. Her face haunted him. He drank from the highest motives,

to deaden his sensibilities, drown his memories and forget his conscience. Alas, she had become that horrible thing to him, a
conscience.

It was her fault, too, that he ran after women. He was used
to the courtesan type and she would not play the courtesan. He
accused her of failing to give him the pleasures of love, of forcing him to seek those pleasures elsewhere.

When a man feels like being good he naturally craves the love
of an angel. But when he feels like being bad an angel is a bore.
It was all very well for George to take care of him when he felt
like being cared for, but now he wanted to escape from the
guardian angel, and there she was, remembering his appeals to be
saved. Even if she said nothing, her very presence was a reproach.

George, who could never blame Alfred, blamed her illness for
their temporary estrangement. This illness, she always contended,
was the beginning of the end.

Poor boy! Poor poet! She understood, she was sorry, but what
could she do? She could only wait until he had exhausted his
mood of dissipation. Then he would come back to her and adore
her again as he had adored her before. She waited, and her waiting was a fresh source of irritation.

Before she was strong again George was steadily writing in bed.
After two weeks she was able to sit at her desk. Whenever Alfred
returned to the hotel he found her absorbed and apparently contented. He looked at the sheets of paper covered by her firm,
close writing. The sense of her achievement filled him with secret
rage. He tried to dissuade her, as he had always dissuaded her,
from working. But now she refused to yield to him because, she
explained, she had given her word of honor to send some manuscript to her publisher.

Alfred told her that such language from a woman to a man
was humiliating and that it seemed to him that she was trying
to usurp his place. A woman, it seemed to Alfred, should be a
creature of emotion. By all the books, plays and poems that were

ever written, by all his traditions and all his desires, a woman should be passionate, instinctive, personal and jealous. This woman outraged all traditions. If she had wept and made scenes and begged and entreated, he could have understood her. But in her attitude to her lover she unsexed herself. She was calm and patient. She never stooped to jealousy or reproach. Worst of all and most unwomanly, she used reason. She told him quite reasonably that after she had mailed her first bunch of manuscript she would devote herself to him again. She was irritating, she was arrogant. He had known it from the very first day.

He was angry and suffered from self-reproach. The more he reproached himself, the more he drank and gambled and played with women. He offered to share part of his gayety with her. But she hadn't the strength or time for these interruptions. So it happened that each went back to his own old habits. Each devoted half the night to an interest which the other could not share. They lived in a tangle of miscomprehensions.

Alfred saw George as his mistress. He was blind to the other sides of her. He undertook to make his mistress happy. But he wanted to do it in his own way, the only way that he could understand, by giving her excitement. These were the things that upset her life, disturbed her tranquillity, and made her a stranger to herself.

George in turn saw Alfred as an unbalanced genius. She undertook to restore his balance, quite unconscious that if she restored his balance she destroyed his genius. She tried to cure him of dissipation so that he could do his best work, but he wrote best when he was recovering from debauch. Then, in a fierce rage of self-disgust, his soul awakened and he felt inspired. George was bent on making a man of him. But he was not meant to be a man. He was meant to be an eternal bad boy. To make a man of him would have spoiled his poetry and broken his spirit.

As a woman she wanted him to need her. As a worker she expected him to allow her to have several hours a day alone. As a poet he wanted her to leave him to his poetry-inspiring dissipation. As a man he wanted her to concentrate on him. He wanted her to give him all her capacity for emotion, yet he expected her to remain unmoved while she watched him go to the dogs.

When they tried to get out of the tangle they only intensified the snarls. Silence did not untie them, words only made the knots worse.

One evening as they were lingering over dinner, Alfred began to express his resentment and pour out his grievances against his companion. She was so good she got on his nerves. He hated her serenity, her steadiness, her capacity for work. She was preachy, she was interfering, she was stupid, she was religious. She ought to take the veil and stay in a convent. Finally his accusations came to a head in a definite attempt to break with her.

"I beg your pardon, George," he said. "I have made a mistake. I do not love you."

George wavered for a moment, rose from her seat and walked away from him. But before she left the room she flung back proudly:

"We no longer love each other."

Back in her room she tried to think. But the pain that tore at her nerves made thinking impossible. She would act and act quickly to ease the suffering that left her dizzy and weak. She lifted her gowns from the hooks and began to fold them. She would pack and go back to Paris. She would leave him alone. She pictured him alone in Venice. Alfred the helpless, the self-indulgent, penniless and forsaken in a strange land! She could not forsake him. He had jilted her, it hurt cruelly. It struck at her pride, it bruised her heart. But she could not leave him to feel deserted as she now felt deserted by him.

She tried to decide on some plan of action. If only she could shut off for a few moments the sharp-edged force that was cutting at her like the drive of little knives. She sank on the floor unable to move. She closed her eyes and began to remember. She had felt the same stabbing pain before, some time long ago—when was it? She thought back—desertion—deserted—a little girl, an old coach moving into the distance, in the coach a loving passionate woman, her mother, going away forever, to live somewhere else forever. The child Aurore running, screaming, "Mother, mother, take me with you!"

And now grown-up George was feeling the same sense of desertion, the isolation of spirit, the fear of life that had agonized the child. The child Aurore had promised to be good, she had hidden her grief. George also had made a promise and was trying to keep her promise.

What was this insistent thing in her that made her keep her word and feel responsible? Why didn't Alfred have it? He couldn't even keep his word to Buloz. Why couldn't he be a man? She needed a man to lean on. Whenever she tried to lean on him he was a broken reed.

No matter, he would have to lean on her. She had enough money to carry one of them to Paris. Could she persuade him to take it and go? She knew too well that in their strained relation his sensitive pride would take offense at the suggestion. They were totally estranged. No, they were only estranged as lovers. They could be friendly, behave as friends, go on speaking decently, ignore the broken romance. They could do all this if she were able to conceal her suffering. She owed him something as a friend. She was older, her love had always been maternal in part. Could she make it wholly maternal? That was the one solution. No use thinking of escape. She must wait for money, work for money to carry them both home. So much emotion was making her ill. If she fell ill again he would hate her worse than ever. To-morrow, no doubt, they would be dining together and she must be able to talk and smile. No emotion, no tears.

There was a door between their two rooms. The key was in his room and the bolt was on her side. George rose quietly and very quietly bolted the door.

6

From this time on the door between the two rooms remained closed. They did not dine together the next day nor for many days. To escape facing her, Alfred took his dinner elsewhere. Often he came back to the hotel in the morning while she was at breakfast. She would put him to bed, draw the curtains, and return to her desk.

She deadened her emotions and the deadening was successful; it hardened the ache in her heart, it closed the wounds of her spirit. But as soon as she succeeded in ceasing to feel she began to have frightful headaches. She could not eat or sleep.

There was a morning when Alfred came home half crazed with wine and despair. He had gambled and lost his last sou. He owed a strange Englishman a sum of money which he could not pay. Alfred had a very high sense of "the honor of a gentleman." He feared he would be talked about and dishonored. At the time that he confessed his debt of honor, George, who had been paying their bills, had very little money left. She could not help him except by working harder. She worked harder, while Alfred drank to drown his sorrow. He was amazed at her labors. Sometimes he was angry, sometimes he was ashamed. He worked by fits and starts, after a night's debauch, but sustained effort was incomprehensible to the poet.

"We poets," he explained, "are the lilies of literature. We toil not at all and we spin when we please."

He accused her of touching a spring in her head and starting imagination to flow like water from a faucet.

"Oh, my great George," he said to her, "you who earn money so easily!"

Night after night she continued her easy earning of money. Often in the late afternoon she would go to the Place Saint Mark and drink strong black coffee to keep herself awake. Work! Work! Nothing but her work would pull them out of this painful impasse. They decided to return to Paris as soon as possible, but for the present they lacked money for the long expensive journey. Until funds arrived from Buloz nothing could be done.

For two weeks they dragged on together, outwardly friendly, inwardly estranged. Then Alfred began to act queerly. He was drinking immoderately. He talked of suicide, and, more frightening still, he talked of insanity. He repeated his fears all day. "I am going crazy! I am losing my mind!" He threw himself on the bed and lacked strength to get to his feet.

There was only one thing to turn to—bloodletting. Modern science was all for opening a vein; it cured everything. A doctor was called. He was a doddering old man and he could not find the vein. George was distraught. She remembered a physician, a Dr. Pagello, who had attended her two weeks before. He had skilfully opened a vein and had cured her headache. She wrote this man an appealing letter, begging him to come immediately and to bring another doctor for consultation.

Her letter to Dr. Pagello explained Alfred's condition:

"He hardly knows what he is saying or doing. I fear for his reason more than for his life. He weeps and says he is dying or going insane. He is the being I love best in the world. I suffer agony in seeing him in such a state."

Dr. Pagello responded promptly. As soon as he walked into the room George knew they were in competent hands. Dr. Pagello, with his colleague Dr. Juannini, diagnosed the case as "typhoid fever, complicated by alcoholic delirium"; in other words, delirium tremens. That night two strong men could not hold the frenzied poet. He grabbed George and tried to strangle her. He shrieked and went into convulsions. The paroxysms were repeated many times.

Now was the test of George's friendship and her strength. She became a nurse. She became two nurses, day nurse and night nurse. There was no longer any question of leaving an unfaithful lover. He was merely a friend now, but he needed her again. How thankful she was that she had not deserted him. How grateful that this young doctor was so devoted to the patient. Together they would save him.

Dr. Pagello came each evening and stayed far into the night. He was unwilling to leave her alone with a sick man who might grow violent at any moment. George leaned on Dr. Pagello. At last she had found some one to lean on. He helped her through the long ordeal. Together they watched for the crisis on the twelfth day. It passed and the gifted poet was saved for posterity.

On February 4th she wrote to Buloz:

"Your reproaches reach me at a sad moment. I am in despair, overwhelmed with fatigue, suffering terribly and waiting for I know not what. How can you expect me to think of literature, or of anything else, at such a time? I only know that we now have left only sixty francs; that we are spending enormously for drugs, doctors and the necessities of illness, and that we live in an expensive hotel from which Alfred cannot be moved for a month. If he lives I don't know how we shall pay the expenses of his illness and his return. I am sorry you have been inconvenienced by having to wait for my manscript. If Alfred has a few days' calm I will quickly finish my work. But he is in a state of frightful delirium. I cannot leave him for a moment. It has taken me nine hours to write this letter."

Nine days later she wrote to Buloz again, telling him that she must be on her feet at all hours, that she could not undress at night and that she slept on the sofa. Nevertheless she had managed to write some pages each day during the hours that Alfred was asleep.

In one letter she begged Buloz to forward the thousand francs he owed her. In another she entreated him "in the name of the sick poet" to advance Alfred the money he had lost to the Englishman and added, "If as a result of his illness he is unable to work for some time, do not worry, my work will take the place of his."

7

The doctor had given his p~~atient~~ some quieting medicine and had left for the night. George could rest now, without worry. She could write to Madame de Musset, telling her that all was well with her son—her son, not theirs any more. After a few weeks she would take him home and give him back to his mother.

How strange it would seem at quai Malaquais without Alfred! She tried to imagine what life without him would be like. She pictured herself waiting for him, watching for a letter. What if he never came any more to quai Malaquais! The old horror of loneliness swept over her. She rose and looked at her invalid. He was sleeping peacefully. The poor boy was wasted by fever. His white face was pitiful. How bad he was and how maddening, but she wanted him to be happy. Her heart tightened, and the muscles of her throat contracted as she gazed at his still face. The emotion she felt—what was the emotion she felt? She did not know, she could not analyze, her feeling for Alfred. If he had died, she would always have felt that he was the being she had loved best in the world. She had forgotten herself completely in fighting for his life. But now that he was certain to live she would fight for herself.

After the crisis was passed, the invalid required careful watching. George and Pagello watched, drawn together by their common concern. Alfred was weak, he slept a great deal, but he did not want to be alone. He needed the nearness of human beings. Doctor and nurse withdrew to the far corner of the room, where they conversed quietly. Dr. Pagello could not speak French, George spoke but little Italian. She was trying to learn the language and she was eager to know about Italy, its history, its art, its legends. Pagello was all of Italy that came through to her, shut in as she was by the four walls of a room. He was the interpreter, he became the symbol of the land she had traveled so far to study. By the charm and beauty of Italy he was transfigured.

And what a contrast he was to the poet! Alfred, as he grew better, exhibited the impatience and the irritation of invalidism. Pagello was calm and patient. Nothing disturbed his serenity, his well-being, his poise. He was all healing; and Alfred was not the only one who needed to be healed.

George was aware that this young doctor did not find her tiresome and stupid. His devotion to the patient, it became evident, was in part devotion to her. His admiration dated back to the day several weeks ago when he had first caught sight of her sitting on the balcony of the Hotel Danieli. He had observed her as a slim, dark foreigner beside a blond young man. The melancholy face, the great sad eyes, the red kerchief worn turbanwise, the Spanish cigarette, had attracted his attention and had captivated his imagination. All this and more he told her slowly in careful Italian, trying to make his words so simple that she would understand their foreign sound. She was the first important woman he had ever known. Her famous name was familiar to him, to all his friends. He was almost in awe of her. The admiration she excited was shown in his eyes, his face, his whole attitude. He blushed when she asked his opinion and his eyelids fell before her candid gaze. But he did not confess his love. She seemed beyond his reach, like Dante's Beatrice. He spoke with eyes of worship but he did not speak in words.

Night after night she paced the floor, unable to sleep or work. Her brain was weary and yet she could not stop thinking. What did she want? What had she always wanted? Happiness, her own kind of happiness, a single-hearted love. Alfred had promised it and had been utterly unable to give it. His conduct at Venice had been treason to their dreams, it had been treason to their ideal. Yet all men would agree, all women would agree, that Alfred had the right to what they called affairs of gallantry. Strong in his sense of traditional right, backed by his certainty of public approval, he had deliberately betrayed her by playing at love with these Venetian women.

What would he think, what would they all think, if she took one, just one, Italian man? And why shouldn't she? The handsome face of the young doctor flashed on her mental vision. She saw the dark eyes. She felt with a tremor of eagerness that he was always admiring her, desiring her. Pietro Pagello! Perhaps, she was not sure, perhaps the Venetian doctor was her fate. He pleases me, she mused. Perhaps later on I shall hate him, but now he pleases me. Is it only the appeal to the senses? I don't know. What difference does it make? One must take what one can get out of life, as men do. They are happier than women, they know more than women, they are more nearly right than women. And on reaching this conclusion she was soothed and at peace, ready to throw herself down and fall asleep, dreaming of the dark eyes that were always admiring her, desiring her.

8

One evening Pagello asked her if she had ever thought of writing a novel about Venice.

"Perhaps," she said, and smiled mysteriously as she took pen and paper and began to write.

Wishing to obliterate himself he picked up a book of Victor Hugo's and pretended to read. He watched with thrilling interest as she rapidly covered page after page, never looking back at what she had written, never seeming to weigh or consider her words. After a time she finished and gave him the hurriedly written manuscript.

In his timidity he did not dare to assume it was for his perusal. "Whom is it for?" he asked.

She took back the paper and wrote on the outside, "For stupid Pagello."

He carried the precious manuscript home and read it in a rapture of intoxicated senses. It purported to be a chapter of a novel. It revealed to him a woman disillusioned, disappointed, reaching out to a new love.

"I do not know, I shall never know, whether you really love me. You speak only a few words of my language and I do not know enough of yours to ask such subtle questions. Perhaps I cannot make you understand me even when I do know your language. We have thoughts, feelings and ideas that we cannot explain to each other.

"Perhaps you have been brought up in the belief that women have no souls. Do you know whether they have or not? Do you understand companionship, patience, friendship? Shall I be your companion or your slave? Do you desire me or do you love me? Do you know what I am? Are you dissatisfied at not knowing? Am I something which you search and dream of, or am I merely a woman like any woman, like those who grow fat in harems?

"If you were a man of my own country I could ask you questions and you could understand them, but then [if you were one of my countrymen] I should be still more unhappy because you would deceive me.

"You at least will not deceive me with words. You will not offer me empty phrases and false promises. That which I have searched for in vain in others I may not find in you, but I can always believe it is there. I can interpret your reveries as I please and make your silence speak the words I need.

"Looks and caresses have always lied to me. Let me explain yours in my own way and do not add to them any lying words.

"Let us remain as we are. Do not learn my language. I do not wish to find in yours the words which convey doubts and fears.

"I would like never to know your name. Hide your soul from me so I may always believe that it is beautiful."

This is a part of the remarkable letter in which George revealed to Pagello that she loved—love.

On the following day George and Pagello walked and talked for three hours. Pagello's journal explains how she made love to him. A strange love-making! She talked about Alfred. She told Pagello the history of the last few months. She related the story of her wrongs. She poured out all her passionate resentment in poor Italian or in rapid French. He did not understand half of it. That made no difference; what she needed was relief. And Pagello, who was a doctor and who knew how to bleed sick bodies, apparently knew nothing of bleeding hearts. With all his medical training he did not realize that he was but a clean rag applied to a wound.

He forgot that first letter written when George was afraid that Alfred would die or lose his mind, the letter in which she said, "He is the being I love best in the world." He forgot the last letter, full of complaints of Frenchmen and the French attitude toward women. All that Pagello saw was that George seemed almost to hate Alfred. He had perhaps never heard that hell hath no fury like a woman scorned, or that hatred is the reverse side of love. It was not in vain that George had inscribed her letter to "stupid Pagello."

In his journal he stated, "On that day we came to an understanding. It was not until three weeks later that we became lovers."

They waited because Alfred needed them. George and Pagello would have liked to go away together. They would have liked to take an apartment and leave Alfred at the hotel. But all their wishes were put aside for the sake of the poet's recovery. It was not only that he needed their physical care, he would have languished without companionship. He was a sick child who demanded constant attention.

George stayed on at the Hotel Danieli. It was this good that she did which made her conduct seem so bad.

9

Into this situation came Alfred Tattet, Musset's best friend. Tattet was a man about town, rich and dissolute. Traveling through Italy with his mistress, an actress, he called to see how the other Alfred and the other mistress were getting along. He found Musset dressed and sitting up in an arm-chair. He admitted that the poet was more in need of a nurse than a sweetheart. He admired George in the new rôle and he was shocked at her appearance. He found her looking battered and worn.

It did not occur to either of these two Alfreds that there was anything unusual in George's ministrations. If they had witnessed such devotion on the part of a celebrated author whose time was important they would have been deeply impressed. But they did not see a celebrated author whose time was important. They saw only Alfred's mistress or ex-mistress, it did not matter which. She was a woman who belonged to Alfred. Her sacrifice of self, her personal devotion, her paying of bills, her service as a nurse, all these things had no bearing on her conduct. There was only one question of ethics in a woman's relation to a man. Did she keep her body for him and for him alone? Alfred had the sex ethics of a Turk. Even though a Turk is through with one of his women she still belongs to his harem. Tattet and Musset shared the same viewpoint. Musset had no money and Tattet had no genius. Otherwise they were as congenial as two peas in a pod.

With the appearance of Tattet it would have seemed natural for Alfred to find a solution of what was in fact his chief problem. Here was his opportunity to lift their financial burden from George's shoulders. He might so easily have set her free by borrowing money from his rich friend. But even though Tattet was his best friend Musset did not ask him for a loan, nor did Tattet offer one.

Both men were obsessed by the question of sex. Tattet felt it his duty to tell the invalid that George was getting interested in another man. Musset was made to see the situation through Tattet's eyes, the eyes of the world. As long as George stayed with him he "passed as her lover." Therefore appearances were on his side. Musset and Tattet, siding with appearances against

George, agreed that something must be done about the poet's honor.

Alfred's first impulse of honor was to kill George. In his confessions he relates the scene in which he threatened her with a knife. She smiled at him, saying, "Come, my child, these horrors will make you ill. You have a fever. Give me the knife." He adds, "I fell into a complete delirium. She ran out of the room."

Alfred's second impulse of honor was to kill Pagello. He wished to fight a duel. Tattet succeeded in dissuading him, for which he earned the gratitude of George. In a letter written to him after his departure, George tells Tattet that she does not blame him for taking sides with Alfred. That was quite natural. She thanks him that the poet's precious blood had not been shed.

After the upheaval of Tattet's visit Musset thought back into the period of his fever. There had been a time when he scarcely knew the difference between reality and hallucination. He tried to remember whether during his delirium George and Pagello were not embracing each other at his bedside, or even while sitting on the bed. He decided that they were. He accused her of these rather tactless embraces, which she firmly denied.

George wrote to Pagello that she wanted to tell the poet frankly of their love for one another. "He will weep for a time and then get over it." Pagello, as Alfred's physician, forbade her to do so. If Alfred were a normal human being they could talk to him frankly, but jealousy made him insane. Concealment was a matter not of choice but of necessity, since scenes of violence were not conducive to the invalid's recovery.

George was caught in a situation which would cover her with reproaches no matter which way she turned or in what direction she moved. Her new love affair did no violence to her own feeling of fair play. She was indifferent to appearances but she hated concealment.

Later when Alfred was far away from her, he saw himself as "a miserable coward" for having called her deceitful. "Even if

all my suspicions were true, in what did you deceive me? Did
you tell me that you loved me? Was I not warned? Did I have
any right? Oh, my dear, when you loved me, did you ever deceive
me? What reproach did I ever have against you during the seven
months that I was seeing you day by day? You do not lie, that
is why I love you. You are as sincere as you are noble and proud."

But this was later. His present mood was one of tyranny, the
tyranny of an invalid whose weakness is his chief power. He used
his sickroom as a trap in which he caught George and held her,
and his sickness as a chain by which he tied her to his side.

"My life beside Alfred is terrible," she wrote to Pagello. "All
our conversations are full of bitterness and we cannot speak of
the past, of the present, or the future without reproaching ourselves directly or indirectly for the harm we have done. I hope
that in a few days he will have the strength to occupy himself or
seek distraction and that our intimacy will become more bear-
able. While waiting, boredom and sadness devour me. Help me
to be patient. This morning you were sad, you spoke words of
discouragement which I understood. My friend, my friend, I beg
you, hide your sufferings from me. It takes a great deal of stoi-
cism not to yield to my own and not to claim and take back the
liberty which belongs to me. This evening when I was obliged to
refuse to go out with you my heart was torn, and when you left
I felt so much like crying that it was torture. But I saw so much
coldness and sadness on Alfred's face that I felt forced to make
the sacrifice. However, our relations are so spoiled and poisoned
that everything goes wrong with us. When he saw that I was
staying at home he reproached me for being sad and for not
knowing how to conceal my displeasure."

If she put on her hat and coat he would burst into bitter accusations. She was going to meet her lover. Let her try to escape
him. He was sick now and helpless, but she would find out some
day that he could create a scandal that would ruin her. He
would tell the world that she was an unmentionable name of a

woman. He would write it on her tombstone for every passerby to see. The doctor had forbidden excitement, and her invalid was evidently starting a brainstorm. She removed her coat and hat and stayed at home.

As she looked back upon her passion for Alfred it seemed to her that it had meant slavery and the slavery had always made her suffer.

"What can I do?" she wrote to Pagello. "I cannot feign a love which I no longer feel for him. The love which he shows me at present and which would have given me so much joy a month ago touches me no longer and convinces me still less. What is such a love? When I was his slave he loved me feebly, now that I am once more in possession of my reason his wounded pride clings to me and pursues me as though I were a difficult conquest. . . . He does not know real love. It does not require quarrels to keep itself alive. It is neither languishing nor sick, it has no need of excitations; it is healthy and strong. Happiness does not put it to sleep, peace and trust do not kill it, it knows neither jealousy nor anger. It never asks pardon, because it never gives offense. . . .

"I have gone as far into despair as a human being can go. I have thus taken on a strength of inertia which is above heroism.

"A hundred times I have been told that love is a chimera and that happiness is a dream. I have said it to myself a hundred times, but as long as I feel within me the force to desire happiness and love, I shall have the force to hope for them. You are so loyal and good that you believe in many people. As for me I distrust the whole universe excepting you alone."

Whenever George went to lie down, Alfred tiptoed into her room to make sure she had told the truth. He spied on her day and night. He crept to her bedside when she was asleep to feel and see if she were really there.

"It will be very difficult for me to meet you," she explains to

Pagello. "You see what scenes it leads to. Because of a few hours' absence he quarrels with me three days and three nights, for he does not sleep, he wakes every few minutes and comes to see what I am doing. This surveillance is odious to me. It seems to me that I live in a cage which suffocates me and at night I wake up with a mountain on my chest."

If she protested, Alfred had an attack of nerves which led to fever and violence. She sacrificed her liberty to ward off these relapses, but as time went on she grew resentful and in resentment she dreamed of Pagello; he at least was neither jealous nor suspicious. Alfred, in playing the part of persecutor, left to Pagello the rôle of deliverer. Pagello seemed almost godlike in his simplicity and poise. Everything was done to make her idealize the good-looking stranger. She never had a chance to see his imperfections. Her fancy, fed by opposition, became infatuation.

"I have delayed too long in giving him his liberty and in taking back my own. Oh, my liberty, my sacred liberty, which it has been so difficult to conquer and which I have sworn to keep! Well, I want it only in order to suffer once more. My heart breaks this chain only to forge a stronger one. It is madness, I know it, but it is impossible not to have blind faith in you and not to believe that happiness is enfolded for me in your love. If you knew my life and if you really understood my burdened heart, perhaps you would tell me yourself that I am reckless. . . .

"If unhappiness comes to us, if some day our affection makes us suffer, or if sickness, misery or human weakness assails us, never mind, we shall have loved, we shall have been happy. I still feel the courage to suffer. Come what will, happiness is worth paying for."

Alfred's condition was aggravated by drink. When he began to go out again he found occasion to buy the wine of Cyprus of which he was excessively fond. Drinking was followed by delusions and delirium. After the poet had indulged in too much wine, Pagello was in the habit of seeking him out and leading him back to George.

"This poor sick child whom you have brought back to me this evening . . . I well know that this madness will not be the last . . . Nevertheless I cannot help feeling despair when I see him abandoned and in need of care, friendship and help. . . . Poor young poet, he has a feeling for great things, but he has not the force to execute them. . . . He obeys all his bad impulses and suffers from them; he is to be pitied."

In spite of protestations, George was so emotionally involved with Alfred that she could not pull away. Pagello was kind, unselfish, devoted. But George would rather talk about Alfred's faults than Pagello's virtues. Watching the excitement with which George complained of Alfred, Pagello, if he had known anything about psychology, would have said, "How you love him!" What he did say was, "Forgive him." George consented to forgive and forget the insults and injuries Alfred had heaped upon her.

"But when I see the injuries begin again after the tears, the repentance which follows once more seems to me merely a weakness. His heart is not bad, but his soul has neither strength nor true nobility. You tell me to be generous, but I fear that will only make all three of us more unhappy than before. Anyhow, I don't believe in repentance. I don't know what it is myself. I have never asked forgiveness of anyone."

This letter was written when George was suffering from her spoiled child's worst behavior. He seemed possessed by a devil, and there was no one about who could cast the devil out. Pagello stood by helpless. Bleeding did not seem a proper remedy. George waited with the wisdom of experience. She knew Alfred. His bad moods swung back to their ultimate reach and then came to an end, after which there was nothing left but reaction. His good moods would force him forward equally far in the opposite direction. She expected the poet's better nature to assert itself. And finally, assert itself it did, overwhelmingly. One could almost see a shining halo hovering over the poet's blond hair as an angel came to take possession of his soul.

The angel was as excessive as the devil had been. In the place of meanness it breathed magnanimity, in place of selfishness it exulted in renunciation. The change began, as always, by repentance. Alfred heaped reproaches upon himself. He blamed himself for all George's suffering. As soon as he blamed himself George stopped blaming him. Her heart melted into tenderness. Her sublime child was restored to her heart. Resentment disappeared.

Alfred, grown suddenly sympathetic, asked George to confide in him. Was he not her best friend? Could she not tell him frankly whether she loved Pagello? George, who had been longing for frankness, was not quite sure whether the new mood had come to stay. She dared only say, "That is my secret."

Alfred insisted upon being taken into the secret. In the evening he turned to Pagello and with the same tender sympathy asked if Pagello loved George. Pagello, seeing his patient's calm demeanor, told the truth. Alfred's face, so long distorted with jealousy, was now transfigured with ecstasy.

"You love each other, and yet you love me!" he cried exultantly, and putting their hands together in the manner of a priest he blessed their union, exclaiming. "You have saved me, body and soul."

A scene like this reveals better than any description why women fell in love with Alfred. Life at his side was always exciting. His nerves, his emotion, his imagination, lent him a divine madness that subjugated all judgment. His excited ego exalted himself and everyone else. He was not merely persuasive, he was overpowering.

One might imagine that George and Pagello would feel uncomfortable, standing with hands joined beneath the young man's blessing, but, no, he carried them along—not George alone but even the stolid Pagello entered into his vertigo. They found him magnificent. They enjoyed being blessed.

The remainder of the evening was spent by George and Pagello in admiring Alfred. It was spent, in fact, by all three of them in admiring Alfred. He was superhuman and he knew it. In a voice trembling with emotion he gave George into Pagllo's keeping. In making him the gift of his own former sweetheart he declared that the Italian was the better man and more worthy of her.

Poor Alfred, who could not see that a woman has a right to give herself! Poor George, who had already given herself! Did Alfred know it and ignore the fact? She could not ask. It would spoil the beautiful scene and disturb his happiness. It was so moving, so dramatic, that Alfred, touched by his own magnanimity, wept, but his tears were tears of joy.

And now their plans were changed. George had expected to go home with Alfred, but the poet would not accept the sacrifice. The martyr rôle was for him alone. He had made her suffer and now he must make amends. After some discussion it was finally agreed that the faithful servant, Antonio, should accompany him to Paris. George was daily expecting money from her publisher. She begged Alfred to wait, but the hero was impatient. On the following day he went away forever.

But forever was not very far away, it was merely to a neighboring quai where Alfred hired a gondola and a gondolier. The gondolier was not engaged to propel the gondola. He was merely to act as messenger and carry to George a letter of supreme farewell. The poet sat in his gondola resting while he waited for his answer. In his letter he said:

"After the first step that I took away from you, with the thought that I had lost you forever, I realized that I deserved to lose you, and that no punishment is too severe for me. He who did not know how to honor you when he possessed you, now sees the truth clearly through his tears and honors you in his heart, where your image will never fade."

The answer was scribbled by George in pencil on the back of an envelope:

"No, don't go away like that. You are not well enough, and Buloz has not yet sent me the money necessary for Antonio's traveling expenses. I cannot bear to have you go away alone. My God, why do we quarrel? Am I not always your brother George, your old friend?"

Alfred returned for another more lingering farewell, and to let George pack his trunks and buy him a few presents and a new traveling bag.

The whole last day they spent alone together. She went with him as far as Mestre, where he was joined by Antonio. Alfred, gentle and affectionate, now seemed to George to express his true nature. He was, had always been, would always be, an angel. One last farewell and then the pain of separation. She kissed him sadly and watched the post-chaise carry him away.

10

When George left Alfred at Mestre and turned her face toward Venice, her nerves broke and nothing in the world about her looked normal. She found herself suffering from an optical illusion. She saw the bridges upside down with their bases stuck into the air. The houses along the canals behaved in the same way. She winked her eyes to see if the illusion was due to tears. No, the upside-downness continued for hours, it was the result of nerve strain. In the turmoil of life at the Hotel Danieli she had not known a moment's release from tension, and now the tension ended abruptly. She was like a horse whipped uphill with a heavy load. The pulling was over and the result was collapse.

Under the strain of Alfred's goading, she had thought it would be heaven to be left alone with her lover, Pagello. She was free to be alone with him now but she did not go to him. She went to the home of two new friends, Mr. and Mrs. Rebizzo. They invited her to spend the night and rest. She stayed with them, but she could not rest without news of Alfred. The first day after his departure she was unable to move. On the following day she went to Vicente, the neighboring town, which had been Alfred's first stopping place and where Antonio had promised to leave a note for her. On arriving at Vicente she was disappointed. The careless travelers had left no word, and her second return to Venice was as wretched as the first had been.

Seeing her sick lassitude, Pagello insisted on a trip into the mountains. He arranged a week's outing. They walked several miles a day, slept in little mountain inns, and tried to stop thinking about Alfred. But George only remembered him the more. Her monthly installment for Buloz weighed on her mind. She was too tired to write fiction, so it occurred to her to send the magazine a long letter describing her travels. Because she was obsessed by thoughts of Alfred she could not limit herself to descriptions of scenery. She described the poet, his corrupt youth, the curse of his temperament and his gift of genius. This letter, dedicated "To a poet," she forwarded to Alfred, telling him to keep it in his portfolio, put it in the fire, or give it to Buloz for publication, as he pleased. It was published as first of a series of *Lettres d'un Voyageur*.

The third return to Venice found her improved in health but still suffering from nervous strain. For nine months she had been living in and through another being. For two months she had watched over a sick man, and now her nerves craved their accustomed habits, and her attention, so long riveted on the invalid, refused to turn immediately to other things. She slept badly, waking to listen for his voice that was always calling her.

Pagello was self-reliant and unselfish. Determined to make no demands upon his weary sweetheart, he tried to take care of her and thus missed the chief appeal he might have made to her strange maternal egoism. He neither wept at her feet nor asked forgiveness. He never was ill or unreasonable or crazy. He was kind and devoted and left the mother in her to utter loneliness. In her first letter sent to Alfred at Milan she wrote: "Ah, who will take care of you, and whom shall I take care of! Who will need me and whom shall I feel like looking after now! How shall I get along without the good and the harm you have done me!" She worried at not hearing from him. She felt the strain of uncertainty "in this country where letters so often get lost or are six weeks en route." She received a short note from Padua and finally a long letter from Geneva. He still maintained the new tenderness shown before his departure. He was well, comfortable, almost happy, but had wept many times in the dreary hotel rooms.

"I love you still with real love," he wrote. "At this distance I neither grow violent nor have attacks of nerves. Tears fall on my hands as I write, but they are the sweetest, most precious tears I ever wept. I did not want to write before I was sure of myself; so many things have passed in this poor head of mine! I seem to awaken from a strange dream. Poor George, you deceived yourself. You thought yourself my mistress, you were only my mother. Heaven made us for each other, but our embrace was too intense, we committed incest."

He told her how he ran around Geneva looking into the shops, and how he bought a new vest which delighted him. He put it on and looked at himself in the glass. Suddenly he realized what a child he had been. As he looked at his image in the mirror he asked, "Was that the man you wanted to love? For ten years you suffered. For ten years you carried in your heart the inextinguishable thirst for happiness, and that was the reed on which you tried to lean! I left you so worn out, so exhausted by those two months of suffering. I made you so unhappy! For a long time to come I shall see your face, that has grown so pale with watching those eighteen nights at my bedside."

George was deeply touched by the discovery that the self-absorbed poet was capable of such sympathy. Why could he not have given it to her when he was there beside her? How she had needed it then! It would have meant balm and healing. But sympathy is always welcome even when it comes too late. How close he seemed now that he was far away. She was impelled to open her heart to him and expose the feelings she had been too proud to express.

"Do not believe, never believe, Alfred, that I can be happy in the thought that I have lost your heart. Whether I have been your mistress or your mother is not important. Whether I inspired you with love or friendship, whether I was happy or unhappy with you—all that does not alter my present state of mind. I know that I care for you and that is all."

She refers to the happiness she used to feel in doing for him, surrounding him with diversions and guarding him from harm. "What fatality has changed into poison all the healing I offered you? Why did I become to you a torment, a scourge, a spectre? When these terrible memories assail me (and when do they leave me in peace?) I am driven mad." She tells him that except for the appeal of his youth and for her own weakness caused by his tears on a certain morning, they would have remained brother and sister. "What difference does it make, after all? We have been lovers, and we know each other to the bottom of the soul. So much the better! Oh, what misery it would have been for us if we had separated in a moment of anger without understanding each other, without explaining ourselves. It would have poisoned our whole existence. We would never have believed in anything again."

The farther away he goes the more completely she forgets all her injuries. Was he unkind or cruel? Did he call her offensive names and cease to love her? All that miserable period is obliterated. She does not remember any wrongs. She does not want him to ask her forgiveness. She would rather ask his. She does not remember anything except that they were very unhappy and they separated. "But I know—I feel—that we shall always care for each other until the end of our lives."

More and more she wrote about this faith, that there was something left from the wreck of their love affair—a fraternal friendship that would endure throughout old age. Always they must be able to say to each other, "We have loved, we have suffered, and now we esteem each other." She encouraged him to find another sweetheart. He must not fear, he must have trust, he must be willing to take the risk. It is better to suffer and to be mistaken than to live without love. When he finds that sweetheart, perhaps she will say, "Do not speak to me about Madame Sand. She is an infamous woman." If such is the case she will stay away from him, she will understand.

So they agreed that each should find another love-life, while maintaining an affectionate friendship that would endure throughout old age.

II

Gradually George absorbed the shock of Alfred's departure and settled down with Pagello. She even felt at times a sense of liberation and freedom. She reasoned with herself. After all, what she really wanted was a husband. She hated changes, upheavals, unfaithfulness, uncertainty. She longed to be united to a manly man in a changeless, restful bond that made for permanence and peace. For this she had stayed with Casimir long after her hopes had been broken. For this she had taken Jules. In this hope she had taken Mérimée and now again Pagello. And Alfred? No, she had not taken Alfred as a husband. Marriage was not Alfred's vocation. That she had taken him as a lover was her great mistake. She loved him. She continued to love him, but only as her child. Pagello would make a model husband. He was faithful and devoted. They would spend their life together, at least part of their life; of course not all of it. One half of each year she would give to her children, the other half to Pagello and Italy. At Venice, and with

Pagello, she could work without interruption. It would be a sort
of marriage. She was really a moral being. It would satisfy her
moral ideas.

And so they began their new life. Pagello had a brother Robert
and a half-sister Julia. The two men shared the second floor of a
shabby old house, the Casa Mezzani. The two women occupied
the apartment beneath. The room which was to serve them all as
salon was bare, and George furnished it. She made the curtains
and cushions, upholstered all the furniture in chintz and slowly
succeeded in embroidering tapestry for six chairs, re-upholstering
them one by one as the work was completed. Although she spent
most of the day in writing, during her odds and ends of time she
was domestic. She helped their one servant prepare meals. She
knitted socks for the two men, and presented brother Robert with
four pairs. She renovated her own clothes and trimmed her hats.
On Sunday she went to church with Pagello. The music and the
slow intoning of Latin always stirred her emotions. Thinking of
her children, her three children, Maurice, Solange and Alfred, she
wept with loneliness.

There were long family evenings. Julia sang and George accompanied her on the piano. Pagello looked on with husband-like pride,
approving these feminine accomplishments, extolling George
to the skies. He anticipated her needs, ran her errands, sympathized with her headaches, felt her pulse often and bled her occasionally to keep her in good health. He found that George herself knew a surprising amount about medicine. The professional
physician and the amateur exchanged stories about their cases.
Pagello was amazed at his sweetheart's versatility. There never
was a woman who knew so much about so many things, nor one
who was so active and industrious and serviceable. It seemed to
Pagello that she was made to be the good wife of a good man.

He could not do enough for her. When she wanted flowers and
he felt too poor to buy them, he started early in the morning and

ranged the countryside, bringing home great armfuls of wild-flowers with which to decorate her rooms.

He was solicitous about her work and protected her from callers. Literary Venetians, who had discovered that the author of *Lélia* was in their midst, were keen to meet her. They sent invitations, wrote letters, applied to the French consul for introductions. Pagello answered the letters, refused their invitations, and kept them away so that his Lélia could write in peace. How wonderful she seemed to him! He was too modest to intrude his own affairs and his own ideas upon the marvelous mind of his beloved companion. His part was to listen while she talked about whatever she pleased.

It pleased her to talk about Alfred. She spent the happiest hours of her day talking to Pagello about Alfred, his bad conduct, his magnificent behavior, his future, his genius, his wit, his wickedness, and how much she missed him.

Pagello was not jealous. Why should he be jealous of a man who was far away, who was, besides, only a child? Pagello could proudly measure himself against this infant. He was thirty years old, a trifle older than George. He was so good he did not need to be saved, so strong he did not require protection, so grown up he did not demand indulgence. It seemed to him natural that George preferred him to Alfred. He was not conceited, but anyone could see that he was the better man of the two.

Was George in love with Pagello? She was very fond of him, she appreciated his faithfulness, but—there were so many buts. He was "a mute who would cut off his head for her," but she did not like mutes. He lacked enthusiasm and she was accustomed to enthusiasm. He saw her only as a wife. He was used to Italian women and he liked them stupid and good. He had not read *Lélia*, could not understand it, did not understand romanticism. In short, he was not Alfred. No one but Alfred had ever given her the illusion of complete oneness. She had been the mistress of a poet. She was now the wife of a general practitioner. It rested her, it was conducive to work, but it did not satisfy the soul.

There was something substantial about Pagello. All his habits were different from Alfred's. He was out all day as a husband should be, he came home to dine as a husband should, and spent his evenings at home. He was a lump of solid virtue. And since George never went anywhere and since Pagello hesitated to intrude his affairs, they were soon talked out. Besides, it tired Pagello to try to talk French, and, although he would not confess it, it was almost equally tiring to listen to George's Italian. Her soothing embroidering made him feel drowsy, so that shortly after dinner Pagello would fall asleep. At first he merely dozed in a chair, but after a time, as he felt more at ease with George, he would throw himself down on a sofa and fall asleep there.

George would gaze for a time at her model husband, so good, so devoted, so fast asleep, and then her thoughts would go to Alfred. She would re-read his letters to relieve her loneliness, and answer them to create in herself a sense of companionship.

Her one link with the outside world was Alfred. Her mother disapproved of her stay in Italy and did not write to her. Hippolyte did not write, Casimir sent brief family letters at long intervals, Boucoiran, who had charge of her affairs, was a poor correspondent, and her other friends had long ago been alienated by her exclusive devotion to one man. Her only real letters came from Alfred. He alone knew her surroundings, her associations, her contacts. He alone would care to hear about the little happenings of every day or the thoughts and emotions of her inner life. That he cared to hear, that he hungered to hear, became more and more evident as his letters grew longer and more impassioned. They arrived by every post. Each letter that penetrated into her humdrum workaday life lifted her into exaltation, and while this mood continued she would answer, pouring out her soul.

It seemed that at last they had found the right relation to each other, that of mystic spiritual union, which left each one free.

Pagello was not self-centered. He was willing to revolve about George. He deferred to her and let her take the lead. To please Pagello, George tried to be interested in herself, to dwell on herself, to be self-centered, but the effort went against her nature. It made her restless, filled her with vague homesickness for someone more demanding, more assertive, someone upon whom she could spend herself. Each of these two natures was outgoing, each needed an egoist. They often wished Alfred were with them. They recalled the delightful trips the three had made together to the islands and neighboring quais, days on which they had spent long hours in the gondola. On those occasions they had never been bored, because Alfred talked and they listened, feeling between themselves a secret silent sympathy which drew them together.

Alfred had related them to each other. Without him they fell apart. How they longed for their little egomaniac! He was exciting, absorbing, upsetting, exhausting. How time had flown when they listened to Alfred while he talked about himself! How time dragged now that they were left alone to talk about each other!

12

While George was adjusting herself to new conditions in Italy, Alfred was readjusting himself to old associations in Paris. He returned home hungry for pleasure and diversion. He found himself an object of curiosity and interest, fêted like a prodigal son of whom everyone was a near relative. Two weeks before his arrival everyone who was anyone in Paris had been told his whole sad history. The poor poet, so they said, had been preyed upon by an infamous woman, who had carried him away to Italy where she had ruined his health, broken his heart, and eloped with another man. His youth, his beauty, even his vices, made him in the eyes of the world a fascinating figure.

Every afternoon he would dress with extreme care for his appearance in public. He would draw on his white gloves, put a flower in his buttonhole, pick up his ornate cane. Then, with his hat carefully set over one ear and a tuft of blond hair sticking out over the other, he would saunter along the boulevards or the Champs Elysées, conspicuous, romantic, a sad smile playing about his full red lips. Picturesque he was, and, in the light of his sad history, pathetic. He was invited everywhere. He was pitied, petted and admired.

In the midst of new distractions he forgot George, forgot to send her any word of his safe return. He did not even instruct Antonio to send her a line. On the 21st of May he mailed her a letter which was dated the 19th. He had arrived in Paris on the 12th. In this letter he repeats to George the calumnies that are being circulated about her, and assures her that his voice will always be raised in her defense. The faithful Planche defends her, he says, so do Jules Sandeau and Boucoiran. Sainte-Beuve and Buloz seem non-partisan or non-committal. The women blame her, and kind friends run to Madame de Musset with tales against "that wicked woman." Alfred tells Madame de Musset how devotedly George nursed him. That should be enough to pacify a mother's heart.

"I have thrown myself head over heels back into my old life. I have come home with the firm intention of amusing myself and of seeking a new love. I have not yet dined with my mother."

One has visions of Madame de Musset overseeing the preparation of Alfred's favorite dishes, the waiting of dinner, the nightly disappointment, the daily hope that he will stay at home. But the fond indulgent mother knew at least that her son loved her. She has the last letter preceding his return in which he had written, "I am bringing back to you a sick body, an exhausted soul, and a bleeding heart which still loves you."

That letter was written by the poet at a distance from his mother. Again at a distance from George the poet wrote, "It is not my mistress whom I miss. It is my comrade George. I do not need a woman, I need that rapt attention which I used always to find at my side ready to respond to me. Adieu, my first and last love, my friend, my only mistress. Write to me, above all, write to me."

Alfred's escape from the vampire seemed to have excited the hopes of other would-be vampires. Many women made overtures to him. One said with a sigh, "The day you were born, be sure a woman was born to be your mate." He agreed with her politely, decided that she was not the born mate, and went home and wrote about it to George.

On another occasion when a woman asked him three times in succession whether it were true that Madame Dudevant was adorable, he smiled and said nothing, while he thought to himself and wrote to George, "I will not deny my savior."

He tells George he has made up his mind to fall in love again as quickly as possible, but is determined to find a woman who is young and who has a virgin heart. Never again will he give his trust to a woman who has loved another. He cannot bear the thought of a predecessor. It is not enough that his sweetheart should belong to him in the present. All her past must be his. He does not care about beauty as much as he used to.

For some reason personality seems more important to him now than physical allure. But the one thing he cannot get along without is brains. When he finds himself at dinner next to a chorus girl she bores him to extinction. Yet there was a time when her type delighted him. Now he demands "a lofty intelligence, youth, and a virgin heart." This exact combination is exceedingly rare, but nothing else will do for Alfred de Musset. He knows himself corrupted by dissipation. Nevertheless, or perhaps therefore, he requires a fresh untouched nature. Youth and virtue are all about him, but in his yearning for a pure young girl he finds himself facing a great danger. All pure young girls have set their hearts on marriage. He must of course protect himself from falling into that trap. And where are the women with lofty intelligence? He cannot discover them. His thoughts keep returning to George. How she understood him! How tolerant she was and how forgiving! She alone recognized the poet in the lover. She saw his idiosyncrasies as part of his genius. What he wants is another George Sand, one who will give up her work and concentrate on him and use her lofty intelligence in his service. It ought not to be impossible to find another younger, fresher, more virginal George.

He was always on the lookout, and yet in all Paris, perhaps in all the world, he could not find another George Sand. He was surprised and hurt by his failure. He was dazed at his own insistence on intelligence. Why had he changed so in his attitude toward women? He was a year older, that explained it. A year ago he had seen women merely as bits of decoration or creatures of sex. Now he saw them as beings who could respond to and understand a man of genius. Yet no one was fully responsive to him, no one understood his genius, no one appreciated how different he was from other men. Everyone seemed to lack sympathetic imagination. What had happened to make him so fastidious? It must have been his illness. That was it, illness had made him more serious, more discriminating about women.

All this he wrote to George and she sympathized. "Tell me that you are happy and I shall be," she repeats again and again.

He wept often and always told George about it. He went to her rooms at quai Malaquais, where he found some cigarettes she had rolled and left there. In a mood of intense suffering he smoked the cigarettes that had been touched by her fingers. He found also a bit of broken comb and carried it in his pocket because it had touched her hair.

Notwithstanding all that was childish, vain and snobbish, he sent her poetic letters full of tenderness, loneliness and longing; and George, in spite of excessive solicitude and many little preachments about health and moderation, answered with motherly letters full of a great love that gave all and asked in return "a corner of your heart."

She had found in him, now that he was no longer in love with her, an ideal lover freed from possessiveness and jealousy. And he, now that she belonged to another, had found in her the perfect mistress, always desired and desirable because she was beyond his reach.

It took ten days at least for mail to travel between Paris and Venice, and the post was often delayed. The letters went their slow way back and forth, carrying their exaltation of soul, the ache of their hearts, and the inconsistencies of their shifting moods. There was much fine language and flowery speech, since that was the manner of the times. There was the exaggeration of romanticism, since that was the romantic period. And woven with the artificial literature they made for each other there was the simple appealing story of two human beings who struggled to understand each other and themselves. One reads of eagles and mountain peaks and heaven and ecstasy and God, and perhaps the very next paragraph will relate to practical matters that are handled—by George at least—with businesslike dispatch.

George, when she descended from the mountain tops, was occupied with two overwhelming, ever present anxieties, her children and her debts. During all her stay in Venice she had worried over her children. She had written for news of them to her husband, to her mother, and to Boucoiran, and she had written often to her son, Maurice. Her letters to Casimir were surprisingly wifely. Casimir wanted to rid himself of Solange as once before he had rid himself of Maurice. George begged him to postpone his decision until she returned to Nohant for the autumn holidays.

She was concerned also about Maurice. Boucoiran had not written about the boy for two months. Her worry and suffering were constantly growing greater. She dreamed of Maurice at night. Often she dreamed he was dead. When Alfred left she asked him to call at Maurice's school and send her word of the boy. But Alfred wrote that he could not obey her because to see Maurice would awaken painful memories, since the boy had his mother's eyes. Whom else could she ask? Sainte-Beuve was not an intimate friend of that sort, and Planche has been alienated.

"It is ages since I asked Boucoiran if they are satisfied with my son at school and if he has seen his reports. I have received no answer. Forgive me for speaking of my anxieties, but for the love of God go and see my son; tell me how he is and if he remembers me."

After this appeal Alfred went to see Maurice. He found the boy well and in charge of his two grandmothers.

As for the ever present problem of money, George owed Buloz and La Rochefoucauld and her rent bill in Paris. In Venice she had borrowed from her Italian friend Rebizzo. She would not take money from Pagello. "That would be too odious." Buloz would not pay her until she had finished *André.* Very well, she finished it, and probably Buloz handed the money to Boucoiran, who had charge of her business affairs. But no word had been received from Boucoiran. She had earned the money and it did not come. She was sleeping on a bare mattress. She would have to economize on her food. Finally, in desperation, she told Alfred about her money worries. Alfred rose to the emergency. "Remember that in all circumstances my life belongs to you and you will be doing me a service in asking me to perform one for you."

He then told her to borrow some more money from Rebizzo.

On June 15th she was almost in the position of one who hesitates whether to steal or beg, thanks to the indifference of her friends Buloz and Boucoiran, who had left her since April 1st with only a hundred francs. She had worked enormously and had earned enough to pay her most pressing debts and live in comfort. "This extreme misery poisons my life and forces me to continual privations. You have no idea of the economy with which I live and the persistence with which I work. It is getting fantastic, but I prefer an existence a trifle less sublime."

Alfred once more rises to the emergency. "Remember that nothing but your life proves to me that I live. If you tell me to contract a debt for you I will do it gladly, and I will pay it later by my work."

But he did not work, nor did he contract a debt. He could easily have borrowed from his mother—he did not conceal this fact from George. On the contrary, he naïvely confided to her that his mother had offered to give him what money he required. It did not occur to him to take advantage of this offer. Toward his own mother he was sensitive and proud. But, like Casimir, like Jules Sandeau, Alfred had no economic pride in his attitude toward George. Her nature was over-generous and in consequence her men became irresponsible.

In her reply to Alfred she told him that he must wait three years before repaying what he owed her, and that he must work only to amuse himself.

13

George's first disappointment in Pagello was his silence. Her second disappointment was named Arpalice. Pagello, who had so successfully protected his Lélia from callers, did not succeed in shielding her from a visit from Arpalice. For this visit there were no preliminaries such as letters or introductions. With the simple directness of a primitive nature, the woman made her way into Madame Dudevant's room and demanded her lover.

George did not, perhaps, expect that Pagello had no ties to break, although she might have expected him to have broken them more thoroughly before taking up his existence with her. But here was Arpalice explaining her side of the question. She had been deserted, and she wanted Madame Dudevant to give Pagello back to her. There was something about Arpalice that was reminiscent of Jules's laundress and Casimir's chambermaids and Alfred's chorus girls.

A few days later George heard a noise in Pagello's room which sounded "as though he were trying to operate on thirty cats tied together." George opened her door and looked out. She saw Pagello chasing Arpalice from his room with terrible language. George protected Arpalice, who then turned on George and threatened to assassinate her. George replied that she would call the police. Julia took the threat seriously and was absurdly worried about George's safety. Arpalice pulled out handfuls of Pagello's hair and destroyed his beautiful new coat. And George wrote about it to Alfred.

By this time George had disciplined herself to accept the French point of view toward women. She had only to extend her tolerance to include the Italian. But in spite of philosophy, her sensibilities seem to have been jarred. She decided to go away and thought longingly of Constantinople. She wrote home, "I should be very glad to get hold of the small sum of seven or eight hundred francs to make this trip to Constantinople." She could not follow her feeling for the same reason that she could not go home. She had no money. After she had made her last loan to Alfred, at the time of his departure, she was left with one hundred francs and she had received no more. She adjusted herself to the inevitable, reminding herself constantly how good Pagello was, and yet wondering all the time how she could ever have imagined him ideal.

Lonely, homesick, consumed by longing for her children, oppressed by debt, struggling with the fatigue of overwork, she wrote to Alfred, making light of all her troubles. As for health, she is strong as a horse. As for loneliness, she is surrounded by friends and a happy family circle. As for Pagello, she praises his goodness but she cannot restrain herself from confiding to Alfred: "At last I have learned to love with my eyes open. For the first time in my life I love without passion. When we are together I become stupid and good as he wishes me to be."

No golden glow remained about her Italian lover. His ex-mistresses—there were three of them—had destroyed the magic. Her mind reverted to her old preference for friendship. She regarded Pagello as a kind elder brother. If she could not go to Constantinople she could at least leave the family circle. "At the end of a month," relates Pagello, "she decided to move, and establish herself near the Bridge Barcaroli in a side street leading to the bridge. In this house she wrote *Lettres d'un Voyageur* and the novel *Jacques*." George wrote Alfred that Pagello still came to dine with her, but often left at eight o'clock.

She no longer wrote letters explaining to her friends that she expected to spend half of each year in Venice. In a letter to her brother she said, "If I had the money I would go to Paris and no-where else," and she told him, "I am now able to write thirteen hours a day without fatigue, although my average is seven or eight hours." In great haste she completed a short novel entitled *Léone Léoni*. The scene is laid in Venice. Léone Léoni is a fascinating scoundrel. He is about to marry the beautiful Juliette, but on the eve of the wedding he persuades her to elope instead and dispense with the ceremony. Juliette loves Léone in spite of his sins and his disordered life. In the course of time Juliette finds herself de-serted. She then falls in love with an excellent young man who proposes marriage, but on the eve of her wedding Juliette hears Léone's voice calling her. She returns to her wicked lover and leaves her devoted fiancé to undeserved loneliness.

This story of self-abnegating love fascinated George's readers, and was an enormous success. It is asserted that the influence of this novel on the mind of Countess d'Agoult decided her to share the fate of the musician Liszt and follow him into his voluntary exile.

Léone Léoni comprises two hundred and fifty pages. It was completed in one week. What an example of George's capacity for imagination and emotion and work! It may be presumed that during this week of creative obsession George was not very lively company in the evening. Knowing how she identified herself with her characters, one can imagine her gazing at Pagello, thinking how good and devoted he was, and at the same time hearing in-wardly the sound of Alfred's voice which she would willingly follow to the ends of the earth.

Next followed *Jacques*, a long serious work. *Jacques* was the

novel which shocked the world. Even George Sand's ardent admirers apologize for it and beg us to forget it or to regard it as a
work of temporary aberration. She allows her hero Jacques to
criticize the institution of marriage. He prophesies that, as we
grow more civilized, marriage will be outgrown and will give
place to some kind of civil contract or experimental union which
can be dissolved at will. Jacques is a heroic character. Living in
an age which does not permit divorce, he tries to give happiness
to his young wife and the man of her choice. As the only solution
to their problem he commits suicide by falling over a precipice
in such a manner that his death seems to have been an accident.

Jacques outraged public opinion. Husbands especially disapproved. What if every wife in search of happiness should expect
her husband to commit suicide! It seemed to many readers that
the book should be suppressed. However, this excitement was
created later when the book was published.

While George was writing *Jacques* she was wholly absorbed in
thoughts of Alfred, magnanimous Alfred, who went to Paris and
nobly resigned her to Pagello. Alfred is, of course, the idealized
Jacques, whose exalted character is a tribute to the poet's superhuman nobility. If Léone suggests Alfred's fascinating wickedness, Jacques is undoubtedly the prototype of the poet's angel
side.

14

George never wavered from the plan she had made in April to
reach Paris in time to attend the closing exercises of Maurice's
school. She looked forward to the September holidays, which she
intended to spend with her children at Nohant. Toward this she
bent her energies. *Jacques* was completed before her departure.
The first volume reached Buloz in time for him to forward one
thousand francs. With the money received for *André* she paid her
most pressing debts in Paris and all her Venetian debts. With
Jacques she paid her way home and had money to spare for any

emergency. Pagello adds to the universal testimony that George "was prodigal for others but miserly toward herself." Considering this tendency, emergencies were sure to arise.

Pagello was undecided whether or not to go to Paris. George asked him to accompany her, and Alfred wrote urging him to come. "You must come, my friend, or else you must not allow her to leave. Three hundred *lieus* are too long for a woman to travel alone. I know that her answer to this objection will be that she is as strong as a Turk. But I will whisper something in your ear so low that she cannot hear me. The smallest Turk is stronger than the strongest woman in Europe. I who am not a Turk assure you that this is so. Believe me and come.—Alf'd de M't."

Pagello's own account of his decision follows:

"I arranged my affairs as well as I could so as to raise a little money. On the next day I told her I would go with her, but that I insisted on living alone in Paris and did not want to be urged to go to La Châtre, as I preferred to benefit by my stay in the great capital by visiting the hospitals and pursuing my professional studies. I said it rather sadly but emphatically, and she answered, 'My friend, you shall do as you please.' I had understood her and she had understood me. From that time the relation between us was that of friends—at least on her side. As for me, I was satisfied to be only her friend, but I felt that I was still in love with her."

15

George reached Paris completely happy. Not only was she restored to Maurice, but she had beside her, her kind elder brother Pagello and her sublime child Alfred. She felt that the triangular friendship was certain to be harmonious. It had been so when Alfred left Venice, it so continued in all their correspondence, it was so now in their three souls.

Had not Alfred said of Pagello, "Splendid fellow, when I think of him I can hardly restrain my tears!—He is a noble creature who loves you as you deserve to be loved—I love him almost as much as I love you"?

Had he not called Pagello his own better self? Had he not placed George under Pagello's protection? Had he not written directly to Pagello declaring himself one of Pagello's best friends?

Alfred was a changed being. He said himself that his jealousy had been infantilism. It was a thing outgrown. He assured George that he was a man now. And George believed him. As for Pagello, the beautiful thing about the calm Italian had always been his large incapacity for jealousy and suspicion. Toward Alfred he felt as a father. He had sent his love to the poet repeatedly. He had written to him, "Love me as I love you." He had referred to the sentiment which linked them together as "an affection sublime to us and incomprehensible to others."

George believed in both her men. She based her faith on their explanations of their own high-mindedness. It looked as though the dream she had expressed to Alfred might come true: "Why can't I live between you two and make you both happy, without belonging to either of you? I could live like that ten years." She meant it quite literally. She could have lived like that as long as her two men were happy. It may be said that her naïveté was ridiculous, or with equal truth it might be urged that her faith in perfection was magnificent.

But her idealism, whether naïve or magnificent, unfitted her to cope with human nature as it is. She could never see that sex was more important than love. Both men professed to love her. Both had surrendered the sex claim, so why couldn't they all be happy together? It never seemed absurd to her to demand the impossible of herself or others. The fact that each man had been her lover was to her a matter of no great importance. To each of the men it was the most important thing in life.

Pagello took up his residence at the Hotel d'Orléans. He seemed in no hurry to begin his studies. He hung around the apartment at 19 quai Malaquais. He could not tear himself away from George.

When Alfred came to call, Pagello was present. The two men at first meeting greeted each other cordially. But when Alfred inclined his head toward George in that little way he had, and lifted his blue eyes to hers adoringly, Pagello felt like murder. And when Pagello stood stolidly by in his best proprietary manner and would not budge from her side, Alfred shot hot hatred out of his red-lidded eyes. George looked at them, astounded. The passion that blazed between the two men scorched the very soul of her. It destroyed her hopes, devastated her illusions, and laid waste her dream.

After Alfred's visit she was exhausted, and Pagello, who out-stayed him, regarded her exhaustion as proof of her preference for the poet. Alfred, in his turn, wrote a heart-rending note to George. He had counted too much on himself in seeing her again. He was leaving for Spain in order to put the mountains and the sea between them. He would never return to France. He would expatriate himself. And since he was leaving forever, he begged for one last interview with her alone.

George's idealism had led her into an impossible situation. She could not see Alfred alone without hurting Pagello, so at first she refused the interview for Pagello's sake. Alfred wrote again, in more heart-rending phrases, insisting that she see him secretly. She would not see him secretly and yet she could not let him suffer. Pagello agreed to absent himself while Alfred called once more.

George and Alfred met alone. George tried to make him see that his banishment was wholly superfluous, since she was leaving for Nohant in four days. But the poet would not be dissuaded from his dramatic exile. He wanted it understood that he intended to die under foreign skies. George talked to him of his youth, of future glory, of hope and faith in himself, and then, before George had given Alfred his eternal farewell, Pagello walked in on them.

George rose to the emergency. She kissed Alfred on the

forehead, and then, in French fashion, once on each cheek. She did it so simply that jealous Pagello did not seem to mind at all. There were moments, evidently, when George was able to lift men to the level of her dream.

Alfred left France "forever." Was he trying to win sympathy, to attract attention, or merely to dramatize the situation? Whatever his motive, he accepted the money from his mother, packed his bags and left. But he did not go to Spain. He went to Baden, and there he stayed. He did not work for glory as George had urged, nor did he write for Buloz as he had promised. He moped in solitude and wrote a long letter to George. He had put her beyond his reach and he loved her to distraction.

Before her departure for Nohant George turned her attention to Pagello. The Italian doctor was introduced to several eminent physicians and was given the run of the Paris hospitals with admission to the clinics. Buloz presented him with a free pass to the theatres, and Boucoiran promised to take charge of his welfare. But Pagello preferred Alfred Tattet, whom he had known at Venice; Tattet, who, next to Alfred's brother, Paul de Musset, was George's worst enemy. After George went away, Pagello was lonely and began to feel injured and critical. Influenced by Tattet, his eyes were open at last. He saw clearly that George was a vampire. He forgot that he had fallen in love with her at first sight. He persuaded himself that she had dragged him into a love affair, broken his heart, sucked his blood and ruined his career. She had lured him from his duty to his father and his patients and his prostitutes. He had been respectable until he had met her. His father had always told him it was unchristian and immoral to live openly with a foreigner. Now he saw that his father was right and that his affair with the Frenchwoman was a scandal. Pagello remembered Musset's cordial letter urging him to come to Paris. He thought of all the time and attention he had lavished on Musset in Venice, and felt hurt that the Frenchman had shown no hospitality in return.

Poor Pagello! He longed to hear his own language and see his own people. He wanted to go home and devote himself to his career and Arpalice. But he could not leave Paris because he had no money. He had brought with him four oil paintings by Zugarelli which he had hoped to sell. But art dealers set no value on them and no one wanted to buy. If he could not sell his paintings he would starve. His meals became more meager every day.

George had felt in Italy that she would rather die than borrow from Pagello, and now Pagello in Paris proved himself equally proud. While waiting for George to come back and solve his problem he felt increasingly bitter toward her. Pagello had admired and adored his mistress, but he had not been clever enough to hold her. Naturally he blamed the mistress for her failure to be held.

Alfred at Baden was trying to write a book about George, but he was surprised to find that he knew very little about his loved one. What had they talked of when they were together? He could not paint a picture of her life. Perhaps, after all, the story would have to be about himself and his own life. He could put her in as the object of his affections. Still, this was hardly fulfilling his promise—"I shall build you an altar with my bones." He decided he was unable to write at present; he was unhappy; it was her fault.

Alfred had lost the only woman in the world worth possessing. He had once possessed her, and had thrown her away, had blessed her union with another. He saw his mistake and regretted it, and quite naturally blamed the woman.

Meanwhile George at Nohant was in a family turmoil. Casimir drank and scolded and resented her presence. He flew into violent rages before the children, and Maurice was old enough to be hurt and disturbed by the discord between his parents. What could she do about this terrible mistaken marriage? Casimir declared he hated Nohant and wanted to live in Paris. But when George agreed to stay at Nohant with the children and maintain it at her own expense, he was angry and refused. She assured Casimir he would always be welcome to come back and stay with them. His answer was that he would never set foot in a house where he was not the sole master. Unhappy Casimir had never tried to do anything or be anything since his marriage. He had lived on his wife. He was a failure and he had to blame someone, so quite naturally he blamed his wife.

George, the woman, wife and mistress, naturally blamed the three men because not one of them was meeting her ideal. She felt weighed down by responsibility for three ruined lives. She did not know what to do about any one of them. They seemed helpless, weakly willing to let their lives be ruined, while she was struggling with greater burdens than had been laid on them. They seemed free and unappreciative of their freedom.

It now appeared that Pagello had deceived her as to his true character. His lack of jealousy had been the security of absolute possession. "From the moment he set foot in Paris he no longer understood anything." He had lost all his simple goodness and had become suspicious and unreasonable. George, who had thought him strong, now considered him a weak creature. She was disillusioned, but she was determined to remain his friend. When she tried to stop thinking about Pagello she worried over Alfred. If she took her thoughts off Alfred they returned to Casimir. She did not know which of the three men worried her most.

One afternoon at Nohant, feeling the need of solitude, she left the children to their naps and Casimir to his black humor and went into the woods near the château. It was a soft September day and she tried to find healing in the soothing influence of trees and birds and flowers. She took with her paper and pencil and the little album in which she pressed her flowers. She was in no mood to write to Alfred, but she realized his impatience. She knew he was watching the post, counting the days. How could she bring herself to write to him when her mind was burdened by her own problems? She brooded over her children, her hopeless future, and her miserable past. She thought of Casimir and his resentment, of Pagello and his unhappiness.

Then she re-read Alfred's letter.

"My dear soul: You have the heart of an angel. I want to talk to you of my love. Ah, George, what a love! No man has ever loved as I love you. I am lost, do you understand, I am drowned, submerged by love; I no longer know whether I live or eat or walk or breathe or speak; I only know that I love you, my life, my well-being, my well-beloved. Say to yourself that you are loved as much as God is loved by his priests and worshippers and martyrs! I love you, O my flesh and my blood! I die of love, of a love without name—mad, desperate, lost! You are loved, adored, idolized to the point of death! No, I shall never be cured. No, I shall not try to live. I prefer it this way, death for love of you is more precious than life. I know only too well what they say. They say you have another lover. I know it. It is killing me, but I love you, love you, love you. No one can prevent me from loving you! I said to myself that I must live, that I must take another love, forget yours, have courage. I tried, at least I made an effort. But now, listen to me, I love my suffering better than life. Oh, my betrothed—think of your child who is about to die! Try to forget everything else, re-read my letters if you have them, or my little book; think—let your heart go out to me—weep for me—and then take your pen and give an hour to your poor friend. Give me all there is in your heart for me. Even force yourself a little; that is no crime, my child. Tell me even more than you are feeling. I won't know the difference —it won't be a crime—I am lost! But let there be nothing in your letter but your friendship for me, your love, George, don't you call it love? Let me have a letter in which there is nothing but your love—and tell me that you give me your lips, your teeth, your hair, all—all that head of yours which I have had, and tell me that you kiss me, you—me! O God, O God, when

I think of it, my throat contracts, my eyes fill, my knees tremble. Ah, it is horrible to die, it is horrible to love like this. What thirst, my love—oh, what thirst I have for you! I beg you, let me have that letter. I am dying! Farewell! Oh, my life, my life, I press you to my heart. Oh, my George, my beautiful mistress! My first, my last love!"

This adoring, impassioned letter awakened no response in her. Its appeal only increased her melancholy. Why could she not respond to him? Pictures flashed across her mind of the devastating influence of his passion. She tried to imagine Alfred in her apartment, belonging there as he used to do. No, she could not go through it again. She did not want to lose the mystic union of the last five months. She preferred it to frenzied love. It was not Alfred alone she feared. She knew herself. She could not stand out against him. She would yield, submit, be subjugated again. It was her fatal way of loving. She could not love in any other way. Her heart cried out for the exalted moods of her mad poet, but her reason told her that she must not yield to his tyrannous love. She did not want to be a slave again.

Just at the moment reason was uppermost. There had always been a conflict between her love for the poet and her love for her own children. Now her maternal need was satisfied, she was with her children. They had the prior claim and they absorbed her attention.

There was one part of his letter which especially wounded her spirit. She read the passage again. So he wanted her to deceive him! Yet at Venice this was the one thing he could not forgive. Now he begged her to pretend to him, and for the same reason for which she had been obliged to pretend to him at Venice, to save him from suffering. Now, pretending was no crime; yet at Venice it had been a crime. What did he mean? How was she ever to know what he really meant about anything? He was coming back to Paris. He did not even mean what he had said about going to Spain. Decidedly, she could not rely on this capricious passion. She was happier, much happier with the love he felt for her in absence. Her answer to his letter conveyed all the reproach she felt.

"Alas, alas! What does this mean? This is passion and not friendship. Nevertheless I do not worry over these expressions. I know they are only your poetic way of using language. But now you go to extremes, and Pagello does the same. He complains of my sadness and my failing health. Can't he appreciate that I have other things to worry me besides you two men? When you were leaving, you said to me, 'Are you unhappy?' and I said, 'Yes, on account of my children. I cannot bear to lose them even though to keep them I must break from everything in my life.' Poor Pierre, he suffers and I must try to console him, and you will help me, won't you, for I feel that these emotional upheavals are killing me. Each day I find myself more ill and more discouraged with life. I feel that we three must separate without bitterness and without violence. Do not love me any more, do you understand? I am worthless—I doubt everything. My heart is frozen —I am telling you all this because if we are to see each other in Paris you must not have any idea of renewed intimacy with me. We must leave each other, do you understand? We must do this because you are persuaded that you cannot be cured of this love which you nevertheless so solemnly abjured at Venice before and also after your illness.

"Farewell, then, to the beautiful poem of our exalted friendship and of this ideal tie which was formed between us three. Was it all romance? Yes, it was only a dream, and I alone, imbecile child that I am, accepted it in good faith. Now, after this awakening, I see that one of you desires me and that the other abandons and affronts me. Am I still expected to believe in ideal love? No, there is no such thing in this world. Those who mock at everything are right. If it were not for my children I would willingly throw myself into the river."

In his response to this frozen, reproachful letter, Musset told

her there were many pretty women at Baden who would be very
glad to receive him. He had only to put on his shoes and his coat
and go make love to them. Certainly they would not leave a
lover merely because they feared to be misunderstood. He made
no reference to George's worries over her children and her marriage. As for helping her with Pagello, he told her that at Paris
Pierre opened a letter George had written to him. The wretched
Italian was so mad with jealousy that he broke the seal, then closed
it again with his thumb.

"If he suffers, very well, let him suffer, this Venetian who
taught me to suffer! I give him back the lesson he taught me.
As for you, be forewarned, I give you back your own words:
I have written this so that if you hear of my return, you need not
have any idea of renewed intimacy with me."

In spite of these haughty recriminations he pleads with her
to see him again in Paris. This is the chief emphasis of his letter.
Will she see him again, will she, will she? He lives only to see her
again.

George accepted this letter of petty childishness as she did the
letter of poetic passion, saying to herself that one must not take
Alfred too literally, the meaning under his words showed that
he was deeply wounded by her coldness and preoccupation. She
realized that she must not expect help for her own problems
from Alfred, nor from Pagello, nor from Casimir. She must go
on working, waiting for her children to outgrow Casimir's legal
control. In the meantime there remained loneliness—the loneliness she could not endure.

Each one of these three tortured souls sought his own escape
from suffering. Casimir, who wanted to be important, found
oblivion in his wine cellar. Alfred, who wanted to prove his
genius, and who had promised Buloz to employ his solitude in
writing a novel and some poems, rushed back to Paris and its
devastating attractions. Pagello, who wanted Italy, devoted himself to the study of surgery.

And George, who wanted nothing in the world but love, started a new novel in order to earn money.

It was, as always, terribly necessary to earn money. Casimir had bought land he could not pay for, and had stocked his wine cellar at great expense. She was concerned to pay his debts. She had also to meet obligations of her own. And there was Pagello, penniless and unable to get home. Buloz had just paid George two thousand francs. She had earned it by working from eight to ten hours a day. Pagello was informed through Boucoiran that a purchaser offered 2000 francs for his four paintings. Pagello was exuberant. His pride being satisfied, he asked no questions. He was given George's hard-earned money and felt so rich that he immediately bought a box of surgical instruments for which he paid 500 francs. He then purchased some clothes and a number of new books and began to live in comfort.

Early in October George took the night and day journey by diligence to Paris. She brought her children back with her and gave Pagello another 500 francs to pay his fare home.

Pagello was beginning to feel more hopeful about the future. The dangerous Frenchwoman had not succeeded in ruining him. He had proved himself too intrepid and too resourceful. He would return to Venice with all the prestige of Paris, with his modern instruments and many valuable contacts. His career had never looked so promising. His trip to Paris had been of inestimable advantage. His fatal passion had not hurt him, it had helped him. True, he had learned that Madame Dudevant was a vampire, but no vampire could destroy a strong man.

A few days after George's arrival in Paris Alfred returned from Baden. It was still a fortnight before Pagello's intended departure. Alfred was now in the position which Pagello had occupied in Venice. He was in love with another man's ex-mistress. The situation was identical and the ethics of the situation were the same. But Alfred's point of view was different. He now felt that George had a right to take a lover and he had a right to make love to her. He wanted her and he intended to get her, but he did not intend to tell Pagello. It would have seemed quite absurd for George to feel obligated to tell Pagello. Alfred still felt, however, that George had lied and deceived in Venice in concealing her new love affair from him. More than once Alfred had been the lover of a married woman whom he held blameless so long as he profited by her deceit. In his philosophy all sex infidelities were justifiable except those that made him suffer. The woman who made him suffer committed the unpardonable sin.

Just at present George had put an end to his sufferings, she had consented to see him.

Alfred to George:

"My love, I am here. You wrote me a sad letter, my poor darling. And I also have returned in a sad mood. You agree that we shall see each other, and I, how I long to see you! But, dear child, do not fear from me the least word or the smallest thing that could make you suffer for one moment. When once we see each other, beloved, you will have absolute confidence, and you will realize to what extent I belong to you, body and soul, you will see that my own suffering and my own desire cease to exist when you are to be considered. Confide yourself to me, George, God knows that I shall never do you harm. Receive me, let us weep or laugh together, let us talk of the past or the future, of death or of life, of hope or of sorrow; I am no longer anything but what you make me. Do you know the words of Ruth to Naomi in the Bible? I can say no less to you. Whither thou goest, I will go; where thou lodgest I will lodge; thy people shall be my people; where thou diest there I will die and there will I be buried.

"Send me one word, set your own hour. Shall it be this evening? To-morrow? Whenever you choose, whenever you have a moment, an hour to lose. Send me a line in answer. If it is for this evening, so much the better. If it is for a month hence, I

shall be ready. Let it be when you have nothing else to do; as
for me, I have nothing to do but love you.

Your brother,
Alf'd."

This message of tenderness appealed to George as completely
as the letter of frenzied love had repelled her. In vain now did
reason tell her that she must not yield to capricious passion. She
heard only the cry of her heart. Alas, the children had been placed
in their schools and she was alone again. She was more afraid of
loneliness than of Alfred. She persuaded herself that there was
nothing to fear, no occasion for doubt or misunderstanding. He
was gentle and unselfish—who could distrust a poet who quoted
the Bible? In an ecstasy of love and longing they met and fell
into each other's arms.

Then followed this letter from George to Alfred:

"I might have known that the happiness so long dreamed of
and promised would be followed by those reproaches, and that
you would regard as a crime what you had acknowledged was
my right. Try to remember your despair and all that you said
to convince me that I was necessary to you, and that without
me you were a lost soul. Once again I was mad enough to long
to save you. But now you are more lost than ever, because hardly
were you satisfied when you turned against me and poured out
on me all your anger and despair. My God, what can I do! I
am through with life! What do you want? What do you ask of
me? Questions, recriminations, suspicions, so soon, so soon! And
why do you talk about Pierre when I have forbidden you to
discuss him with me? Besides, what right have you to catechise
me about Venice? Did I belong to you at Venice? Didn't the
breach between us date from the very first day? My child, my
child, I don't want to remind you, but you forget the facts so
easily and you must remember these things. Then, on a certain
evening which I shall never forget, those terrible words were

spoken in the Danieli Casino—'I beg your pardon, but I do not love you.' I would not, I could not, leave you alone in a strange land, without knowledge of the language, and without one sou. We tried to take up our former life as good comrades. But even that was impossible. You were bored—I never knew in what condition you would come home at night, and one day you told me you feared that . . . [four words obliterated by George with blue pencil.]

"Pierre came to bleed me—you did not think of being jealous then, and certainly I did not think of caring for him. But if I had loved him from that moment, if I had given myself to him then, what obligations did I have to you, you who called me boredom personified, silly dreamer, stupid animal, nun, and I don't know what besides? Very well, at present you want the history, day by day and hour by hour, of my association with Pierre, and I do not recognize your right to question me. I would feel degraded if I allowed myself to confess to you as though I were a woman who had deceived you. Believe anything you like, in order to torture us both; I have only one reply to make: since I was no longer yours, I was free to be his, without accounting to you for my actions. At Venice I did not allow you to ask me the least detail, whether on a certain day we kissed on the eye or on the forehead, and now I forbid you to pry into a phase of my life where I have a right to draw a veil. Now that I have once more become your mistress, you should not try to tear away that veil. If he had asked me questions about our intimate life, do you think I would have answered? Do you think it would be in good taste for my brother to ask me questions about you? But you say you are no longer my brother—alas, do you understand now why I shrank from resuming this fatal bond? Didn't I foresee that you would behave this way, and that you would agonize over this past? It exalted you like a beautiful poem so long as I refused myself to you, and it seems to you a nightmare now that you have once more succeeded in possessing me.

"We see now how it is with us, so let me go away—we are about to be more unhappy than ever. If I am loose and perfidious, as you seem to say, why do you want to take me back and keep me?

"I don't want to love any more, I have suffered too much. Ah, if I were a coquette you would be less miserable! It is necessary to lie to you, to say I did not love Pierre, I never gave myself to him. What prevents me from making you believe that? You suffer merely because I was sincere with you. We cannot love each other under these conditions. And all my efforts to regain your friendship were illusory. What is left to us of this tie that seemed so beautiful? Oh, God, neither love nor friendship!"

16

"I can't understand what it is he accuses me of," she wrote to Sainte-Beuve. "His injustice is eating out my heart. It is terrible that we should separate because of such things."

"What do you want? What do you ask of me?" she had written to Alfred. She knew that she would give him whatever he wanted and asked, but she could not make out what it was, and poor Alfred did not know either. Her indignant letter seemed to break his heart. He answered the letter but could not answer her questions.

"My child, my child, I am so guilty toward you! How badly I treated you. Oh, I know it! And you, do you want to punish me? Oh, my life, my well-beloved, I am so unhappy, I am going mad. I am stupid, ungrateful, brutal. Oh, George! George! Listen: Don't think about the past. No, no, in the name of heaven! Don't make comparisons, don't think it over. I love you as no one has ever loved before. Oh, my life, listen, listen, I beg of you, do not condemn me! Oh, God, what shall I do if I have lost her! Oh, how I suffer, my friend. What a night I have just passed. Tell yourself that I love you—believe it! My child, punish me, I beg you to do so. I am a miserable madman. I deserve your anger. Punish me, but don't condemn me. Wait, I don't know what I am saying; I am in despair. I hurt and offended you, I exhausted you, and how I left you, oh, madman that I am, and I had hardly taken three steps outside your door when I almost fell down in the street. My life, my supreme good, forgive me. I beg you on my knees! Think of the beautiful hours I am holding for you in my heart. They are bound to come. I feel them there. Think of happiness. George, I have never suffered like this. One word, not of pardon, I don't deserve it; but only say 'I will wait.' My life, do you doubt my poor love? Oh, my child, believe in it or I shall die!"

When George's reply did not follow promptly, the poor suffering poet was ill, genuinely ill, in bed and helpless. He wrote again and asked her to come and nurse him. He had arranged it so that she would be admitted. His mother would never know, or, if she did know, she would pretend not to. Her spoiled darling must have whatever he desired.

Would she go and nurse him? Does a fireman spring to his feet at the sound of a fire alarm? Just so quickly and automatically would George answer the appeal of weakness and need. She sat up all night with him. She forgave him, and, as he was too weak for reproaches, they were reconciled.

These three letters tell the story of the next few months. How many times she went back and forth between Nohant and Paris does not matter. How often Alfred stayed away from her and then returned is not important. The real drama was not concerned with outward happenings. It took place in their inner lives. It had to do with the emotions of three characters, a hero, a villain and a victim. The bright shining hero was Alfred, the black ruthless villain was Alfred, and the woman between the two was George. From November until March she went back and forth between Octave and Coelio. That was her tragedy. He loved and exalted her. He hated and degraded her. He drew her into his arms in tenderness and pushed her away with violence.

According to Alfred's own confession: "A quarter of an hour after having insulted her, I was on my knees. As soon as I stopped accusing her, I asked her pardon. As soon as I stopped reviling her, I wept."

In the words of Arvède Barine: "Musset dragged with him a libertine past which stuck to him like a shirt of Nessus and forced his mind to torture his heart. He did not believe [in women] and he had a desperate need to believe. He dreamed of a love which was at the same time a delirium and a cult. He spent his time in trying to scale the heavens and in falling back into the mire, and he blamed George Sand for his downfall."

He was helpless in the conflict of his two natures. He could not love, he could not believe.

She could not stop loving. She could not cease believing. She was equally helpless in the grip of her instinctive will to give and forgive. He was exactly the man who suited her, because in him there was so much to forgive.

When Boucoiran expressed disapproval of her infatuation she answered, "There are so many things between two lovers which they alone in all the world can judge."

As for leaving her lover, where could she go? To whom could she turn? She could find no substitute for the great emotion he gave her. He seemed her only hold on life.

Meanwhile Alfred could not forgive her for Pagello and for what he called her deceit. He went over and over the past situation, hammering in the heinousness of her guilt, her treason, her perfidy. She grew less proud, less resentful. In order to come close to him and reach accord with him she stopped defending herself. What difference did it make who was right and who was wrong? She was willing to be wrong if it made him happy. Perhaps she was wrong. Probably she was. Anyone who made Alfred suffer must be wrong. She had made him suffer. Yes, she was wrong.

By such stages she changed her point of view to suit Alfred, because after all nothing mattered but Alfred. He talked to her for hours about his suffering, and his need of happiness. She agonized over his suffering. To answer his need of happiness became her obsession. He wanted passion, she became passionate. He wanted jealousy, she became jealous. He wanted her to focus on him, he became the centre of all her thought and emotion. She obliterated herself for him, absorbed herself in him. Her state of being became a trance. Just as she had once become Indiana, and again Valentine, then Lélia, then Jacques, she now became Alfred, hearing with his ears, seeing with his eyes, using his senses instead of her own.

So moved was she by his mental torment that she crossed the bridge between her soul and his. She sunk herself into his consciousness until she felt with every fiber of his being. She knew his jealousy, his masculine guiltlessness, his conviction of the woman's sin. To heal his suffering she brought the guilty woman to her knees. The fact that the woman was herself seemed unimportant.

But all her yielding was useless. She lacked the one essential. He wanted a woman whose past belonged exclusively to him. She could not reconstruct her past, and so in spite of her devotion she failed him.

Poor Alfred! She blamed herself, she bowed her head in sorrow. She could give him only her life, her body, and her soul. She could not give him her virginity. She tried to make it up to him by every possible self-sacrifice.

He demanded repentance. A few months earlier George had declared, "I do not know the meaning of repentance—I have never had occasion to ask forgiveness of anyone." And now she repented. What she had called his insults were accepted as the punishments of a just God.

He demanded confession. A few weeks earlier George had written, "I do not recognize your right to question me. I would feel degraded if I allowed myself to confess to you." And now she confessed. She was no longer herself. She was a woman obsessed by Alfred, expressing Alfred. It was as though she had said to him, "Thy prejudices shall be my prejudices; thy vanity, my vanity; thy pride, my pride."

This repentance and this confession were written down in a journal to Alfred. But after she had expressed them in writing she could not give them to Alfred to read. Conscious as she was of being a slave, some integral part of her being refused to proclaim her slavery. She clung to this pride or this integrity by refusing to show him her journal.

17

Whenever Alfred turned against George he told his side of their story to his brother Paul and to Alfred Tattet. They made him promise to stay away from the dangerous vampire and he obeyed. When his mood changed and he wanted to see her they were watching him, holding him to his promise, and, because he was sensitive to what they might say, he stayed away.

While he was refusing to see her, George grew desperate. She tried to think of something more to give him. He had loved her long, luxuriant hair. He had praised it and caressed it. Had he not written from Baden, "Give me your hair, give me all that head of yours which I have had"? In a mood of utter abandon she cut off her hair and sent it to him as a symbol of subjection. He wept and wanted to go back to her, but Tattet would not let him.

There was an hour or two of every day in which she half awoke from her trance. She thought of her work, her children, her self-respect, her pride, and longed to be rid of her tyrant. But all the other hours of every day she hugged her chains.

In her shabby old apartment every association spoke of him. His sketches on the walls, his books on the table, his music on the piano, made the place his own. The arm-chair seemed to belong to him. The rug by the sofa was where he had knelt and wept on the day she first promised to love him. He had knelt there and wept there many times since that day, begging forgiveness for his sins. The whole room, the walls, the floor, the ceiling, seemed listening for his voice. The arm-chair was waiting to receive him. She looked at its emptiness, and in an agony of apprehension she listened with the silence of the room and waited with the patience of her inanimate possessions.

She was always expecting him. He might appear at any moment. The door-bell rang; she started to her feet. Her heart, that had been dead, began to beat again. No, no, it was only two shadows who entered. They moved about the room, sound came from their mouths, but they had no more reality than ghosts. They did not arouse her from her trance. She regarded her callers with the calm impassive gaze that made them call her the sphinx. She looked at them but did not see them. A mist effaced their features, a haze shut them away. She saw one face, the "divine profile" of her poet. Was she to see him forever? Was he to intervene forever between her gaze and the world of men?

In her journal to Alfred she wrote: "I cannot suffer like this! I am young. I am still beautiful. Among these men around me there is more than one who would be proud and happy in my love. Why can't I choose one of them? Where is that life urge I felt at Venice? What has become of that fierce vigor which took hold of me like an excess of rage, and which lifted me from the waves in which I was drowning? This man who caused my despair finds his amusement in trying to kill me. But I do not want to die! I want to love again, be young again. I want to live! . . . Ah, but you say that one cannot love two men at the same time. Nevertheless, that is what happened to me. But when you say that because it happened yesterday it will happen again to-morrow, when you believe that I cannot set foot outside the door without succumbing to temptation, you are crazy.

"Am I stupid or insensitive? Can't you see that women like me learn by their mistakes? . . . Poor Alfred, if no one knew about it you would forgive me. But there is M. Tattet, who would say with a disgusted air, 'God, what weakness!' And there are others who would say, 'How pitiful! How ridiculous?'—Oh, this miserable, masculine self-love! . . .

"I can still make a man happy if that man will honestly help me. I need strength to rest in, a heart without vanity to receive and hold me. If I had found such a man I would not be where I am now! Oh, God, did I commit a crime at Venice in turning from love and death to love and life? Is the love of life a crime? If so, if indeed I committed an involuntary crime, thou hast punished me as much as human judges punish a premeditated assassin and still more, because a parricide is killed but once, whereas I for the last ten weeks have been dying day by day. It is too long an agony!

"And you, cruel child, why did you love me after having hated me? What mystery takes place in you each week? What is the meaning of this crescendo of dislike, disgust, aversion and fury, culminating in cold and scornful contempt, then suddenly melting into tears and tenderness? Torment of my life! I would give all that I am for one day of your ineffable love."

But writing in her journal did not bring her faithless lover to her arms. Then she made a trip to Nohant, and absence so endeared her to the poet that when she returned to Paris Alfred took up his residence again at 19 quai Malaquais.

George was sufficiently human to write to Tattet announcing that Alfred had again become her lover. "There are certain surgical operations," she added, "which are successful and which do honor to the surgeon's skill, but which do not prevent a recurrence of the illness."

During the time that George was living on her emotions and writing her journal, Alfred was also exclusively occupied with his own sensations. The paradoxical poet hated her for making him suffer but he loved his suffering, hugged it to his breast, told Paul and Tattet where it hurt most and made poetry out of its throes.

So long as George made him jealous he enjoyed himself. When she yielded to his caprices he was bored because there was nothing left to make a scene about. He pretended to be jealous of Liszt just to whip up excitement. When no more thrills were provided by George he produced a few on his own account. He talked to George of a new mistress, whom he praised outrageously. George rose above jealousy and hoped he would be happy and that the woman would teach him to believe in love.

He throve on misunderstandings and reconciliations. Excessive emotion kept him in fit condition. But George went to pieces and grew pale and thin. The wrinkles gathered around her eyes. She had often talked of being old, now she was growing old in fact. The portrait of her by Delacroix, painted at this time, shows her emaciated face and great sad eyes.

Her last letter to Alfred conveyed no expressions of passionate love. It breathed utter weariness. She was tired, tired to her very soul.

"No, no, I have had enough, unhappy being that you are. I have loved you as my son. It is a mother's love. I still bleed from it. I pity you. I forgive you everything, but we must part. . . .

"You say that I ought to beat you when you behave so outrageously toward me, but I don't know how to fight. I am naturally gentle, that is the way God made me, but I am proud, nevertheless. My pride is broken at present, and my love is only pity. We must part. Sainte-Beuve is right. Your conduct is deplorable, impossible.

"My God, to what a life I am about to leave you! Drunkenness, wine and women, over and over forever. But since I can no longer do anything to help you, why prolong what is shame to me and punishment to you? Even in the midst of all this suffering, your mad jealousy is directed toward everyone and every-

*George Sand, painted by Delacroix during the period when she was
writing her journal to Alfred*

thing. The more you lose the right to be jealous the more jealous
you become. It is like a punishment from God on your poor head.
But my own children! Oh, my children, my children! Good-by,
unhappy one. My children, my own children!"

And so George ended it.

Like a sick animal that needs to crawl into a hole, she longed
to hide herself away from Alfred. She could not face another
scene with him, so she arranged to escape by stealth. The faithful Boucoiran was summoned to aid her, and was given full in-
structions. On the day of her premeditated flight, Boucoiran
reserved a seat in the diligence which was to leave the Tuileries
at six o'clock. Then, late in the afternoon, still obeying her in-
structions, he went to her apartment and announced in the
presence of Alfred that Madame Dupin was ill and needed her
daughter. Boucoiran furtively grabbed the traveling bag. George
put on her hat and bade Alfred a hasty farewell.

The poet, in no wise disturbed, waited for her return. But there
was no return.

George stayed quietly at Nohant, bearing as best she could a
sense of terrific defeat. During long days of solitude she tried to
face herself and retrieve her failure. Her losses were many, and
the only gain she counted was the conviction that she had relinquished the mad search for love.

At first reflection she almost wished she could go back to the
old simple faith of her girlhood; but religion and law had but one
command for her—submission to the mastery of Casimir. That
submission had long since been outgrown. No, she had not been
wrong to choose her freedom. She had been wrong in the use she
had made of it. She had misused it and abused it.

The books she read, the men she knew, the leading spirits of
her time, had all practiced and preached romanticism. They believed that artists, writers, and all superior people were free to
live as they pleased. Each one was a law unto himself. She had
accepted this cult. She had related herself in this way to the men

of her generation. And in so doing she now believed she had been guilty of arrogant pride.

In a long letter to Sainte-Beuve she revealed a new humility:

"Everything in the world outside has seemed to summon me to a life of presumptuous irresponsibility and impudent heroism. Living for myself alone, and risking nothing but myself, I was always exposing myself and sacrificing myself on the theory that I was a free being, useless to others and mistress of herself. I almost reached the point of committing suicide out of sheer self-indulgence. . . . Cursed be the men and the books that influenced me by their sophisms. I might better have stuck to my Franklin, who up to the time that I was twenty-five gave me such delight, and whose portrait is hung near my bed. I shall never again return to Franklin, nor to my Jesuit confessor, nor to my first Platonic love, nor to my collection of plants, nor to the pleasure of nursing my children, nor to fox-hunting or galloping on horseback.

"Nothing that once was, will ever be again. I know that only too well. I wish to resign myself and wait until Providence, in some natural way, sends me the means of doing good. I do not know yet whether there is any such means, because what we agree to call goodness, the general sort which we all practice more or less, does not seem to me to deserve such a fine name. . . .

"Ah, I see clearly at present, you may be sure, and that is the punishment of my mistakes. The idea of another love for me such as you suggest is like a dream which will never be realized, and indeed I shall use all my energy to prevent its realization.

"No, no, I don't want either one of the loves you describe, neither the tender and enduring kind, nor the sort that is blind and violent. Do you think that I could inspire the first, or that I should be tempted now to experiment with the second? Both are beautiful and precious, but I am too old for either. This side of my life is struck by a sadness and a terror which is like death, which is death, no doubt. . . .

"I wish to give to my children a respectable old mother. If I do not succeed in this, my friend, you may be sure I shall not allow my life to be a drag on theirs. For the last three years I have lived in dread of a sort of death which I do not wish to be forced to give myself, because I love life, however bad it is. Nevertheless I shall know how to renounce it if my way of life should shame my son or injure my daughter.

"I am resolved to use all the strength that remains to me in repairing the harm I have done myself. If I cannot do this I would rather put a bullet through my head than begin again the life that I have led these last two or three years.

"Write to me, and do not fear to treat me frankly and rudely. Treat me as though I were a man."

V

GEORGE AND MICHEL

GEORGE recovered from her love of Alfred.
Those who had watched her agony felt that she owed it to Alfred to make a slow recovery. But her convalescence was brief. She lived out of doors with her friends the birds. She tramped the unpathed places of the Nohant woods. And the good brown ground which her feet touched gave her strength. The earth was her mother and nature was her nurse. They received her and healed her.

After a crisis George often yielded herself to this primitive healing. Aurore Dupin had behaved in the same way. When as a child of thirteen she had been hurt by Madame Dupin's revelations about Sophie, Aurore had run wild in the woods. Madame Dupin, far from understanding her grandchild, had called this behavior reversion to barbarism. But it was, then as now, Aurore's instinctive means of recuperation after a shock.

Gradually, as George felt her vigor renewed, the woman who had been wrecked by a great and fatal passion was sloughed off and abandoned, while George felt within herself the creation of a new personality.

She had so many selves. She had left several behind her and did not care to sit and weep over their outgrown shells. She did not whine or indulge in remorse. She started again with the present and turned her back on the past.

She was willing to accept the consequences of every act of her life. But acceptance meant to George something different from orthodox submission. It meant facing and, if necessary, grappling with inevitable consequence, never lying down under it, but standing up to it, as a fighter prepares for combat.

She was going somewhere, and no cruel consequence was to be allowed to crush her or keep her from moving freely on her way. She bent all her energies toward the woman she intended to become. In this courageous spirit she was ready to solve her present problems and go on to new life—to many new lives.

Her immediate problem was her marriage.

What should she do about this Baron Dudevant, the father of her children, this man whose violent language drove one child from the table in frightened tears while the other cowered for protection at his mother's side, this spendthrift miser who speculated in land and expected her to meet his notes when they came due?

"Our debts," she said to Duteil, "exceed our revenues." Since the debts were Casimir's and the revenues were hers, this was tactfully expressed.

Duteil, who was equally the friend of both, advised her to live with Casimir as his wife. By so doing, Duteil believed, she would gain an influence over the father which she could use for the children's sake.

George was shocked at Duteil's advice. Did he not realize that she was a moral being? Did he think she would stoop so low as to live with her husband—she who had hitherto kept her sex relations pure? Did he believe that she would give herself for ulterior motives to a man who hated her? She had made mistakes, it is true, but she had never done anything to justify such an unworthy suggestion. Duteil, so it seemed to George, had strange ideas of what constituted virtue. She talked to him for hours to make him see the difference between right and wrong.

She turned from Duteil to Alphonse Fleury.

"Why not consult a lawyer?" was Fleury's suggestion.

"What lawyer?" asked George.

"Louis Michel, of course, the greatest lawyer in Berry."

"The man they call Michel of Bourges? I thought he was an editor."

"He is—the greatest editor in Berry."

"At least," conceded George, "he seems to be quoted by every-one. I'm always hearing 'Michel says'—'Michel thinks'—'Did you see what Michel wrote in to-day's edition?' I've never read his paper, but he must write forcefully."

"Wait till you hear him talk!" Fleury exclaimed.

"Ah, yes, he's a politician too, isn't he?"

"The greatest statesman in Berry. He is three men in one."

"He must be very strong," said George.

Fleury's advice seemed more practical than Duteil's. Perhaps also it was pleasanter to contemplate. And since Fleury was on his way to Bourges, George climbed into the diligence and went along.

2

At Bourges, at the hotel, George and Fleury registered and took rooms for the night. It did not occur to either of these old friends that they were violating any rule of propriety. It was well established by now that George was a wholly exceptional person. Everyone who knew her conceded her right to make her own rules. So Madame Dudevant and Alphonse Fleury took their dinner in the hotel dining-room and did not notice whether they were noticed or not.

After dinner Fleury went in search of Louis Michel. He found the great man tired and ill and about to retire for the night. Would Monsieur Michel care to go to the hotel to meet George Sand? asked Fleury timidly.

"George Sand!" Michel forgot his fatigue. "George Sand here in Bourges!" Michel sprang to his feet. "Not the great George! Not the author of *Lélia!*"

"Yes, yes," nodded Fleury.

"But I—" cried Michel, striking his breast. "I am infatuated with *Lélia!*" He seized hat and coat and started down the street so rapidly that Fleury, who had eaten heartily, could scarcely keep the pace.

They found George smoking in her room.

Michel looked at her and felt a shock. Not because she was smoking. That was odd, but he did not object to eccentricities. No, his shock was due to the discovery that the author of *Lélia* was a woman. He had known it vaguely as a fact. Yet he had always thought of George Sand as a magnificent intellect, therefore as a man. And here George sat in skirts. Strange! Thrillingly strange! Michel blinked his near-sighted eyes at her, then feeling a queer sensation, like a rushing in his ears, he turned away his head.

She began to talk in matter-of-fact fashion of her marital troubles and the legal aspect of the case. She told him of her two or three—it was three, wasn't it?—unhappy love affairs, disposing of these faminine secrets with a frankness that seemed to Michel amazing and unprecedented. As he listened, Michel felt a mild concussion of the brain that went from his head to his heels and paralyzed his celebrated powers of speech.

"I am through with men," he heard George saying. "There is not a man on earth before whom I shall ever bow my head again in submission or in sorrow."

Michel approved these sentiments. That such a woman should devote herself to one man, any man, seemed a sacrilege. No man was worthy of the author of *Lélia!*

Michel drew closer to the marvelous being, so incongruously seated in a commonplace hotel room. He placed his spectacles more firmly on his nose and dared to stare at her. As he stared he was aware of a frail body, a pale face, and two enormous eyes, the widest, deepest eyes he had ever seen. Their subterranean depths reminded him of fire smouldering underneath volcanoes.

A lost soul, thought Michel. Then in a flash of insight he saw himself as a savior. He made a silent vow to win her soul and intellect for the republic, for France!

After this sudden revelation and this sacred vow he was bored by George's troubles with her husband, impatient of the history of her lovers. All that personal side of life was insignificant to Michel. He was a prophet in search of apostles. He was the leader of a cause.

George was still discussing the legal aspect of her case.

"Are you a republican?" Michel interrupted.

"I have always been a republican, always, even as a child," George answered quietly.

"Then you will help us?"

"But how could I help?" George asked modestly.

"With your brain and your pen, with the fire that is in your soul. Join the movement. Be one of us. Devote your life to the cause."

George was silent. She had always disliked politics. Indeed, she found its feverish activity ridiculous. She could not imagine herself drawn into a political campaign to change the form of government of her country.

"Oh, let me alone!" she laughed. "I am nothing but a song-bird. Let me sit on my branch and sing in the sun."

"No, no!" protested Michel. "Be serious."

"Very well then, without metaphors, I am a poet who needs solitude, and since I have no home I intend to travel. Please settle my affairs for me so that I can go away and dream by myself while you labor to regenerate society."

"But you say you are a republican!"

"I think with you," she admitted.

"Thinking is not enough. You must act."

George shook her head. She saw that her personal affairs were forgotten. She did not refer to them again.

Michel, like a fanatical Savonarola, exhorted his new acquaintance to forsake her selfishness and give her heart and her life to France. He drew a vivid picture of his republic. It seemed to

George that Michel's republic resembled Utopia. It was the kingdom of heaven on earth.

As she listened she observed him. The strong man of Berry appeared to be a dried-up old man. Fleury had told her that Michel was thirty-seven. He looked sixty. His face was wizened, his eyes were hidden behind ugly spectacles. He was almost completely bald. What little hair he had was displayed on his cheeks in short sideburns. But the ostentatious thing about Michel was his head, which seemed to be two skulls soldered together. She could almost see the seam between.

This phrenological phenomenon impressed George favorably. It appeared to her that Michel's dome-like forehead provided extra room for his high faculties. They were duplicated, no doubt. He was probably a mental prodigy, a superman.

His dress was strange. He wore wooden sabots and a long loose coat of coarse homespun. This costume was evidently affected to prove that he was not ashamed of his humble origin. Michel had been a peasant and had risen by his own efforts into the professional class. What an achievement! What a history! As George looked at Michel a story began to take form in her brain.—Chapter I. Michel as a boy.—Chapter II. Michel's early education. —Chapter III. Ambition overcoming obstacles.—She would call the novel *Simon,* an excellent title. Simon, like Michel, would hate all aristocrats. Then by some subterfuge he must be made to marry a countess. A dramatic situation! Simon could never forgive his wife for belonging to the privileged class. He would love her as a woman and hate her as an aristocrat. He would—

Michel's monologue and George's novel were interrupted by the arrival of friend Planet, the republican leader from La Châtre.

Someone opened a window to let the smoke out. Although it was a warm spring evening Michel felt chilled. He asked permission to cover his bald head. George handed him his hat, but he refused to wear it in the presence of a lady. Taking from his pocket several large bright-colored kerchiefs, he knotted them together at the four corners.

"With your permission," he said politely, and covered his head.

His skull was so slippery that the improvised cap kept falling into his lap. He replaced it gracefully, but at the first gesture it fell off again. As he went on talking he was perpetually catching it, waving it, and patting it back upon his prodigious double head.

Sometimes the cap posed picturesquely, making him look like a gypsy. At other moments it landed grotesquely, trailing a knotted corner over an ear or an eye. He was oblivious to his appearance, and his three auditors were so in awe of him that he seemed magnificent in his homespun and his sabots and his queer headgear. It was as though his costume proclaimed to them—thus should we all dress, thus *shall* we all dress in the republic that is to come.

Michel's appearance was not important so long as he talked. He talked with passion. He thought with passion. His inner force overflowed in an intensity that was like nothing human. His eloquence was both primitive and sublime. It was rhythmic. It inspired thought that might have been set to music, but that could not be conveyed in words.

George enjoyed Michel's eloquence as she might have enjoyed the sound of an organ touched by a master's hand.

True, he contradicted himself. And with the music of his eloquence there was an obvious lack of logic, or say rather there was too much poetry in his arguments.

George disagreed with him often but she disagreed silently. She had lost all desire to argue or interrupt. Besides, she was touched by the evidences of suffering in this successful leader of men. Years of illness had left their devastating effect. Looking at his emaciated face one felt that the man was doomed.

Yet, dying as he seemed, he poured out a vitality as exhausting as it was inexhaustible. George, Fleury and Planet waited in amazement for the orator to show fatigue. Michel had arrived at seven. Not until the clock struck midnight did he arise to go.

Then, since he was in the midst of an explanation, he asked them
to go along with him toward home. When they reached his door
he was so absorbed in talking that he walked back with them. At
the hotel, as he had not finished his argument, they escorted him
to his home again. They made the trip back and forth nine times.

It was a warm spring evening. The full moon lighted the nar-
row streets of the sleeping town. Whenever they passed a stately
building of the Renaissance they paused in front of it, admiring,
gesturing, arguing, questioning, stirred by Michel's prophecy of
the perfect government soon to replace the tottering throne of
France.

The moonlight, the massive architecture, the fiery eloquence
of Michel, the sense of something approaching conspiracy, were
all so exalting to the four reformers that they could not part until
dawn.

As soon as they left Michel, Planet turned to George.

"What have you done to him? He has poured out his soul to us.
It is you, your effect on him. I have lived by his side for a year
and I swear to you he has never been like this before."

"It's proselyting," said hard-headed Fleury. "He thinks George
will be valuable to the cause."

"He will never rest until he has converted you," said Planet.

George was too exhausted to protest. Michel was undeniably
noble, but she needed sleep.

The next day she felt it necessary to escape from Bourges before the great man made another nine-hour call. She left with
Fleury on the early coach. When they reached Nohant in the
afternoon she fell into bed and slept until noon of the next day.
Scarcely was she awake when the maid brought an enormous envelope containing a letter from Michel.

Fleury was right. Michel was determined to convert her. His
ways were masterful. The letters came thick and fast. He never
waited for an answer.

How could the great man of Berry spare so much time for

writing letters? Was he neglecting his labors as editor, lawyer and leader of the province? Were all these duties insignificant in comparison with the one soul he was determined to save?

3

George could not answer Michel's letters. Her writing had to go to Buloz or she could not pay Casimir's debts. However, this difficulty was easily adjusted, for what could George give to her readers more stimulating than a discussion with the great man of Berry? By concealing his identity and addressing him as Everard, she could write to him and to her public at the same time. The *Lettres à Everard* passed directly from Michel's hands to the Buloz magazine. By this arrangement George turned from fiction to the question of the hour.

It was the time of ferment leading to a second republic. Louis Philippe seemed securely seated on the throne, but a growing number of thoughtful men were preparing the minds of the people for a change of government. All society was divided into two camps, for or against the monarchy. So long as reform was limited to theory it was allowed, but if the theorists attempted action they were shot.

At Lyons an industrial uprising had resulted in a massacre. The leaders were arrested and sent to Paris for what came to be known as the "monstrous trial." Michel, as a leading republican and a brilliant orator, was engaged as one of the counsel for the defense.

Planet accompanied Michel to Paris. Fleury and George soon followed. Thus, not long after the moonlight meeting at Bourges, the four friends found themselves together in the excitement of a political crisis. Public interest was seething. Nothing was talked about but the trial. Michel was an important figure and his followers were numerous. George, converted to political action, was drawn into the centre of things and met dozens of Republicans. They were a strangely assorted mixture of artists, politicians, workingmen and intellectuals. The great musician, François Liszt, was among them, also the brilliant ex-abbé and Christian socialist, Félicité Lamennais.

George lunched with one group of men and dined with another. Michel made demands on her time and energy. When he had writing to do or speeches to prepare, she gave him invaluable aid. She had found what she had asked for, a life of ideas.

In his attitude toward his disciple Michel was impersonal and paternal. Like Prince Murat at Madrid, he called her his aide-de-camp, and, as in Spain, she dressed at times in masculine attire. Indeed this was the only condition on which a woman could take active part in politics. No women were admitted to the trial, but, passing unnoticed as a man, George was able to attend the meetings at the Palais de Justice and the trial in the audience hall of the Luxembourg.

At night after their meetings the group of men, including George, often tramped the boulevards as far as the site of the old Bastille. Sometimes they boarded one of the little steamboats that puffed up and down the Seine. Or they sat to a late hour in a café, discussing the happenings of the day and planning the next step.

Michel made a great deal of his protégée. The great man had always been sorry that he had no child of his own, so he adopted George as his son. He adopted Planet also, but George he regarded as his youngest son. He called her Benjamin.

More than he needed a son, however, poor Michel-Everard required the services of a nurse. He was wretchedly ill. Physicians could not diagnose his mysterious ailment. He was subject to sudden attacks of excruciating pain. As long as they lasted he screamed in agony and when the pain ceased he fell into a torpor of exhaustion. Then, after sleeping for two or three hours, he emerged strong and vital, ready to make a speech or tramp the streets.

Michel's insistent dominance over his miserable body appealed to George's sympathy. She got in the habit of writing his letters to save his strength. When he was ill she brought his friends to call on him. Often her children spent their day of vacation with Michel, and learned from him the principles of his faith. George neglected her work to help Planet watch over the master. The two adopted sons were constantly running back and forth between George's apartment at quai Malaquais and Michel's near-by lodgings at quai Voltaire.

It seemed to George that Michel's unselfish devotion to humanity deserved the faithful service of his friends. George called him a Roman. She considered him the noblest man she had ever known.

4

One evening the three friends, George, Planet and Michel, were standing on the bridge Saints-Pères. His Majesty, Louis Philippe, was giving a ball in the royal palace, and through the trees of the Tuileries gardens came reflections of the palace lights and the subdued sound of music.

Suddenly George, who was plunged into reverie, heard Michel's voice declaiming:

"Civilization! Yes, that is the great word of you artists! Civilization indeed!" and Michel hit his cane against the balustrade of the bridge. "I say to you that to renew your corrupt society this beautiful river must run red with blood, this cursed palace must be reduced to ashes, and this vast city must become a strip of barren ground."

George, thoroughly aroused, listened in amazement as Michel continued his appeal to the torch and the sword. Had the man gone mad? Was he, after all, then, not on the side of the moderate republicans? Was he a follower of the guillotined Robespierre or of that dead fanatic, Babeuf?

"The perversity of courts," Michel was declaiming, "the corruption of great cities," "the enervating influence of art"—having destroyed all these influences by the consuming fire of eloquence, he dumped them into "the smoking ruins of the old world."

Finally the orator turned to George and asked:

"Do you agree with me?"

"I thought I was hearing Dante after his return from hell," was George's answer. "No, decidedly we do not share the same ideas. I have listened for two long hours while you have defended the cause of death. Now let me say a word for humanity," and George began to vindicate civilization and art.

But Michel refused to listen. He was furious. He walked away from the bridge through the gardens and broke his cane against the old walls of the Louvre.

George turned her back on him and started homeward with Planet. But Michel followed to her door and tried to prevent her from entering.

"If you leave me before you agree with me," he threatened, "I shall never see you again."

"Good-night, Planet, good-by, Michel," and George smiled at them. But as soon as the door was closed between them she stopped smiling. Why, in heaven's name, did he always lose his head when she differed from him in argument? What was the meaning of this frenzied desire to seize and subjugate her mind and impose his own opinions? Violence! Blood! Revolution! The man was mad!

Before she fell asleep her last conscious feeling was relief. She was cured of hero-worship. She felt free now to live her own life. She would start on her travels—Switzerland, Constantinople, the Orient. Solitude, peace, dreams.

5

The next day George applied for a passport for foreign travel. She felt exceedingly light-hearted and carefree. After all, she reflected, she was not fitted for politics or any kind of collective action. She would seek her own truth in her own way.

Returning home, she found Michel waiting in her apartment.

She looked at him strangely. When she addressed him, her voice sounded strained.

"What's the matter?" asked Michel nervously.

"Did you mean what you said last night?"

"I meant every word of it."

"So all this time you have believed in violence and you have hidden it from me, from all of us? Blind leader of the blind! Go your own way, then, and I shall go mine. I'm leaving Paris to travel abroad."

The bombastic Michel grew suddenly quiet. He drew his chair away from the window and sat in the half light, looking at her, listening to her outburst, marveling how it had happened that their positions were reversed. George was the orator now, and he it was who feared to interrupt.

"I have listened to you," she was saying, "I have admired you. But I have not surrendered my right to think for myself. We have discussed certain questions of which you think you have the solution. You have not given me the solution. You have no solution. I cannot reproach you with that, but I do object to the claim you make on my intelligence. You are irritated every time I disagree with you. When I oppose your theories you act as though I were doing you a personal injury. You are not the sort of person who expects politeness or hypocrisy. Let me speak frankly—I have had enough of your republic."

Michel looked at her in wonder, too stunned to respond as she continued to reproach him.

"I took you as my guide. You are not content to be a guide, you want to be a despot. But whether as guide or despot I cannot accept you, I cannot follow you."

Then, as Michel started to speak, she turned to him accusingly, her dark eyes flashing anger.

"Don't tell me that you have a solution, that you hold it in your hand! You haven't anything. You hold nothing. You don't know any more than I do."

"May I speak now?" asked Michel meekly.

"Speak! Speak all you please! But you cannot dissuade me, I am going away."

As Michel began to defend himself his face still bore the look of wonder, as though he were amazed at hearing the words he let fall.

"I have made a discovery"; Michel's voice had a new appealing quality. "Souls have sex. And you are a woman. Will you believe me when I tell you that I never realized this before? When I read *Lélia* and the *Lettres d'un Voyageur* I thought of the author as a young man, a poet. When I saw you for the first time I was astonished, it was as though no one had ever told me that you wore a woman's dress and that in private life you went by a woman's name. I was actually disappointed. I wanted to keep my dream. I tried not to let your feminine appearance destroy the mental image I had made of you. I seldom observed your face. I observed your mind. I interested myself in your ideas. I am so near-sighted anyhow that the only thing I was keenly aware of was your voice." Michel spoke more softly as he continued to explain. "Your voice, George, has none of the flute-like quality that belongs to a woman. You speak in a low tone like a boy, and your words are not like a woman's words. You don't exclaim or interrupt—at least, you have never done so until to-day. So that, since my sense of hearing received more of you than my eyes did, I always thought of you and talked to you as though you were a young man who had studied philosophy and history, a young man who understood me; yes, I thought of you as my son."

Michel removed his glasses, wiped them carefully, and replaced them, then scrutinized the face of his companion.

"It seems to me that I now see you clearly for the first time. You are a being of pure sentiment and pure imagination, in one word, a woman."

It was said with so much tenderness that George felt no temptation to argue, and even as he preached to her she felt no offense.

"Let us discuss you as a woman, or rather let us talk of something more important than yourself, your duty. You dream of individual liberty, but it cannot be reconciled with social duty. You say that your person belongs to yourself and that your soul also belongs to you alone. That is a sophism worse than all those for which you reproach me. You belong to your country, your soul belongs to the cause. If all lovers of truth said farewell to their country, their brothers and their task, truth would not find a single follower."

Michel rose to his feet and walked to the window, where he stood facing George with his back to the light. She noticed his bent shoulders, his worn face, his bald head. She pitied him.

He saw her great eyes fill with compassion. He felt insignificant, and to magnify his importance he spoke in a loud tone, gesticulating, shaking his fist.

"You are unjust and exacting. You don't know anything. You say so yourself. Then suddenly the fever of knowledge takes possession of you and you demand that absolute truth should be handed to you. *Quick, quick, give the secret of God to George Sand, who doesn't want to wait.*"

George felt moved by Michel's persuasion, not so much by his words as by the deep feeling underneath. She in turn made an effort to assert herself.

"I must go away, Michel. I need solitude. I can think better when I am alone."

At this unyielding attitude all Michel's proud anger collapsed.

"Oh, George," he answered sadly, "no one can find the truth alone. Let us seek it together. I do not ask you to follow me as an infallible guide, for I do not know the road. I ask you to go with me, to warn me of obstacles, to lead me back to the way when I have lost it. Do not scorn me because I am not a god, and do not curse me for having pointed out a destination which I do not know how to attain. The way that I cannot find alone we may find together. Don't leave me, George. I have given you my—my affection. So much the worse for me. You have not asked for it, you have no need of it. I have no right to ask you for yours."

Michel paced the floor and gave vent to his emotion in explosive sentences.

"You are a dreamer. Truth is not found in solitude. You are a woman, you don't understand politics. Violence is a necessity of politics. You don't agree with me, very well then, leave me. Certainly you are free to do so. No, George, don't go, I need you so!"

In the midst of his agitation a distant clock struck the hour. Michel paused abruptly, brought back to his vaunted sense of social duty.

"Four o'clock!" he cried, distracted. "I'm late for the meeting. I have to make a speech!" He seized his hat and ran into the hall.

In a moment he was back again to ask, "Is the maid out?"

"Yes—why?"

No answer. He closed the front door.

George thought she heard a peculiar sound. She followed to the door and tried to open it. He had locked her in.

She returned to the sitting-room and sank exhausted on the couch. She never realized how tired she was until Michel had left her. She drew her feet under her, and reaching for a pillow she touched Michel's overcoat, left forgotten on the couch. With a sigh of contentment she leaned her cheek on the rough homespun. Thus she would lean on him who was henceforth to be her master.

She pressed the coat closer. She imagined him there wearing it. His coat, his shoulder, his arms. How masterful he was!

So his will to dominate was his way of loving her! All his despotism was love. Now that she knew herself necessary to his happiness, nothing else mattered. She had often thought that if she could find a strong man she would be happy in subjecting her will to his. She had found her strong man.

A delicious dreaminess stole over her. The seeker after truth could not hold her own against the seeker after love.

6

"I beg your pardon, George, for locking you in." It was three hours later and Michel was explaining shamelessly. "I was afraid you might start on your travels in my absence. As soon as I have convinced you that you must stay, I shall leave you free to go. Until then I must keep this," and he held out the key.

"Put the key in the door, Michel. I have decided to stay—on one condition: you must never again talk of revolution."

"Agreed!" cried Michel joyously.

Thus it was he dominated her.

After this talk Michel's attitude changed. Instead of being brusque and rude, he was courteous and gentle. She was no longer his equal comrade, she was that weak thing, a woman. The discovery made him tolerant and tender.

George was touched by this new tenderness. It transfigured her comrade. His ugly face became illumined. His near-sighted eyes, looked at more closely, showed they had caught and held the beauty of his soul. The bent old body became majestic. She had always called him Roman, now he seemed a Roman god. He was Jupiter come down from Olympus. His homeliness was but the form that Jupiter chose to wear in winning an earthly woman. She saw the god beneath the disguise.

Imperial Jupiter, disguised as pompous little Michel, became the perfect lover of the dreamer's most extreme imaginings. Her mind had first craved him, then created him. George's imagination was as opulent as a fairy godmother. It gave her everything she asked for. At the time that she was writing *Lélia* she had dreamed of a poet; *Lélia* was scarcely finished when she called forth from the unknown an incarnation of her dream. After the break with the poet she had demanded a life of ideas; almost immediately she met Michel. He became the symbol of a new mental interest.

She had not intended to carry over into this new phase of ex-

perience any pursuit of personal happiness; her emotions had been
nobly submerged. But her need of love, seemingly dead, dumbly
persisted in the silence of her being. This hidden need demanded
an object that was totally different from past experience, because
she herself was a different woman, more developed, more mature.
She was consciously seeking a mental interest, while unconsciously
she was also seeking a mental affinity.

Then suddenly, as though he had discovered her secret need,
Michel revealed that he loved her. And Michel became the symbol
of the new supernal ideal.

"I love you," she wrote to Michel, "because when I picture
grandeur, wisdom, force and beauty, it is your image which comes
before me." Again she wrote to him:

"It was you I loved through all the phantoms in which for a
time I believed I had found and possessed you."

Alas for the symbols which had once conveyed illusion! Aurélian, Pagello and Alfred no longer seemed real.

7

Michel, like all prophets and reformers, expected the speedy
arrival of his utopia. He expected also to be one of the cabinet of
the new republic. It was not enough to be the leader of a province;
the strong man felt that he was called to lead the destinies of
France.

Was his love of humanity mere ambition and vanity? No test
of his ambition had as yet been made, but his vanity was becoming
more evident.

The monstrous trial ended disastrously. The men of Lyons were
not acquitted, and Michel was sentenced to a month's imprisonment for contempt of court. One of the other lawyers had been
given a year in prison. This humiliated Michel. Was his colleague
regarded as more dangerous than the great man of Berry? Michel
was jealous—George had all she could do to pacify his fury. He
fell ill. Because George could not allow the sick man to endure the

misery of prison, she succeeded in having his sentence postponed for several months. The fact that a woman had intervened in his behalf was carefully hidden from Michel. His pride would have suffered from the criticism of men. Luckily it did not hurt his pride at all to let a woman nurse him, so although a novel was due in a few weeks' time, George abandoned her work to devote her days and her nights to the suffering man.

Later, when Michel did actually languish in prison, George's devotion was unfailing. She wrote to Liszt:

"Michel is in prison. I have not yet seen any of our acquaintances. The old republican is more ill than ever. I am so busy taking care of him that I am almost never at home."

For the present, however, Michel was scarcely able to travel. As soon as he could be moved, Planet accompanied him to Bourges. Liszt departed for Switzerland, and George was left in Paris during the month of June to finish a novel due the first of July.

She started manfully, but her rooms under the roof were uncomfortably hot. Facing the court on the ground floor was an empty apartment that had been under repair and was now temporarily deserted by the workmen. It seemed invitingly cool. George moved in and used the carpenter's bench for a desk. Here, surrounded by sawdust, mice and spiders, she worked all day and part of the night. The maid brought her meals and told all callers truthfully that her mistress was not at home.

The novel George was engaged in writing was entitled *Simon.* Since Simon was Michel, George could write about her hero while thinking about her lover. Under these propitious circumstances the manuscript was ready for the printer in time.

During July George made a visit to Bourges. She stayed in a house offered by a friend. She lived quietly, writing as steadily as ever, and seeing Michel, Planet, her hostess, and one or two friends. She was rewriting *Lélia.* It had been the wish of Lamennais, Liszt and Michel that she should cut out all the curses and put in their place her hopes for humanity. It was a splendid idea and it satisfied Michel, Liszt and Lamennais, but unfortunately it spoiled the book.

For George and Michel the visit at Bourges was different from the weeks they had spent together in Paris. There was no activity they could share and no excitement to stimulate their minds. Michel appeared to George in a new light. During the first week of her visit he was reading Montesquieu and he preached moderation. During the second week he was reading Plato and he preached Platonic ideas. Then he read Aristotle and forgot Plato. He was always under the dominance of the last book he had read. As fast as he changed his theories he wanted George to change with him, which she sometimes found it difficult to do.

Like Madame Dupin, Michel often found George obstinate. Nothing could make her other than she was. She never took on any thought that was not fundamentally her own.

When she had read Rousseau she had become his disciple because she had previously agreed with his theories. In the same way, when she met Michel she became his disciple because she had always been a republican. Her mind refused what was alien to her convictions. Lamennais, Liszt and Michel all believed that they had influenced her mind. But they had merely fed her own convictions. No one ever persuaded her away from herself.

Sometimes, in a mood of humility, Michel cried out to her, "You think more logically and see more clearly than I do!" While he turned like a weathercock, George remained straight and solid as a tree that has deep roots in the earth.

Michel continued to be a despot, and his despotism did not always seem the expression of godlike love. When he took part in conversation as one of a group, he liked argument and criticism and seemed stimulated by the opposition of men. But if George sided against him before others, he exhibited the anger of wounded vanity. However calmly he might accept criticism from men, he looked to his woman for sympathy and praise.

When George and Michel were alone the situation was even

more difficult, because then if George differed from him he lost self-confidence, called himself a failure, and talked of living in the desert or becoming a monk. Any least objection from her left him crushed.

Most of the time Michel was like an inflated balloon soaring above George's head. But as a balloon that is pricked falls to the ground, so Michel, if George hurt his vanity, fell flat. In this position he looked so pitiful that George, in compassion, patched him up with praise and filled him with flattery until he could soar again above her head.

It became evident that Michel did not have a strong mind. Nevertheless he was a virile personality. He dominated his illness by will power and his followers by eloquence, he was a brilliant lawyer and he had masterful ways. Despite the weaknesses which made him less godlike, he continued to fulfill George's symbol of a strong man.

Michel's happiness depended on the belief that George agreed with him. Every time he said "Yes" he wanted her to say "Yes, indeed." Then he felt complete.

Secretly he was not sure of himself and he relied upon George to supply the confidence and conviction he lacked. He demanded her presence on all occasions. Without his chief disciple he could not preach. George saw this greediness for agreement as vanity, but it went deeper. He was not so much asking her to flatter him as he was asking her to supply his lack of motive force. He had not the slightest intimation that George said "Yes" just to please him and added "indeed" when she really meant "perhaps."

George never asked Michel to agree with her. Her mind was self-sustaining and self-sufficient. She did not care what he thought or said or did, so long as he loved her. It was her heart need that made her dependent and weak.

Did he love her? Did he love her? It was the only question that affected her happiness.

He loved her in order to get her to agree with him. She agreed with him in order to hold his love. So they parted with this mutual deception, which made them both quite happy as long as each was successfully deceived.

8

George could bear with Michel's despotism of love, but she could not endure Casimir's despotism of hate. She therefore postponed her return to Nohant until the presence of the children made it possible for her to live under the same roof with her husband.

She stayed with him during the children's vacation. Her status in the family had grown less from year to year. It was now completely lost. She was not allowed to speak to a servant or use a horse without asking permission of the head of the house. She took the children for all-day jaunts and picnics, heard their lessons, lived in their lives, and pretended that she had a home.

She was waiting for Casimir's departure. As a consequence of their complete estrangement husband and wife had decided to separate. After many discussions as to which of the two should remain at Nohant, Casimir had chosen to live in Paris and resume his bachelor life. A friendly agreement had been drawn up and signed, whereby he was to receive the Narbonne house in Paris, together with an allowance from his wife. The definite break was to take place in November, when the children were to be sent back to school.

On October 11, 1836, a day which was to be memorable in the life of Madame Dudevant, Duteil drove over from La Châtre with three other friends. They remained for dinner. Everything went off very pleasantly until Maurice found the cream pitcher empty and asked for more cream. What was there in that to enrage his father? Did it seem to Casimir, who had been drinking heavily, that the child was giving an order?

"Leave the room!" commanded Casimir.

Maurice was intimidated by his father's tone. He ran to his mother and pressed his quivering body against her arms.

Casimir had told the child again and again that he was master. He had told his wife that he was master. He had told the servants. And it seemed to him that no one believed him, no one obeyed.

"Obey your father," Aurore repeated quietly, hoping to avert a scene.

Another order! Or so it must have seemed to the angry man.

"Leave the room yourself!" And Casimir rushed toward his wife with upraised arm. It was the same gesture he had used against her in the home of James Duplessis one summer evening long ago.

But this time the blow was averted.

Duteil caught Casimir's arm and held it. The others came forward and helped. Casimir shook them off and left the room.

Everyone was relieved and the guests talked loudly about the weather. Before the topic was exhausted, back came Casimir bringing a gun. He pointed the gun at his wife. The men were out of their chairs in an instant. They surrounded him, pulled the weapon away, and pushed the enraged man into his chair. Casimir, apparently pacified, resumed his dinner.

That was all. And that was everything. Aurore's emotions were now shaken from the moorings of habit. She was no longer satisfied with the friendly arrangement that left Baron Dudevant free to return to Nohant and threaten her with a gun.

Michel agreed with her. She went to Bourges for his counsel, and he now advised a judicial separation. In order to avoid a public trial, a second amicable agreement was made whereby Casimir was given one half of his wife's property on condition that he stay in Paris and allow Madame Dudevant to secure judgment by default. Having consented to this arrangement, Casimir went to Paris. The children were sent back to school, and George remained at Nohant.

For the first time in her life she was allowed to live alone in her

own house. How she reveled in her home! She dismissed all the
servants except the gardener and his wife, who lived in the lodge
at the entrance to the estate. She put away everything that reminded her of Casimir, and felt great satisfaction in having the
furniture changed until each chair and table and picture was
placed as it had been in the old days. This seemed to remove Baron
Dudevant's influence and bring back the spirit of Madame Dupin.

In the evenings she lighted all the candles and walked through
the reinstated rooms, from the boudoir where she had written
Indiana through the bedroom where her children had been born,
across the great hall where she had played as a child, into the dining-room and the salon that were filled with memories of her
grandmother. In the salon she lighted a fire and sat in front of it
brooding, remembering, saturated with contentment.

At last she had entered upon the inheritance Madame Dupin
meant her to enjoy. She abandoned herself to the luxury of a life
without Casimir. For the first time she appreciated the beauty
and value of married life. She could so easily imagine a man, the
right man, in the house with her. Now that Casimir had left she
was moved to write a story of happy married life. She would call it
Mauprat. It would describe a husband who was always devoted,
always faithful to his wife.

9

Into this contentment came Michel of Bourges. He was wholly
the lawyer now. He wished to confer with his client, to give her
his best legal advice. He was determined that her conduct should
be above criticism.

"If you expect me to win this case for you," he warned her,
"you must be good."

"But I am good," George protested in surprise.

"It isn't enough to be good when you have a law-suit on hand.
You must seem good as well."

"Then I don't seem good to you?"

"To me you seem too good for this earth. I'm talking about the public. You must be discreet."

"What is there to be discreet about? I am perfectly willing that my whole life should be read by everyone like an open book."

Michel groaned at his client's obtuseness. "Listen, George, be a good boy and mind me. You must not ride horseback, nor smoke, nor wear trousers, nor have a love affair."

"But a good boy may do all these things."

"A good boy may. A good woman may not. I meant to say be a good woman."

"I won't give up smoking."

"Don't be stupid. I only mean that you must not let it be known that you smoke. In the public mind it isn't what you do that matters, it's letting it be known."

"I hate deceit and I hate concealment. There is nothing in my life that needs to be concealed."

"George, George!" sighed Michel hopelessly.

"My self-respect means more to me than other people's opinions. If a thing is right it does not need to be concealed. The things I do seem to me right or I wouldn't do them. I am the only judge of my own actions."

"When your case comes to trial you will see that there are other judges with authority over your actions. They can ruin your life. They can take away your property and your children and leave you penniless and alone. This law-suit is a serious game, George. The judge is umpire, and in order to win you must obey the rules that others have made."

"I see what you mean, Michel. To keep my children I must make sacrifices. Very well, then. Let the people in the town of La Châtre think of me as a repentant Magdalen. My horses will remain in the barn. I shall smoke behind closed doors. I shall wear the longest, fullest skirts that are made. I shall never see you alone. But I hate such subterfuges, and I warn you that as soon as this case is decided I shall pull on breeches and leggings, jump on my horse and gallop all around town."

"I don't think you show the proper spirit."

"Are you speaking now of the proper spirit for a boy?"

"No, for a woman."

"There we are again. Two codes of morals for two human beings whom God has made with the same needs and the same desires."

"Your principles, my dear George, are made for a world that will never exist."

"They are made for a world that will exist some day as surely as there is a just God."

"Nevertheless your ideal world does not exist in the year 1835, and your case will be tried this year."

"You are right, Michel," George assented meekly. "I yield to your advice. What else must I not do?"

"You must not live here at Nohant alone."

"Oh, but I love it so! It's the first time—"

"You must have a chaperon."

"A chaperon!" George laughed. "That is the height of absurdity. I who have lived as a bachelor for four years! Now, Michel, how would you like to have a chaperon?"

"That's different."

"Why is it different?"

"You ask questions like a child. When a man and woman are in litigation, the president of the court appoints a guardian for the woman so that her virtue may be preserved."

"And in the meantime Casimir is allowed to live his gay life in Paris! Why not give Casimir a chaperon?"

"Casimir belongs to himself. You belong to Casimir."

"I do not."

"In the eyes of the law a woman belongs to her husband until the law says she does not. While the question remains unsettled, the husband's property must be protected so that it may be returned to him intact. This is the usage of our courts. The president of the court is very friendly, he consents to appoint Madame Duteil as your chaperon. You must leave Nohant and live under her supervision until your case is won or lost."

George laughed. Then as the seriousness of her situation overwhelmed her, she spoke under her breath, more to herself than to Michel, "My children, my children, I will do this ridiculous thing for you!"

The house at Nohant was closed and George moved over to La Châtre and spent the winter under the kindly eye of Madame Duteil. There were days when George felt bold and audacious and wrote gay letters to her friends describing her predicament. But more often she laughed softly at the customs and usages of a society in which she lived as an outsider.

Ill adjusted as she was to society, George felt very much at home in Madame Duteil's family. There were fourteen members of the family, of whom seven were children. George worked at night as usual, and since she was supposed to live in retirement, she spent most of her daytime with the children, longing always for Maurice and Solange, who were separated from each other and from her. Would the day ever come when she could have them at Nohant, have both her children and her home?

10

In December, 1835, and February, 1836, two judgments were pronounced in favor of Madame Dudevant. She wrote to Madame d'Agoult:

"Thank God, I have won my law-suit. My children belong to me."

Hippolyte and Duteil wrote to George that they would answer for Casimir. She need feel no uneasiness about his promises. He had given them his word of honor that he would not interfere with his wife's suit.

But scarcely had Madame Dudevant been given her freedom

when the man of honor changed his mind and brought counter-suit against his wife. This meant a public trial, the thing that Michel had tried to avoid.

The case of Dudevant versus Dudevant went to the newspapers and became exciting scandal wherever the name of George Sand was known. The people of La Châtre found it difficult to take sides in the case which was making their town notorious. They did not blame Casimir for his failings, but they did blame him for forcing a public trial—a thing almost unheard of in the province —and for bringing slanderous accusations against his wife.

Feeling was strong for Madame Dudevant, but traditional prejudice was against her. In this conflict between sympathy and tradition, public opinion reached the conclusion that Madame Dudevant was immoral but good. People had heard she was immoral, but they knew she was good. They could not help knowing it. She had been a good mother, and until she left Casimir she had been a good wife. She had always been a good neighbor. The people of La Châtre stood on the street corners to discuss the reputation of Madame Dudevant. She was the talk of the town.

On May 10th and 11th the trial was held in the civil court at La Châtre. Everybody who could crowd into the court-house went to hear the case.

Casimir's lawyer dwelt at some length upon two main arguments. First, the husband accused the wife of every kind of moral depravity. Second, he wanted this hated and despised wife restored to his arms.

Then Michel took the floor and, with all the eloquence for which he was famous, pointed out the contradiction of these arguments. "There is not a judge on earth," he contended, "who after reading this man's accusations against his wife would condemn her to live under the heavy weight of such hatred." Turning to Casimir, he addressed him directly: "The outrage which you have offered her is ineffaceable. This outrage proves that you do not want her, you are not asking for your wife. But you oppose a separation. Do you wish then all the benefits of marriage without bearing its responsibilities?"

Casimir's lawyer replied that his client did not claim that he was passionately attached to his wife at present, but he would forgive her and gradually restore her to his favor as she proved true repentance and submission.

Casimir's lawyer laid stress on the fact that Baron Dudevant had generously given his wife three thousand francs a year, although she earned a great deal by her work. He claimed that the baron refused a judicial separation because he wished to conserve his wife's fortune for the children's sake. Michel, in his turn, contended that what Casimir really cared for was his wife's possessions, not the possession of his wife.

To prove his contention, Michel told the story of the marriage. He showed that the marriage contract was under the dotal régime, which meant that the wife was not obliged to pay the husband's debts. But she had paid them, nevertheless. He dwelt upon her long patience of nine years and her intellectual isolation. He spoke of Dudevant's brutality, drunkenness and infidelities. He related how Aurore, with the knowledge and consent of her husband, had led an independent life, had been almost entirely self-supporting, while Baron Dudevant was enjoying his wife's revenues and was living in his wife's house; how the Baron saw nothing reprehensible in this way of life so long as his wife stayed away; how he had written her friendly letters and had never once in their long correspondence of four years expressed the wish to have her return home; how, on the other hand, the moment she entered her home the friendly relation which existed in the letters immediately ceased on his part and gave place to irritation and violence. He described the scene when Casimir before five friends and other witnesses had threatened his wife with a gun. Michel pointed out further that according to French law a husband could sue his wife for adultery under any and all circumstances, whereas a husband's adultery gave the wife no ground for complaint unless the husband lived with his paramour under the same roof which sheltered his wife. Michel then brought forward witnesses to prove that Casimir had brought his women into his wife's home.

This behavior established Baron Dudevant's guilt. The court of La Châtre pronounced a verdict in favor of Madame Dudevant, and ordered her to support the children and pay the expenses of their education.

Casimir appealed to the higher court. In July the case was heard again in the royal court of Bourges. Now came the sensational stage of the trial.

Bourges, the capital city of Berry, differed greatly from the provincial town of La Châtre. It was more antagonistic to Madame Dudevant. The people of Bourges were well read and well informed. They were acquainted with her writings and they were familiar with the gossip of Paris, where enormous influence was ascribed to her novels and her life. Stories were current that certain women, no longer content with a convent education, demanded more knowledge as though they were men. Then too, examples were quoted of unmarried women who asserted their right to live alone instead of in the family of a male relative. These improper demands were attributed to the example of George Sand.

Her writings were considered more dangerous even than her life. Young girls who read *Indiana* wished to marry for love instead of in obedience to parents, while those who read *André* and *Valentine* considered it right to marry beneath their station.

The name George Sand had become a symbol for all rebellious women. Were not all pretensions to independence on the part of women called "life à la George Sand"?

As for her influence on married women, one had only to read *Jacques*, the story of the husband who committed suicide that his wife might be happy with another man.

And anyhow, should a woman who wore trousers be trusted with two innocent children? Consensus of opinion said no!

Meanwhile George, who was staying with friends in Bourges, was occupied in perfecting a plan of her own. If the case were decided against her and the children given to Casimir, she had made up her mind to emigrate to America with the children. With this purpose in mind she had given securities which enabled her to borrow ten thousand francs. She had sent for Solange, who was held in readiness, and she had arranged to have Maurice taken to meet her at the boat.

At the time of the trial the law held that a woman convicted of adultery could be put in prison and then condemned to return to her husband's arms. George did not expect to be put in prison, but she did face the possibility of losing her children or of being sent back to Casimir. Rather than accept either of these alternatives she was willing to steal her own children, in a legal sense, and live with them in a distant land.

This decision brought peace of mind to the harassed wife and mother. The night before the trial she felt such deep peace that she composed a prayer.

"Son of man, it is in thy name that they slay the lamb at the moment when thou hast placed it upon thy shoulders. Thy cup of suffering is no longer bitter, since it has been touched by thy lips. In our nights of agony we search for the trace of thy foot-steps in the Garden of Olives. We hope, because thou hast en-nobled our sufferings, because thou hast given us God as a refuge against men."

Having arranged to evade the law, and having written her prayer, George awaited her sentence with a clear conscience. She slept soundly the night before the trial.

11

Although George faced the ordeal with calm confidence, her friends feared the outcome. They had assembled at Bourges and had gathered around her. There was her dearest friend, François Rollinat. There were Duteil, Néraud and Planet, together with the two Berrichons from the first Paris days, Alphonse Fleury and Gustave Papet. Aurore's former confidant, Emile Régnault, was present. And from the south of France came Jules Boucoiran, ready to testify in her defense.

Men friends, how loyal and brave they were! Not a woman came to help her. One could not blame them, poor things; they dared not tarnish their reputations. George had written to Zoé Leroy, her once devoted friend, but Zoé could not countenance a judicial separation. It was too unusual, too conspicuous a stand for a woman to take.

George had also written to Aurélian de Sèze and had asked for permission to use her journal to him and his letters to her. Aurélian was now married and the father of several children. He would have been justified in refusing to be drawn into a public scandal. But Aurélian had answered:

"I still have, among other things, the journal, which I am sending. Oh, heavens! Will this be read before the jury? But I authorize you, let them read it, let them print it, I am willing. . . . Yes, I authorize you to make use of everything you have from me."

It seemed that George was justified in her preference for men as friends.

On the morning of the great day the court room was full to overflowing. No such sensation had ever occurred in Bourges. The best families were represented, even modest women braved the criticism of their men folk and went to hear the trial. They stared at Madame Dudevant as she entered on the arm of her celebrated lawyer. They observed her dress—yes, dress, not trousers. The crowd were disappointed. They had heard, and they had hoped it would prove true, that she wore red trousers, high boots with spurs, and a blue velvet coat. It had been rumored that she would carry pistols in her belt. The women felt that her modish and modest summer costume of white was commonplace and inconspicuous. The notorious woman even wore a half veil to her nose and a flowered shawl.

For this trial Casimir had changed lawyers. He had secured the services of Monseiur Thiot-Varennes. This eminent gentleman read passages from George's novels. He chose quotations that were written in the first person singular. Since George's characters were often villains, he easily found many villainous sentiments. They were all attributed to Madame Dudevant as her principles of life.

Then turning to George, who was looking so ladylike in her white dress, he harangued her.

"Your books, Madame, are full of the bitterness and the regrets which devour your heart. They show your profound disgust with life. The torments of your soul pursue you in the midst of your fame and poison your triumphs. You have sought happiness everywhere and you have found it nowhere. Well, I will show you the road to it. Return to your husband. Go back to the home in which the first years of your married life were passed so pleasantly and peacefully. Resume your position as wife and mother. Walk once again in the path of duty and virtue. Submit yourself to the laws of nature. In all other courses you will find error and deception. In that course alone you will find happiness and peace."

Thiot-Varennes was a clever lawyer. He saw the futility of bringing against Madame Dudevant accusations out of her free and independent life which Casimir's letters had so heartily approved. He desired therefore to find some charge against her which dated back to the early years of marriage. If he could prove that she betrayed her husband while she was living with him, his case was won. For this purpose Casimir had given his lawyer Aurore's written confession of her love for Aurélian. Not in vain had Casimir kept the naïve revelation of his wife's first love. Portions of this long letter were read in court as proof of adultery. The clever lawyer made good use of each extravagant phrase. He emphasized every incriminating word: "I am guilty. I confess my fault. Forgive our sin, our guilt."

As these passages were given to the delighted audience, public opinion was quickly prejudiced against the erring wife of ten years before. The confession was heard with excited attention. The author was self-condemned.

After his learned confrère had finished, Michel also read the famous confession. But he read it all, from beginning to end. Heard thus in full, the confession told an entirely different story.

The expression of guilt became the effort of a girl-wife to win her husband's confidence. The self-accusation was changed to renunciation. The touching appeal became the expression of a soul generous to self-immolation.

A wave of emotion surged through the audience. The confession was greeted by sighs and murmurs of sympathy. Men stealthily felt for their handkerchiefs, women wept openly.

The judge, however, kept his head and instructed the jury that the young wife had been guilty of moral adultery.

Half the jurors were moved to vote for the guilty wife who somehow seemed innocent. The other half remembered *Jacques* and stood by Casimir. After deliberating for three-quarters of an hour the jury was divided and a new trial was announced. The volatile audience received the announcement with hisses and groans.

The two opposing lawyers, unwilling to wait for another trial, met and persuaded Casimir to accept a fair division of his wife's property, so that, in spite of litigation and publicity, the case was settled out of court, and the terms of settlement were those agreed upon at the time of Madame Dudevant's first judgment. Maurice went to the husband, Solange to the wife.

But that was not the end.

Casimir was determined to make his son a soldier. Maurice was twelve years old, and his soul was in revolt. He wanted to be an artist and he hated his military school. He adored his mother and the fear of being taken away from her made him ill. In his delirium he cried continually, "Nohant! Nohant!" His condition became so serious that the doctors, even the school doctors, asked to have the boy removed and taken to Nohant. Casimir was obstinate and refused to give his consent. George was helpless. It seemed as though Casimir would rather assert his authority than save his son's life. So the sick boy was sent to stay with his father. But Casimir found the child's illness so alarming that he sent him to his mother at Nohant, to be nursed until he was well enough for school again.

In the summer of 1837 George was called to Paris by the serious illness of her mother. She left Solange in charge of Mademoiselle Rollinat, who had promised not to leave the child's side.

Casimir saw his opportunity and succeeded in kidnapping Solange. He used physical force against Mademoiselle Rollinat, and snatched the screaming child from her arms. When George heard that Casimir had taken Solange to Guillery she was far too frenzied to wait for letters or send an emissary. She remembered the new invention called the telegraph, which was in use by the government. She beseiged officials and had the instrument used in her behalf, so that when she reached Guillery after several days' travel, the police assisted her to recover her child.

When Casimir was asked why he wanted Solange he said frankly that he did not want her, he merely wanted to deal his wife a blow, and he knew his best method of hurting the mother was to hit at her children. As a result of these two experiences George realized that although she had freed herself from an undesirable husband, she had not freed the children from an undesirable father.

Not long after the exhausting trip to and from Guillery, Baroness Dudevant died and Casimir fell heir to a considerable fortune. It seemed to George that she might therefore be relieved of the burden of supporting her husband. She wanted the Narbonne house as a dot for Solange, and she desperately wanted to gain possession of her delicate son. She took the case to court again and claimed that Baron Dudevant, having come into his own inheritance, no longer required half of hers.

The court did not deem it just to deprive the husband of his share of his wife's property. Once more the question was decided by the lawyers. George was obliged to sacrifice her capital. For forty thousand francs Casimir surrendered his right to the Paris house and to Maurice.

At last George had bought back both her children. Solange's dot was assured and Maurice could study art.

But what a price to pay! In regaining the home bequeathed to her by her grandmother, she had lost the income by which it had been maintained. Could she earn enough to support her home and children? Nobody seemed to realize how hard she worked to write novels. Her labor was continued in the silence of the night while others slept.

She was very tired.

12

As she looked back over the last two years, it seemed to George that she had made books as a galley-slave propels a boat, chained to her task, whipped by the lash of necessity.

And as she looked ahead to the laborious life that stretched before her, she saw no hope of freedom. Rest and recreation were like sins that tempted her. She fought against the desire to read the books everyone was discussing and to enjoy studies always anticipated and always postponed. She began to hate the life of unreality in which she was forced to live. Her imagination, it seemed to her, had to become an athlete in order to perform stupendous feats in the gymnasium of her mind. Her nerves, excited at night by obsessions of scenes and characters, left her so languid in the daytime that she was exhausted by any attention given to her children or her friends.

Among her letters to Michel are heart-rending pages in which she relates the difficulties of her work. She tells him how overwhelmed she is by domestic duties, constant interruptions, stacks of unanswered letters. Since her material is used as a serial and instalments have to be finished at a fixed date, she is forced to scribble in haste what she would like to write in leisure. By so doing she violates her muse, which takes revenge by freezing her inspiration. Hence her many dull and involved pages and her doubt of her own powers. When she contemplates what she has written she succumbs to despair. Each night she counts the number of hours at her disposal and the number of pages that have to be filled. Then she drives herself to finish the required quantity before she allows herself to sleep.

Quantity, always quantity! There is not time to think of quality.

Pressure of debt—it is as though a creditor stood waiting by the door. Pressure of haste—the manuscript must be finished in a week.

Now there are five days more, four days more, three days, two days, one more day. Now it is necessary to finish before dawn. Hurry! Hurry! The post is waiting. Buloz is waiting. The magazine must go to press. The public, the great greedy public, is waiting for a new novel of love and passion by George Sand.

Come then, pour out romance for a final scene. Look it over? Edit it? Retouch, correct?—there isn't time. The ink is scarcely dry on the paper when she is obliged to deliver the manuscript. A mixed metaphor? It must go as it is. Involved sentences? Let them go.

Hurry or Buloz will be angry—and Buloz is the one who pays.

One hot dawn she wrote to Michel:

"My head is split by working all night in this intense heat. Coffee and tobacco were the only things that could stimulate my failing spirits to the tune of 200 francs a folio. I now have two hours for sleep, then I must ride horseback for fifteen miles over bad roads to settle some business with butchers. The hard work of life is making me old and is putting wrinkles on my forehead.

"To-night I shall have to work fourteen hours again, and next day the same and so on for six nights in succession. I have given my word. Will it kill me? Already I begin to succumb and I have only commenced. I hate my trade and it alone enables me to pay my debts."

In this difficult period of her life George turned to Michel for affection:

"The one thing I have always sought on earth is a soul identical with my own soul, on whom I could concentrate all my desires and center all my joys. Let fate send me this being and let this being be you."

So far in their association she had answered his demands. Now their positions were reversed. She needed him. "I awake and before my eyes are open I reach out my arm to my table to feel whether a letter has come from you. Often I am so worn out by the last night's work that I haven't strength enough to read it. I hold it in my hands. I press it to my lips, and burying head, letter and hands in my pillow, I go to sleep again with my treasure, happy and calm."

But Michel was no Aurélian de Sèze. He could form no conception of a love that lived in letters. When she had been his Benjamin he had felt impelled to write to her every day, but now that she was a lonely weary woman he had nothing to say. Appeals for sympathy bored him. He might have responded, whether or not he understood, just because the need was hers— his woman's—but that was not Michel's nature. He had enjoyed telling George about his troubles and his theories, but he did not want to hear about her worries and her overwork. No one in the world, he often told her, had ever listened to him as she listened. No one had ever given him such complete, concentrated, absorbed attention. She was his best reflection. But when she was absent he turned to lesser reflections of himself in the eyes of other admiring women. So Michel had other love affairs, and to infidelity he added neglect. He stopped writing for weeks at a time, and George was always waiting for the post, hoping, praying for a letter.

What was the matter with Michel? Why didn't he write? She asked the question of his friend Girerd and Girerd informed her that Michel was vain and self-centered. She asked the question of herself and was forced to the same reply.

But it was not selfishness alone which caused Michel's coldness. There was something about George which antagonized her strong man.

13

During the two years of close association with Michel, George had been passing through a crisis in her mental and emotional life. The feminine Aurore and the masculine George in her had never attained equilibrium, and now they were engaged in bitter warfare. Each side of her nature was intensified by the strain of conflict. She had never been so feminine as in her attitude toward Michel. Her meek submissiveness had seemd at times excessive. Then the part of her that had been denied arose and asserted itself. When this happened she talked to Michel as though she were his equal, expressing her own convictions and opinions with the courage of one who does not need to please. When masculine George was thus in the ascendant, Michel could not hold his own against her. She seemed better fitted than he to be the guide.

Now Michel did not fancy himself as a follower, nor did he like the idea of a woman guide. He adored the Aurore in his friend— her devotion, her self-sacrifice, her nurture-sense. But the George in her he abhorred.

George's frankness and independence threatened to engulf her love affair and destroy her happiness. Nevertheless she could not curb her fast developing masculine self.

In the month of July, 1837, she admitted that she was "tired of giving devotion, tired of receiving in return nothing but ingratitude and hardness." She thought she was cured.

But as late as September, when she received what she called a summons from Michel telling her to come to Châteauroux, she rode on horseback alone at night the twenty miles that lay between them, in order to be with him during the two days of his stay.

This was her last act of devotion for Michel. In the same month of September she wrote:

"My terrible anguish has yielded to its own excess. I no longer love. I have arrived at the last stage of disenchantment."

George had lived through her second great passion. She was now thirty-three years old.

After his break with George came the test of Michel's ambition, and the proof whether or not he had ever been the strong man of George's dream. Since the republic in which he had hoped to play an important part seemed indefinitely postponed, he lost enthusiasm for the cause and developed an interest in wordly success. The baldness which George had so admired was concealed beneath a wig. His sabots were replaced by kid boots, his homespun by stylish clothes, and during the rest of his life he devoted himself to making money.

Michel had been an important influence in George's life. He started her on the path which they promised each other to walk together. When he fell by the wayside she walked the path alone. She continued to be a devoted republican, giving her time and her writing to the cause. Eleven years later, in 1848, when the Second Republic was finally established, George was high in the councils of the mighty, but poor Michel was forgotten and ignored. No place was saved for him in the cabinet or even in the upper chamber. The most he could secure for himself was his election as deputy from his province. To-day if the name of Michel of Bourges is remembered it is because of his association with a famous woman, to whose life he gave inspiration for the short period of two years.

VI

MADAME SAND

AFTER her judicial separation George ceased to be Madame Dudevant; she was addressed by everyone as Madame Sand. Her children also came to be known as Maurice Sand and Solange Sand. Thus the queer little pen-name, so casually chosen at a time when she did not expect to be widely known, became the family name and George became the head of the Sand family.

In the eighteen-thirties it was an achievement for a woman to establish a family. It was even more remarkable for her to preëmpt a new name, and so cut herself off from relatives and relatives-in-law. No one was left to be hurt by this unique procedure. The death of Sophie in the summer of 1837 broke the last close tie with the Dupin past, and after the disappearance of Casimir no Dudevants were entitled to comment upon the conduct of Madame Sand. George became master of Nohant, with the prerogatives and responsibilities of a man. These changes in her outer life reached through to her consciousness and affected her attitude toward herself.

As far back as March, 1836, when she believed she had won her law-suit, she had written to her Saint-Simonian friend, Adolphe Guéroult: "My life as a woman is over, and since I have been given a little reputation and a certain influence (which I have neither striven for nor deserved), I may be able to make a place for myself as a young man."

Again, while she was anticipating a judgment in her favor, she wrote to Guéroult in answer to his expressed desire to have her meet his friends: "I shall enjoy making their acquaintance as soon as I cease to be a slave woman and become a free woman, or as nearly a free woman as our wretched civilization permits."

As she came nearer to masculine freedom, Madame Sand became further removed than ever from the women of her day. She felt affectionate and kindly toward women, as a brother might feel toward his younger sisters, but friends to her meant men.

In writing to Michel about her will, she said, "I leave my son to my friends and my daughter to their wives and sisters."

It was in 1837 that Madame Sand's dear friend Lamennais started a radical newspaper called *Le Monde*. He asked George to contribute, which she did willingly, although at some personal sacrifice, as Lamennais was poor and the pay was negligible. Her chief contribution to *Le Monde* was a series of *Lettres à Marcie*.

Marcie was an imaginary young woman of twenty-five to whom life offered no opportunity except marriage without love to a man who wanted her dot. This marriage of convenance repelled Marcie, but on the other hand she was frightened at the prospect of being an old maid. In this predicament she asked advice of George, and George advised Marcie that the misery of a mismated wife is worse even than the shame of spinsterhood. She told Marcie to strive for independence in a life of study or work.

In the letters to Marcie George preached what is now called feminism. She made the startling claim that woman is essentially man's equal, and gave her opinion of the barbarous laws and customs which oppressed her sex.

Like so many of George's writings, the letters to Marcie created a sensation, but this time George had no defenders. All her readers agreed that she was trying to disrupt the family by giving help and comfort to old maids. By the time six letters had been published, Lamennais was deluged with protests. The distracted editor begged George to desist, and Marcie received no more advice.

But it was feared that the terrible Madame Sand had not been stopped in time. It was impossible to estimate the number of spinsters who had been influenced to hold up their heads and respect themselves, even to the extent of refusing marriage with men who needed their dots.

Another example of George's protest against feminine restrictions was the novel *Gabriel*, published in 1839. *Gabriel* is the story of a girl brought up as a boy, isolated in an old château far from the world, and educated by an abbé surprisingly like Deschartres. She is taught the use of gun, sword and pistol. She acquires masculine attributes, and her mind is trained to a huge contempt for everything feminine.

When she comes of age Gabriel runs away, falls madly in love, and marries the man of her choice. But for a mind so trained marriage is a tragedy. Gabriel finds that her manly virtues are feminine failings. Conduct that was right in trousers becomes wrong in skirts. The qualities that helped her to success as a man lead to failure in a woman. She discovers that success for a woman is won by feminine wiles, which she despises. Her independent spirit antagonizes her husband's family and his friends; her whole little world turns against her. The one thing which would make her situation endurable is her husband's understanding love and sympathy. He loves her, but he forces her to conform to his prejudices and forbids her to usurp a man's prerogatives. Gabriel is condemned to a life which is as unnatural to her as it seems natural to other women. She falls into despair. Why, asks Gabriel, are men and women given two moral codes, which are not only different but opposed? So trained and so judged, she asks, how can men and women understand each other or find happiness in love? The theme is carried to its logical conclusion in the death of Gabriel.

In this story George revealed her struggle with masculine prejudice, her contempt for coquetry, and her despair of finding a male intelligence that could meet her own.

2

In the spiritual dissolution that followed the rupture with Michel, George once more became a pagan and all her ways of life were changed. At three in the morning she left her work and roamed the countryside. Sometimes she walked eight or nine miles, returning home at noon. On these walks she followed the course of the river Indre. When the day grew hot she bathed in the stream, then fell asleep in the sun. Deep in the woods she dreamed she was in Greece, or for hours at a time she imagined herself in America. Such moods were the secrets of her happiness. Lifted above loneliness, she seemed to leave the earth and travel through immensities of space, where she tried to understand the meaning and the mechanism of the universe. These flights of imagination left her impersonal and detached. Her writing became more philosophical. She was less occupied with problems of the individual, more concerned with social wrongs.

As summer gave way to autumn her mood grew calmer. She contented herself with studying nature in flowers and stones and birds. In these pastimes the children and their tutor were always with her. She shared with the tutor the task of the children's lessons. They spent their evenings together reading or playing games.

The tutor, Félicien Mallefille, was youthful but imposing. His air of maturity was due in part to a formidable beard. Ambitious to become a writer, he showed his eagerness for suggestions and advice. He seemed to feel that by sitting at the feet of an acknowledged genius he could catch the inspiration that led to success.

Part of the time Mallefille acted as Madame Sand's secretary. In this capacity it was his duty to copy her manuscript. The material was, as always, appearing monthly. Under pressure of the approaching date of publication, the author was accustomed to ask her copyist to sit by her side at a large table, so that as fast as a page was covered with her fine handwriting it was pushed along to the copyist to be written in larger script.

The first time that he found himself in this thrilling proximity to the great Madame Sand, Mallefille was amazed at the rapidity with which his literary idol was able to create. He looked at the pages which accumulated at his side. He struggled manfully to keep the pace. But his struggle was unavailing.

"I can't keep up with you," he gasped.

"That is natural," George explained. "You lose time looking at my writing, while I never give it a second glance."

"But don't you ever change a word?"

"There isn't time," George answered, writing steadily on.

Scratch, scratch went Mallefille's pen. Scrape, scrape went George's pencil. Along toward two in the morning, Mallefille, exhausted, dropped his bearded face on his arms.

"Go to bed," said George kindly, "you need sleep."

"But the copy must go by the morning post."

"By writing more carefully I can make my script plain enough for the printer to read."

Mallefille could not restrain his admiring interest. "When," he asked timidly, "do you prepare all this?"

"But I'm preparing it all the time," George answered. "This afternoon while we were in the woods the last chapters took shape in my mind, so that when I sat down this evening I knew exactly what I would say though not exactly how I would say it; that comes as I write."

"It all seems so easy!" cried the aspiring young author with envy in his voice.

"No, it is not easy. It takes my life."

"But why, if you will pardon the question, do you work so hard?"

George lighted a cigarette and leaned back in her chair. "I used to work in order to stay away from home. Now that I have my children I work that I may stay at home. In other words, I have always worked, and still do work, in order to live as I please."

"But," the young man stammered, as curiosity got the better of discretion, "you seem under such pressure of haste. Yet I understood you had completed a three-volume novel called *Engelwald*."

George's face became a mask. She spoke coldly. "Ah, yes, unfortunately, I was obliged to burn the book."

"Michel of Bourges was the hero, wasn't he?"

"Unfortunately, as I say, I was obliged to burn the book. And Buloz had paid for it, so of course he was furious. Now I must write three more volumes to take the place of those already paid for."

"I see," said Mallefille. Then he rose, bent over her, and impulsively kissed the back of her hand. "I wish that I could help you," he murmured.

As George pulled away her hand she smiled at his gallantry.

"Be careful, young man, or my cigarette will burn you."

After Mallefille had taken his leave, George forgot her writing for a moment. Strange, this bearded youth had sympathy where Michel had none. He listened to her as she had used to listen to Michel. He admired as she had admired. Perhaps he idealized as she had done. George was so weary of adoring Michel that she wondered how it would seem for once to be adored.

At four o'clock in the morning the manuscript was finished. George felt cold: it was the hour, she realized, when everyone was beneath warm blankets. She was hungry, yet the thought of food repelled her. Her eyes ached and her head was heavy: but she felt able to resist drowsiness for an hour or two more. Taking fresh paper she wrote a title at the top of the page. After jotting down a few notes she began the opening chapter of a new novel.

3

George's love for Michel had been a long time dying. Perhaps that was why she could turn so abruptly from Michel to Mallefille. The young adorer's sympathy became more precious as the days passed, until she wrote to Girerd comparing Mallefille with Michel:

"I think that I have finally slain the dragon, and that this tenacious passion, so destructive to all my faculties, has at last been cured by another affection which is sweeter, less enthusiastic, less harsh, and I hope more durable."

During the following winter George, Mallefille and the children were shut away from the world in the isolated country house. George was still rebelling against the drudgery of her work. She wrote to Jules Janin:

"You cannot imagine, my friend, the disgust with which literature inspires me at present. (I mean my own.) I am passionately fond of the country and, like you, I enjoy everything that belongs to family and home: dogs, cats, and above everything children. I am no longer young. I need to sleep at night and to loaf all day. Help me to extricate myself from the paws of Buloz and I shall bless you as long as I live."

George spent a great part of her day in the education of her children. In her mood of reaction against her own literature she felt that she had mistaken her trade, she ought to have been a schoolma'am. Mallefille, on the contrary, longed to be a writer. What a pity they could not change places!

Mallefille used his leisure to complete his first novel, *Le Dernier Sauvage*. It went the rounds of several publishers and came back unaccepted.

"It's because my work is unknown," he exclaimed one day. "If my book were signed George Sand all the publishers would jump at it."

George looked at him thoughtfully. "And which do you care for most," she asked, "the pleasure of seeing your name on the title page or the satisfaction of earning money?"

"It's money I need at present," he said. "I have plenty of time in which to strive for recognition."

"In that case, suppose we try signing the book George Sand. Of course it might not be accepted."

"Oh, it would be!" he responded eagerly. "But you must read the book first to see whether it is worthy of a name as great as yours."

"Read your book? But I seldom have time to read over my own books! Yours can't be worse than some of those I've written. Sign it George Sand if you like."

"No, no, you must consider your reputation."

George smiled. "I never consider my reputation."

"Your fame, then."

"What you call fame has no reality for me. I never asked for it or sought it. All it has taught me is that the world is full of envy. I do not live in my fame or my reputation. I live in the affection of my friends."

Le Dernier Sauvage, signed by the name George Sand, was published the following summer, and Mallefille was enabled to pay his debts.

George never said anything more intense about Mallefille than that she loved him with "all her heart." Her heart alone, not her imagination, was engaged in this calm affair. Mallefille was not the lover of her dreams, he was not the symbol of an ideal or the symbol of anything. He was a young man whose devotion consoled her for the passionate idealism she had lost. She wrote to Grzymala, "He is the only man who has never made me suffer one single time for one single minute through his own fault."

But if he never gave her a moment's suffering, neither did he give her an instant's ecstasy. As she observed him adoring her, admiring her, interesting himself in her work, she envied Mallefille.

"He is the only man in the world who ever gave himself absolutely to me. . . . He is malleable as wax on which I can print my seal. And when the time comes that I want to change the imprint, by using care and patience I can do it."

She had given to each of her lovers the kind of woman he desired. She had studied each one's need and had answered it. But she never discovered what Mallefille wanted in a woman, because she never put her mind on the matter. She considered what she wanted from Mallefille and set herself to get it. She had achieved her ambition to love as she thought men loved. But she did not find happiness in man's way of loving. She needed to feel love rather than receive it.

When spring came George was tired of Mallefille. As she made this fact evident, he exhibited a masculine temper that was more like steel than wax in her hands. He grew jealous and tried to fight duels with her friends. During the ensuing three months it was difficult to make him see reason. However, his term as tutor expired, and George never saw him again.

VII

SAND AND CHOPIN

FREDERIC CHOPIN had been introduced to Madame Sand by François Liszt. During the winter of 1836 George had taken rooms at the Hotel de France, which was the temporary home of Liszt and Madame d'Agoult. The two women sharing in common their reception room, had a salon and received the intellectual world of Paris. Among Liszt's friends who called on them was the young musician Chopin, who was then twenty-six years old. He had not attained the wide popularity enjoyed by Liszt, but was already known to the musical world as a gifted composer and artist.

Chopin was of mixed parentage. His mother was Polish and his father French, but Chopin loved his mother's tongue and country and counted himself a Pole. He was homesick for Poland and was also suffering the pangs of frustrated love. His interesting pallor, frail physique, and the secret sorrow by which he seemed consumed, made his personality an expression of his own meloncholy music. The melancholy and the music appealed to George; she wanted to know him better. But he shrank from new contacts. Besides, there was something antipathetic to Chopin in a woman who wrote books, wore plain clothes, and was active in politics. His feminine ideal was a clinging and submissive woman like Marie Wodzinska, whom he loved. However, it was the feminine submissiveness in his Marie which had destroyed Chopin's hopes of happiness. Count Wodzinska refused his consent to his daughter's marriage with a poor music teacher, and Marie had obeyed her father.

As the sorrowful Chopin grew better acquainted with the taciturn Madame Sand he gradually felt less intimidated. The strange woman with stupendous eyes and low magnetic voice understood his music. More than this, she seemed to divine his suffering. He felt her friendliness. She invited him to visit Nohant with Liszt and Madame d'Agoult. He half consented, half refused. He wrote home: "Perhaps I shall visit Madame Sand."

After George left Paris Madame d'Agoult, who was inclined to be feline, wrote to her: "Chopin coughs with infinite grace. He is an irresolute man. There is nothing permanent about him except his cough."

Chopin did not go to Nohant in the summer of 1837; he went to London instead. But the timid musician and the virile writer were destined to know each other better.

In May, 1838, George went up to Paris on personal business. A year and a half had passed since she had seen Chopin. But she had not forgotten his melancholy appeal, and he had not forgotten her sympathy. He was at least interested enough to call.

From the first day he felt at home with her. He had expected to feel embarrassed. She had sent him messages of disconcerting levity. "Tell Chopin I adore him. Tell Chopin I idolize him." But however bold she had been in letters, now that she was face to face with him she had nothing to say.

Since Chopin could express himself only in music and George could express herself only in writing, they were somewhat at a loss for conversation. George seated herself in an easy chair and lit a cigarette. Chopin almost mechanically went to the piano. As soon as his fingers found the keys he felt like speaking, so he poured out his sorrow and longing in sad improvisations that rent the heart of his listener. When he had finished he was afraid she would gush, but she only smiled and sat looking into the fire. So he played again and again with more self-revealment. Her silence pleased him. They suited each other. They were secretly glad that cordial, talkative Liszt and charming, lynx-eyed Madame d'Agoult had at last left them alone to know each other in their own way.

As Chopin called more frequently he forgot to be homesick for Poland. This new presence in his life took the place of home and family. He acquired the habit of calling on George every day. Whenever he was away from her he felt like a lost child.

Chopin was suffering, as was usual each spring, from the after-effects of the winter's influenza. He coughed continually. One of his sisters had died of consumption, but he refused to believe that he was a victim of the family inheritance. He always called his throat attacks bronchitis.

In his illness and weakness he was morbidly fastidious. He could not have endured a masculine woman, but on closer acquaintance with Madame Sand he felt that what had seemed masculine in her was merely calmness and strength. She was the very heart and soul of woman. She inspired him without exciting him, soothed him without making him dull. She was like sunsets he did not have to paint or even exclaim about, like rivers he was not required to swim in, like mountains in the distance, mountains he did not have to climb. She was nature, and nature made him feel like playing music.

When he thought of other people and their possible comments on this new fascination, he was self-conscious and irresolute. What would his family say? What would his pupils say if he became the lover of George Sand?

But when he was alone with her all others were forgotten, and he longed to feel her tenderness. He told her that if she would take care of him he thought he could get well again. He needed her devotion, he wanted all her warmth and sympathy for himself alone.

2

Chopin's striking characteristic was an exclusiveness which was shown in his affections and opinions. He had no use for people who did not agree with him. Whoever was careless of dress, familiar in speech, or democratic in principle was shut out from his sympathy—with one exception. George was indifferent to clothes, familiar in speech, democratic in principle, yet Chopin loved her.

George's predilections were different from Chopin's. If he seemed at times a trifle hard in shutting himself away from those who offended his sensibilities, George was equally soft in reaching out to those who appealed to her sympathies. She was inclusive. Her heart received all sorts and kinds of people who seemed to her new friend queer. Her mind was equally receptive. She accepted queer ideas. She did not even believe in a literal hell. That shocked Chopin.

In everything but music Chopin was extremely conventional, and from the niceties of etiquette to the problems of religion, he was orthodox. George did not care for conventional people or orthodox ideas, yet George loved Chopin. She considered him an angel.

But the word that everyone else applied to Chopin was "aristocrat." Chopin was so aristocratic that he called attention to the fact in every visible way. He kept a valet, who curled his hair. He gave meticulous attention to his linen. He followed fashion in clothes, but his taste was so refined that he avoided extremes of cut or color; he liked to dress in pearl gray. He always wore white gloves and an elaborate cravat; he wore them so conspicuously that they excited comment. He hired a carriage for his own use, although he could not afford to do so. He was fussy, uncertain of himself, and anxious to conform.

George never conformed. She did not have to. She was, like all true aristocrats, sure of herself.

Chopin cultivated important people and loved to visit in the homes of wealth and luxury. He liked best to play for a select group of titled people. The bigger their titles the better he played. He was a little brother of the rich. George was a mother of the poor and oppressed.

In spite of these dissonances of taste and opinion, the two artist natures were completely harmonious when they were left alone.

People pushed them apart. Instinctively, therefore, they chose to take their new-found happiness to some delicious desert where, free from interruptions, he might create music and she literature.

In Spain, on the Balearic Islands, there was no society or civilization to separate two lovers. George and Chopin took their romance to the island of Majorca. With them they took Chopin's piano and George's unpublished book, *Spiridion*. And as a matter of course, with *Spiridion* went George's children. Maurice was fifteen now and Solange was ten. Chopin was twenty-eight and | George was thirty-four. |

The visit to Majorca began as a delightful experience. During the first few weeks Chopin's letters to his friend Fontana breathed serene contentment. Free from the distractions of Paris and the interruptions of lessons, he was creating music. He was, as a creative worker deserves to be, saved from all material cares.

But George's letters showed that she was unable to make headway with *Spiridion*. Her time was occupied in fighting for the necessities of life. The people of the island lived in a state of barbarism and their food and wine disagreed with Chopin. No meat except pork and no cow's milk could be procured. Chopin could not eat what the servant prepared, so George turned cook. The servant refused to work, and George turned servant. She taught the children six hours a day, and she suffered from rheumatism. After Chopin and the children went to bed she gave what strength she had to literature.

When the rainy season began Chopin fell ill. The natives believed that his illness was contagious. The "pestiferous foreigners" were treated like lepers and their landlord put them out of his house. They lived then in an abandoned convent about eight miles from Palma. George and Maurice often walked to town in search of supplies.

The rains grew worse and became a deluge. Chopin grew very ill indeed. They wanted to leave, but there was no boat for three weeks. Finally, in February, Chopin was carried to the boat, but, still treated as a leper, he was denied a proper bed and was forced to sleep on an old cot that could afterward be burned. Meanwhile the boat was full of pigs that were tenderly cared for. They were even landed before the passengers were allowed to go ashore. When George and Chopin left the boat they felt reconciled to society.

As soon as he reached Marseilles Chopin revived, and after a stay in the south of France and a trip to Genoa he was himself again.

3

The months at Majorca, however disastrous to George's work and Chopin's health, had cemented their close relationship. George was still infatuated with her invalid, and Chopin had become wholly dependent on George. Separation was inconceivable. Chopin spent the summer at Nohant with the Sand family, and when November came and he was obliged to go to Paris, George accompanied him, and the children accompanied George.

Chopin avoided the appearance of an official lover. At Nohant he was, with entire propriety, merely a guest of Madame Sand. In Paris the two friends—for, according to George, their love affair lasted only a year—occupied separate apartments. George took up her residence with her children at 16 rue Pigalle, in an annex facing a garden back of the house. Chopin tried living at 5 rue Tronchet, but he was desolate and lonely. Very soon he moved into the main house next door to George's house at rue Pigalle.

They settled down to an existence which seemed both sensible and ideal. Chopin was wedded to his music, and George was indissolubly tied to her children. They agreed on a policy of non-interference. Each was to leave the other free to hold his own opinions, live his own life, and make his own friends.

Balzac wrote about George at this time: "The salon where she receives is full of superb Chinese vases that are filled with flowers.

The furniture is green. There is a cabinet full of curiosities, pictures by Delacroix, her portrait by Calamatta. The piano is magnificent. Chopin is always there. She smokes cigarettes and nothing else. One climbs to her apartment by a straight ugly staircase. Her bedroom is brown, her bed is two mattresses on the floor à la Turk. She has the beautiful tiny, tiny hands of a child."

During the morning Chopin endured teaching music. At four in the afternoon he joined George. They received their friends together, in the room full of Chinese vases and flowers.

There was a strange mixture of visitors in that salon. George's literary and political friends were introduced to Chopin's musical admirers and ladies of fashion. The radical ex-abbé Lamennais met the Countess Potocka; Balzac and Heine met the Baroness Rothschild. Louis Blanc, the socialist, fraternized with Chopin's princesses. All the celebrities and social leaders of the day called on Sand and Chopin. So, in spite of their sensible, ideal agreement, they did not lead separate lives. They shared everything.

They even shared the two interests which were to have been treated with non-interference, Chopin's music and George's children. Maurice was a student in the studio of Delacroix. Solange was at boarding school, but spent the week-end with her mother. The presence of the children, however, created no difficulty. Chopin liked them and they adored him.

Their second domicile in Paris was determined by their mutual friend Madame Marliani, who lived at No. 7 Square d'Orleans. George and Chopin took apartments at Nos. 5 and 9 on either side. They dined with Madame Marliani and shared the common expense.

While they were still living at rue Pigalle George began to express that terrible inclusiveness which was so difficult for Chopin to understand. She extended her affection to Eugène Lambert, a boy painter who was in the studio of Delacroix with Maurice. She also made room in her heart for Oscar, the son of her sister Caroline, and for Augustine Brault, who was a second cousin of

Sophie Delaborde. Each week-end Augustine was sent for, to companion Solange.

Solange was a strange child. She did not have the faculty of making friends. She possessed a bitter tongue, which soon alienated those who began by loving her. When she first discovered that her father had a title, she had insisted on being addressed as "the Baroness." This title was now changed by Maurice and Lambert to "the Princess," because she gave herself grand airs. Solange preferred to associate with inferiors. Her enjoyment of Augustine seemed based on the fact that Augustine was a poor relation. She liked to parade her pretty clothes and fine manners to her less fortunate cousin.

Augustine's home life was unhappy; she suffered from her shrewish, vulgar mother all that Aurore had once suffered through Sophie Delaborde. It was inevitable that Madame Sand should feel an acute sympathy for her young relative. She tried to take the place in this child's life which cousin Villeneuve might have taken in her own.

Chopin did not like Augustine. He considered her plebeian.

In the summer of 1842 the four young people were taken to Nohant, where they studied, danced, rode horseback, and played charades. The experiment proved successful, and each succeeding summer Augustine and Lambert were included in the Sand family.

Augustine's father, a workingman, considered Madame Sand a woman of wealth. He complained that she had deprived him of his daughter's wages, so George paid the Braults a monthly sum which was equivalent to the wages which Augustine might have earned.

On several occasions George wrote to friends that she had cherished the hope that Maurice and Augustine would fall in love and marry, but that the two seemed incapable of romantic attachment, for they had known each other since childhood and were accustomed to regarding each other as sister and brother.

4

During the years between 1838 and 1846 George's work, like her life, was growing more serious and mature. Romantic fiction was left behind with romantic ideas. Her early novels had expressed the revolt of the individual. The novels of this second period were a protest against the wrongs of society. In this protest she was influenced by Pierre Leroux, a somewhat visionary prophet to whose ideas she was devoted. Her social novels were less popular and therefore less remunerative than romantic fiction. Leroux also helped to keep her poor. He had a numerous family; at one time as many as thirty relatives were dependent on him. He and his brother were always in debt and often in real distress. George was continually sending them money in absurdly large amounts. She had long known the responsibilities of a man. She now carried the burdens of a seemingly rich man. A constantly enlarging group of people made demands upon her purse. The number of her dependents, however, seemed to increase her strength. Each year she grew more self-reliant. It was as though she foresaw that henceforth she was to be a prop for the men, women and children who made up her intimate life.

In the family group at Nohant the children were thoughtless and carefree. Neither grateful nor ungrateful, they accepted benefits as they breathed the air. Unconscious of the responsibilities that Madame Sand carried, they seemed unaware that they were living off her brain. The half dozen servants would have been surprised had anyone told them that their mistress worked. She slept late, so it seemed to them that she was idle. They did not hesitate to take advantage of her easy ways.

Standing in the midst of these dependent ones was Madame Sand, manager of the estate, hostess, housekeeper, mother, breadwinner, tender friend, and, whenever any one of them was ill, devoted nurse.

For adult companionship the many-sided George had chosen a

dreamy genius. Chopin had his piano in his room. He was allowed his moods. He lived alone for hours or days, and came into the family group when he needed relaxation. George counted it a privilege to care for him. She never turned to him for comfort or advice in domestic worries, because she felt that he should not be bothered and that he could not understand practical affairs.

These years were enriched by human contacts with men the most diverse and eminent in politics, science and the arts. The house at Nohant was always full of company. Chopin's friends were as welcome as George's own. Chopin's intimate friend Delacroix was a visitor, also his pupil, Mademoiselle Rozières. His sister Louise and her husband came from Poland to stay with them a month. George also welcomed Countess Laure, Chopin's Polish friend.

Perhaps it was unusual that Chopin's family and friends should visit him when he was Madame Sand's permanent guest, but everyone accepted the close association of the musician and the writer. No questions were asked and no explanations were made.

Chopin grew to be the fashion in Parisian society. He liked to write to his family about the importance of his friends. His aristocratic taste was shown in those he chose to honor. His music was usually dedicated as follows:

> Opus 30 dedicated to Princess Wurtemberg
> Opus 31 dedicated to Countess Fürstenstein
> Opus 32 dedicated to Baroness Billing
> Opus 33 dedicated to Countess Mostowska
> Opus 44 dedicated to Princess de Beauvau
> Opus 45 dedicated to Princess Czernicheff
> Opus 49 dedicated to Princess de Souzzo
> Opus 51 dedicated to Countess Esterhazy
> Opus 52 dedicated to Baroness Rothschild
> Opus 64 dedicated to Baroness Rothschild

These ladies deserved appreciation. They surrounded him with little attentions. One of them had given him a footstool, another had embroidered him a pillow. It was natural to acknowledge their kindnesses.

George Sand, by Charpentier, 1838

There was never a dedication to George Sand.

As time went on, Chopin's music was known and loved throughout Europe. His name became famous. His admirers found it increasingly difficult to gain an audience with the great composer and virtuoso.

Both Chopin and Sand had to protect themselves from lion hunters. George was easily the most celebrated woman in France. When she visited Switzerland she had written: "I am an object of public curiosity here. I cannot take a step or speak a word which does not give rise to a thousand more."

What was true in Switzerland was true everywhere. Admired or criticized, George was always talked about. As a novelist no one but Balzac rivalled her in popularity. Writers envied her, bigots hated her. She was condemned for her opinions, but she was recognized as a feminine prodigy, an exception to all rules.

5

Poor Chopin was never happy under any circumstances. When he was at Nohant he wanted to be in Paris. When he was in Paris he longed for Nohant. He was equally divided between his devotion to George and his dreams of his lost Marie. He needed George as a strong support, as a mother, and a nurse. At the same time he wanted her clinging and dependent, like Marie Wodzinska. George was anxious to suit him, but she did not know how to cling. She compensated for this deficiency by the intensity of her tenderness. She suffered with Chopin's suffering. Her sympathies were thus drawn upon constantly, as Chopin's illness had many symptoms. He was subject to headaches, chills, bronchial attacks, and insistent coughing which made everyone nervous, including himself.

He was a difficult invalid. He wanted care but couldn't bear to be cared for; neither could he endure neglect.

When his work did not go well George arranged for a day in the woods, hoping that Chopin would accompany her. He usually did so if he were not urged. He would then return refreshed and ready to finish his composition.

Chopin found it impossible to compose in Paris. But he worked steadily at Nohant, where leisure, combined with quiet sympathy, conduced to concentration.

Without George, how much of his marvellous music would have been lost to the world!

One of the favorite amusements at Nohant was private theatricals. Chopin's part was to constitute himself the orchestra. Seating himself at the piano, he would improvise while the young people danced. Sometimes they appeared in costume and Chopin adapted his music to the characters assumed. Or they let Chopin take the initiative, adjusting their mimicry to the music as it led them from burlesque to tragedy and back again to comedy. Pantomime at Nohant gradually developed into an art.

One evening George, in answer to some disparaging comment, spoke in praise of country life, defending its peace as opposed to the turmoil of cities.

"How beautiful you make it seem!" exclaimed Chopin.

"If you feel that way, could you express it in music?" she asked.

Chopin went to the piano and improvised a pastoral symphony.

On another occasion the family was watching with amusement a little dog of George's running around in circles chasing its tail. George turned to Chopin and said, "If I had your gift I would translate this graceful absurd little creature into music."

Chopin straightway created "The Waltz of a little Dog," which became one of his popular encores for concert playing. This waltz, composed for George, was dedicated to Countess Potocka.

In 1844 Chopin suffered from the loss of his father. He was also shocked by the death from consumption of a dear family friend in Poland. The double affliction further impaired his precarious health. When mentally depressed he was victimized by many superstitions. In this his friends said he was more Polish even than the Poles. He had a horror of the number seven and of all dates and numbers containing this figure. He believed in a literal hell and was tormented by the thought of it. The entire Sonata comprising his Funeral March is said by musicians to express the fear of death.

George believed that hell is not a place but a state of mind. Nevertheless she sympathized with Chopin's terror. In the months following his father's death, while Chopin was suffering from insomnia, George moved her writing materials into the room adjoining his and worked there at night, ready at any moment to soothe her frightened child. Thus she relived the experience of her young motherhood when she had spent her evenings in her grandmother's boudoir to be near her children and listen to their breathing while they slept.

In this same year of 1844 George was invited to write for a radical newspaper called *Réforme*. The staff comprised men who were to take part four years later in the cabinet of the new government. At present they constituted a group of important writers and co-workers of whom George became one.

Chopin disliked this public usefulness. He objected to a change of government. Above all, he did not want his faithful nurse and devoted friend to allow her attention to be deflected from himself. He was ignorant of politics and social questions. In music he defied precedent and did not hesitate to create new standards, but outside of his sphere he wanted the world to remain unchanged. He persistently disagreed with George's views, and when he felt irritable he opposed her opinions on matters great or small.

It now seemed to George that Chopin pursued her with polite persecutions. When she allowed Augustine to study music, he objected that women should not be given too much education in the arts. He criticised her for letting Maurice become a painter.

She was wrong to love animals, to prefer blue to white. In his black humors, whatever she did, thought, or said was wrong.

Then the weather changed or the invalid's health improved, and for a time Chopin took his mind off George's affairs and stopped trying to guide her opinions.

But the perfect love that had its beginnings in music and poetry had become an imperfect friendship whose continuance was imperilled by the petty annoyances of everyday life.

6

It was not until the summer of 1846 that the drama of the Sand family began to unfold. The person who played the principal rôle in the drama was Solange.

It had been George's dream to give Solange a happier childhood than Aurore had had. Remembering that Aurore had needed more love, she had always indulged Solange and spoiled her, on the theory that the cure for all difficult characters is love. But Solange was not another little Aurore, she was another little Casimir. Solange did not want love, she wanted importance, and from time to time her nature required her to strike a blow.

While she was a small child she had queened it over everyone. Her attitude in the family was always, "I am master." She easily mastered Maurice, who was gentle and affectionate. If Maurice crossed her, it was her habit to cry out, "I hate you!" She got her own way by displays of temper. She was very intelligent, but no one had ever been able to make her study. She wanted to be courted and admired by everyone. She expected the world to be arranged for her without effort on her part. She was not industrious and creative like her mother. She was, like her father, arrogant and lazy.

And so, in spite of all her law-suits, George never succeeded in leaving her husband. She had perpetuated him in the child she loved. Whenever her dear little daughter was with her, Casimir's character was also there.

All of Solange that was not Casimir was Sophie. Suspicion, capriciousness, hatred and jealous rages—all these were the endowment of unfortunate Solange. George could not understand these qualities. She gathered her young brood about her with an all-embracing attitude which expressed in effect: Let us be a united family. She thought they were a united family. George was still an impossibilist, but she was not as hopeful as she once had been. "I have habituated myself," she wrote at this time, "to love people as they are without hoping or trying to change them."

The three members of the family who were harmoniously related were Augustine, Maurice and George. Solange could not prejudice any one of the three against the other two. She turned to Chopin and tried to prejudice him against them all. If George gave Augustine a dress, Solange complained to Chopin, "Mother dresses her as well as I dress." When Augustine helped Maurice catch butterflies and then worked with him to catalogue his collection, Solange complained to Chopin, "Maurice loves Augustine more than he loves me." She complained to Chopin constantly, and he listened and sympathized. In fact, though no one had noticed it, Chopin also was feeling aggrieved. He wanted and expected to be the sole object of Madame Sand's devotion. She had spoiled and petted him and made him feel that he was first in her affections. Now her two children had become individuals, crowding him out, and he was expected to make room for two more.

Solange, finding Chopin responsive to her hints and innuendoes, fostered the invalid's sense of neglect. Mischievously at first and then maliciously she cultivated in him a sense of injury. She awakened his suspicions. How about Borie, the young man who edited the provincial republican journal which Madame Sand had helped to found. Why was Borie closeted with mother in the salon for an hour? Why was Maurice riding with Augustine? Mother and Borie! Maurice and Augustine! These were the two notes sounded by Solange in whispered confidences with her only friend.

Her only friend! It was thrilling to the invalid to feel that someone leaned on him. Solange aroused his chivalry. George never did that; she always protected him. His feminine ideal was a woman who needed protection, and although he loved George his ideal had never changed.

Whenever Solange appealed to Chopin he put aside his music, forgot his dreaminess, and took part in the family life. But while it seemed to Chopin that he had become a champion, it seemed to George that he suddenly began to dispute with her every decision she made in regard to the children and the household. Her invalid had never been so irritable. George herself was growing irritable. She had lost her serenity. She sometimes spoke sharply. She dismissed two of the servants, and Solange whispered to Chopin, "She does it because Maurice insists."

George could not understand what had happened to herself and her family. It seemed as though they were all caught up in an electric storm. Maurice and Chopin were especially affected.

Chopin burst into jealous rages before her children, before her friends, even before the servants. Maurice grew indignant and defensive. He felt that his mother, at the age of forty-two, was being made to look ridiculous by this friend and guest who conducted himself as though he were her husband and the father of her children.

Maurice was now almost twenty-three years old. He did not propose that his place as the man of the Sand family should be usurped.

The friction between the two men began with pinpricks of criticism, insinuation, irony. It ended in open enmity. On the 29th of June, the eve of Maurice's birthday, there was an explosion. Maurice proclaimed his man's estate by announcing to his mother that he would leave the house if Chopin stayed.

George was panic-stricken. Nothing and no one should come between her and her children. She had always told this to Frédéric, and he had promised not to interfere. George went to Frédéric's room to talk it over.

Chopin politely offered his chair while he sat on the edge of the bed. George spoke with difficulty, she was almost strangled with emotion as she explained that Maurice had threatened to go away. Chopin in nervous agitation fussed at his handkerchief, slowly tearing it into shreds. While George waited breathlessly, he expressed his point of view.

It seemed to him that in a contest between him and Maurice she preferred Maurice. He accused her of no longer loving him, of wanting him to leave. George protested that he needed only to avoid quarreling with Maurice. But was not this equivalent to saying that Maurice came first? Chopin was deeply wounded, but he did not leave Nohant. The difficulty was bridged over, but the breach was not healed.

7

After this crisis Chopin's soul became inaccessible to George. He alternated between moods of petulant criticism and glacial courtesy.

Sometimes he would pass an entire day without speaking a syllable to anyone. He was morbidly sensitive about his illness. If one gave him sympathy at the wrong moment he was angry; if one did not give it when he felt in the mood for it, he was hurt. To satisfy the whims and caprices of the invalid had always required constant vigilance; a trained nurse would have demanded a vacation in six months. George had cared for Chopin for eight years. Now she reached the breaking-point. Not that she broke into tears or hysteria or noisy complaints. Her way of breaking was to seize pen and paper and write furiously for hours. This relief for her bottled-up feelings about Chopin was entitled *Lucretia Floriani*.

Lucretia was an actress. Her admirer, Prince Karol, seemed to the world a perfect lover. But his insane jealousy caused Lucretia untold suffering. George wrote of Prince Karol's love for Lucretia:

"He loved her so much, he was so faithful, so chained to her side, he spoke of her with so much respect, that all this would have been the glory of a vain woman. Yet Lucretia did not hate any woman sufficiently to wish for her this sort of happiness.

"If she breathed the scent of a flower, if she picked up a pebble, if she caught a butterfly for the collection of Celio [her son], if she patted a dog, if she picked some fruit, he would say under his breath, 'What an astounding nature! Everything pleases her, everything amuses her, everything intoxicates her. She finds beauty, perfume and grace in the tiniest details of creation. She admires everything, she loves everything. Therefore she does not love me. An abyss separates us.'

"It was true at bottom. A nature that is rich by endowment and one that is rich by exclusiveness cannot interpenetrate each the other. One of the two must consume the other until nothing but ashes is left."

Prince Karol was obviously Frédéric Chopin, and Lucretia was in large part a study of the psychology of George Sand.

George says of Lucretia:

"She had wished to be a mother to her lovers without ceasing to be the mother of her children, and the conflict between the two feelings had always ended in the extinction of the less dominant passion. The children triumphed."

George, through Lucretia, says of love:

"I know that it is said to be a sensual feeling, but this is not true in the case of intellectual women; with them it follows a regular progression; it first takes possession of the brain, knocking at the door of the imagination. Once it has entered and assumed control there, it insinuates itself into all our being; and then we love the man who dominates us, as god, brother, husband, everything that a woman can love."

Explaining herself by means of her heroine, George makes Lucretia say:

"I have never loved two men at the same time. I have never, even in thought, belonged to more than one during any given

time. When I no longer loved a man I did not deceive him. I broke
with him entirely. Every time I loved it was so ardently and
perfectly that I believed it was for the first and last time in my
life.

"You cannot call me a respectable woman. But I myself am
certain that I am one; I even lay claim to be a virtuous woman,
though I know that according to your ideas and public opinion
this is blasphemy. I submit my life to the verdict of the world
without rebelling, without disputing the justice of its general
laws, but not acknowledging that it is right in my case."

During all the time that George was explaining her suffering
in written words, Chopin away in his room was expressing his
misery in music. He prided himself on hiding his inner life, but
through his music he was telling the whole world that he was
morbid, unhappy and homesick.

Chopin's medium was more discreet than George's. No one
could say whether the erotic feeling conveyed in his music was
caused by Madame Sand or Marie Wodzinsky, but everyone who
read *Lucretia Floriani* could definitely conclude that Chopin's
jealousy caused Sand's despair.

Heine said of *Lucretia Floriani*, "It is a detestible book divinely
written." René Doumic, speaking from the viewpoint of to-day,
says: "The portrait contained nothing that was truly uncompli-
mentary. If it is glorious for Prince Karol to resemble Chopin, it
remains very honorable for Chopin to be the model from which
was drawn this figure of a distinguished neurasthenic."

Evidently this being written into fiction looks differently during and after the lifetime of the victim.

Lucretia Floriani appeared serially during the summer of 1846.
Chopin read portions of it while George was writing it. He praised
the great naturalness of the characters, but did not recognize himself as Prince Karol. The following winter his friends pointed out
the resemblance, and in 1848 he wrote from Scotland expressing
his anger:

"I have never damned anyone, but at present what I feel is so intolerable that it would relieve me if I could damn Lucretia."

8

Toward the end of August Solange fell ill. They called her malady nervous breakdown. George dropped her work and devoted herself to her daughter, taking her on two-week trips to give her the rest and change the doctor had advised. Then, late in the summer, Solange fell in love, and quite suddenly she was well again. The object of her affection was Fernand de Préaulx, the son of an excellent Berrichon family and the inheritor of their wealth. Everyone was delighted with the match. Chopin approved. He considered the young man a suitable *parti*. Secretly he hoped, as he wrote to his family, that both children would soon marry. He wanted to enjoy his home in peace.

As usual Chopin went to Paris early in November. George and her children did not follow immediately, as in previous years. But Chopin's letters to George and her letters to him were as cordial as before. In February the Sand family went to town to conclude preparations for Solange's wedding. The trousseau was ordered and the dot was arranged. Chopin received George joyfully and they met frequently. Solange was radiantly happy.

At this period Madame Sand was often pursued by struggling young artists who sought her patronage. One of these, a sculptor by the name of Clésinger, had dedicated a statue to her. He now asked permission to do a bust of herself. Then, since Solange always wanted any distinction attained by her mother, George allowed Clésinger to do a bust of Solange.

At Easter time the entire Préaulx family traveled to Paris for the signing of the marriage contract. All was in readiness for the solemn occasion, which was only second in importance to the wedding. On the evening before the ceremony Solange drew her mother aside and informed her casually that she refused to sign. This was almost as bad as a bride turning back from the altar.

"But, why, why, what has happened?" George demanded.

Solange smiled and said that she had changed her mind. Then she retired and let her mother face the outraged family and the injured bridegroom.

George met the situation as best she could, and the Préaulx withdrew with hurt dignity.

The reason for Solange's refusal was Clésinger. He had found Madame Sand open-handed and soft-hearted. He considered her rich. During the sittings he had persuaded Solange to jilt her desirable suitor and marry him instead.

In this predicament George insisted that before a second betrothal was announced a decent interval must elapse, if only to save the feelings of the Préaulx family. So back to Nohant went the frustrated wedding party. Meanwhile George proceeded to investigate her would-be son-in-law. She found he was violent in disposition, unreliable in regard to money, and overwhelmed by debt.

But Solange insisted on marrying the undesirable Clésinger, and Clésinger expected the generous dot which had been offered to the desirable bridegroom. The dot was the Norbonne house, valued at a hundred thousand francs.

Love, George conceded, was more important than money, but was Solange really in love with this terrible man? Solange could not marry in any case without her father's presence and consent. Negotiations did not proceed rapidly enough to suit the impatient lovers. Clésinger came secretly to the neighboring town, La Châtre.

One night when George was writing and the household was quiet she heard the sound of carriage wheels in the road, which was close to the house. The sound ceased, the carriage waited, and George went out to see who was stopping beside her gate. It was Clésinger eloping with Solange. When George intervened, Clésinger threatened her with words which made her feel that the marriage should be hastened rather than postponed. She hurried her preparations, sent for Baron Dudevant, and made the best of a heartbreaking situation. Invitations were sent, letters were written, provisions were made ready for the wedding-feast, and a large room was newly furnished as a bridal chamber. George made a brave pretense that all was well. She insisted that Clésinger was worthy and tried to believe that he was. "Since the young people are happy we are happy," she wrote to her friends.

Meanwhile, during the strain of the wedding preparations, George wrote a novel with which to meet the additional expense.

9

Maurice, like Solange, needed rest and change from time to time, so he was taking a trip to Holland, and George was left alone to guard her impulsive daughter. A fortnight before the wedding George strained a ligament in her ankle. She could not walk, she had indeed to be carried to the wedding. In the midst of her personal afflictions she heard that Chopin was ill. Certain of his friends complained of her indifference because she did not go to Paris to nurse him.

On May 12th she wrote to Count Grzymala, "I shall be in Paris for a few days at the end of this month, and if Chopin can be moved I shall bring him back here." She referred to her suffering about the marriage, then continued:

"I think that Chopin must have suffered also on his side at not knowing, not understanding, and not being able to give advice. But it is impossible to take into consideration his advice in the real affairs of life. He has never seen facts squarely nor understood human nature in any respect. His soul is all poetry and all music, and he cannot endure anything that is different from himself. Besides, his influence in my family affairs would mean for me, in relation to my children, the loss of all dignity and of all love. Talk to him and try to make him comprehend in a general manner that he ought to refrain from preoccupying himself with them. If I tell him that Clésinger (whom he does not like) deserves our affection he will only hate him the more, and that will turn Solange against him. All this is difficult and delicate. . . . It is the restless, jealous, suspicious affection he feels for me which is the principal cause of his suffering.

"For seven years I have lived as a virgin with him and all others. I have been so weary of passions, so incurably disillusioned, that even without effort or sacrifice I have grown old before my time. If there were a woman on earth who ought to have inspired him with the most absolute confidence it was I, and he has never understood it. I know that many people accuse me, some of having exhausted him by the violence of my senses, others of having driven him to despair by my coldnesses. I think that you know how it really is. As for him, he complains that I have killed him by privation, while I was certain that I would have killed him if I had acted in any other way. See what my situation is in this miserable friendship, where I have made myself his slave in every way that I could do so without showing him an impossible and culpable preference over my children. . . . As for happiness I don't believe there is any such thing in this world. . . . Burn this letter."

If George's feeling for Chopin was now no more than compassion for his illness combined with irritation at his jealousy, she at least intended to continue her dogged devotion to the end. She expected him back at Nohant, and he expected to return. In April he wrote to his family: "You ask what I expect to do this summer: nothing different from usual. As soon as it commences to get warm I shall go to Nohant."

Chopin also, in spite of distrust and disillusionment, still felt for George the dependent affection of an invalid who needs a woman's care. And she meant more than a tender woman to Chopin. She represented home. Nohant seemed his rightful place. He felt himself the father of the Sand children.

10

As soon as he was safely Madame Sand's son-in-law Clésinger
began to ask for money. He settled down in the comfort of
Nohant. He did not speak of working or of establishing a home
for his wife, and he began to resent Maurice, whom he regarded
as his competitor for all the benefits he hoped to enjoy. Solange
also resented Maurice and began to display an unpleasant cupidity.
The newly wedded pair saw in George nothing but her power to
provide funds.

It was now Augustine's turn to be married. The bridegroom was
young Theodore Rousseau, who had paid his court to Augustine
in Paris. Solange did not relish the fuss that was made over Augustine. Besides, now that she had had her way about her marriage,
poor Solange began to realize that she had made a mistake. She
did not propose that the insignificant Augustine should be happier
or more fortunate than herself. For a long time she had wished to
injure her mother, her brother and her cousin. It was time to show
what she could do.

Drawing Rousseau apart, Solange told him that Augustine was
Maurice's mistress, and that for this service George had for several
years paid a monthly sum to Augustine's parents. The distracted
lover did not question the truth of this loving sister. He broke
the match and ran away to hide his despair.

Augustine could not hide her unhappiness and humiliation.
Madame Sand, when she heard what her daughter had done, was
utterly bewildered. Maurice was enraged. Everyone excepting
Solange was plunged in misery. Solange went about smiling, very
happy over the havoc she had wrought.

Scarcely had this catastrophe taken place when Solange demanded eight thousand francs of her mother as a loan to her
husband. Clésinger's debts amounted to forty-five hundred
francs. George was willing to give Solange an allowance but she
could not attempt to pay Clésinger's debts. She refused the loan

and Solange made haste to inform Clésinger that the refusal was due to Maurice's influence.

The thought that Maurice could deprive him of the needed money made Clésinger half insane. Encouraged by Solange, he went to the studio, where he found Maurice, George, and the village curé. Clésinger took up a large hammer and rushed toward Maurice. George intervened between the crazed man and her son. She seized the hammer, and in the tussle struck Clésinger's face. Clésinger, too infuriated to remember his great strength, then hit her in the breast. As George fell back staggering from the blow, she raised her eyes and saw Solange standing beside Clésinger.

Solange was smiling.

George felt dizzy. As she looked at her daughter she saw Solange's smile freeze and give way to an expression of hatred. Hatred on the face of Solange indicated Maurice. George turned her gaze to see Maurice lifting a pistol which was pointed at Clésinger. The curé, who was standing near, snatched the pistol. How it happened that no one was killed could scarcely be explained.

The Clésingers rushed to their beautiful bridal chamber, packed their bags and went to the hotel at La Châtre, where they waited for an answer to a letter they had sent to Chopin. Soon the answer came, addressed to George. It was a formal request that his carriage be forwarded to Solange at La Châtre. George dispatched the carriage, which Solange appropriated to her use, driving as far as Vierzon, where she took the train to Paris.

Paris meant Chopin. If now she could alienate Chopin from her mother her triumph of power would be complete.

She found Chopin alone in his apartment. He was ill and emaciated, much paler and weaker than he had been at Easter, when last she had seen him. But his visitor was too self-centered for feelings of compassion.

She told Chopin that Augustine was Maurice's mistress. Chopin believed Solange.

She told Chopin that Maurice had tried to kill Clésinger. Chopin believed Solange.

She explained that her mother had rid herself of both of them in order to take a lover. Chopin believed Solange.

11

George had recovered from each of her lovers, but she never recovered from Solange. Until now she had successfully endured the blows of fate, whether of illness, debt, or calumny. But she could not endure the stroke dealt her by her daughter. This blow made her old. She was unable to ease her mind by work, because her brain under successive shocks was dull and empty of ideas. She could not sleep, because when she put out the lights and closed her eyes she saw her child's face. She saw Solange smiling as she broke her marriage contract. She saw Solange smiling when caught in her elopement, smiling as she lied to young Rousseau, smiling as Clésinger struck at her mother. Smiling vengeance! Vengeance for what?

George could not answer. Her powerful imagination, which had written so many novels and analyzed so many women, did not enable her to put herself in Solange's place. Again and again George had said, "I am through with men." And now she tried to say, "I am through with my daughter." She said it to herself and to Maurice, but it was never true. The child she had carried in her arms, the little girl for whom she had written poems and told stories, the young woman who had been her pride, had grown into her heart too deeply to be uprooted. For a time, however, she believed that her love for Solange was dead.

George wrote Chopin her side of the story. She did not mention the attempted elopement and the real reason for the marriage. She felt she must protect Solange to this extent. But she did try to convince him of her daughter's maliciousness. This was in no sense a letter of rupture and farewell. On the contrary, Chopin was intending to visit Nohant. In view of his contemplated visit she warned him in this letter that when he came to Nohant he must not discuss Solange.

When he received George's letter Chopin took it to Delacroix and Delacroix, who knew nothing of Solange's character or the reasons for George's tirades against her daughter, noted in his journal of July 20th that the letter was "atrocious."

Chopin delayed his answer. George waited in a turmoil of emotion. She had always been calm in the face of calumny, but now that the calumniator was her own child she completely lost her poise.

By a turn of the wheel, the positions of George and Frédéric were reversed. A year ago Frédéric, sitting on the edge of his bed and tearing his handkerchief into shreds had, in substance, asked George to choose between himself and her son. Now George, alone at Nohant, had, in effect, asked Frédéric to choose between herself and her daughter.

While expecting him at Nohant and waiting for his decision she wrote to Mademoiselle Rozières:

"July 22nd.

"My friend, I am worried, frightened. I have had no news of Chopin for several days. In the trouble that is crushing me I cannot keep track of time. But it seems too long. He was about to leave and then he does not arrive, he does not write. Did he start? Is he ill, held up somewhere? I should already have left home myself if it had not been for fear of passing him and for the horror I have of going to Paris and exposing myself to the hatred of her whom you think so good, so kind to me.

"Sometimes I think, to reassure myself, that Chopin loves her more than he does me, sulks and takes her part.

"I would prefer that one hundred times to the knowledge that he is ill. Tell me frankly how matters stand. If Solange's frightful maliciousness, if her incredible lies, sway him, so be it. Nothing matters to me if he only gets well."

Then came Chopin's letter accepting Solange's statements as

truth, and refusing to visit George if he were not allowed to continue what he considered his peacemaking and what she considered his interference in her family affairs.

Again George wrote to her confidant:

"While I passed six sleepless nights he was engaged in talking and thinking ill of me with the Clésingers. Very well. His letter has an absurd dignity and the sermons of this good father of the family shall serve as lessons to me. . . .

"I think it magnificent of Chopin to see, befriend and approve Clésinger who struck me—Chopin, who all the world told me was my most faithful and devoted friend."

This was the end. Chopin's love had turned to bitterness. George had become to him, ironically, "the dear Madame Sand." In a letter home written on Christmas Day, 1847, he referred to George with malicious courtesy:

"It is said that she is writing her 'Memoirs.' Indeed it is too soon for that, because the dear Madame Sand will have many more adventures in her life before she grows old, many beautiful things will happen to her, and ugly ones too."

In the same Christmas letter Chopin repeated Solange's accusation against her mother. He offered it as his own idea: "One might believe that she wanted to get rid of her daughter and me at the same time because we were in the way."

Chopin's letters to his family dwelt continually on Madame Sand. But in discussing her and her private affairs he quoted Solange almost verbatim, as though he had no opinions or impressions of his own with which to resist or refute her statements.

When he had lived in the Sand family Chopin had constantly reproached George for too great devotion to her children. Now he depicted her as a hard-hearted mother who treated her children with cruelty. While George was unable to sleep and for the first time in her life was unable to write; while she was, in fact, broken by her daughter, we find Chopin testifying that the strong, insensitive Solange had been "broken in her mother's hands."

Portrait of Chopin, by George Sand

George had consented to whatever Solange asked for: one husband, then another, a trousseau, a generous dot. She had followed after the wild girl, arranging life to suit her caprices, All this Chopin knew, but he wrote to his family that George had "ruined her daughter's life."

Did he perhaps mean that he felt as though his own life had been ruined and broken by George? The unhappy man had lost his home, he was like a child turned against his mother. He pitied Solange, he even pitied Maurice, because he was unwilling to confess his own self-pity.

"Don't let this trouble you," he admonished his family, referring to his estrangement from George. "It is already a thing of the past. Time is a great physician." He then adds pathetically, "up to the present I am not yet cured."

That he was lonesome for George and homesick for Nohant is shown by a plaintive reference to the cause of his self-banishment: "And I could not go to her house because she made it a condition that I must remain silent about her daughter."

Poor Chopin did not wish to have his sisters think that he had played the part of a weak, dependent invalid in Madame Sand's home. He liked to represent himself as a strong personality who had held the Sand family together, and during eight years had prevented the head of the family from resorting to disorderly ways.

"Eight years of an orderly life were too much for her," he wrote to his sister, referring to his beneficent influence on George, and continued: "God granted that those years should be the ones in which her children were growing up. If it had not been for me I don't know how long ago the children would have gone to their father instead of staying with her."

One curious fact revealed in Chopin's letters is that in accepting Solange's jealous accusations against her brother he disregarded his own knowledge of the boy and man. Maurice's most striking characteristic, as Chopin well knew, was his adoring love for his mother. Yet we find Chopin writing, "Maurice also will take advantage of the first good chance to run away to his father."

Another indiscriminating comment made by Chopin was the surprising prophecy, "Maurice will never marry except for money."

When Maurice did marry he chose a girl who brought him not so much as one sou. Her dot, as George explained at the time, was her character. Maurice's obliviousness to money could scarcely have been ignored by anyone living beside him day after day during eight years.

The evil done by Solange reached farther than Chopin. She told to every one her story about Augustine Brault. It quickly spread over Paris and reached the ears of father Brault. Seeing his chance to extract money from his daughter's benefactress, he threatened Madame Sand with publicity unless she paid him forty thousand francs. This she refused to do. Brault then engaged the services of a man named Guilbert to write a pamphlet entitled "The Intrigues of George Sand." When the pamphlet appeared George sent for her lawyer, who put the matter in the hands of the police. The lampoon was suppressed but George refused to prosecute. Augustine was in time happily married to Mr. de Bertholdi, an excellent young man, and they spent their summers at Nohant. The affectionate relationship between Augustine, Maurice and George was never disturbed.

When, thanks to Solange, "The Intrigues of George Sand" was published, the courtly, refined and aristocratic Chopin wrote to his family in far-away Poland about "the dirty story of which all Paris is talking."

Although Chopin had never heard or asked for George's defense, and although the sole authority for the scandal was Solange, he did not hesitate to affirm "The story is true." With a final thrust at George he concluded, "That is the act of benevolence which she thought she was doing and which I opposed as strongly as I could when the girl was brought into the house."

Chopin believed Solange because he wanted to believe her. If he had questioned a single statement, the whole fabric of the phantasy she wove for him would have been destroyed.

Chopin the musician was a highly developed genius. But it is necessary to distinguish between the musician and the man. The man was undeveloped, immature. When George, absorbed in outside interests, seemed to him lacking in devotion to himself, his vanity was wounded, his jealousy was aroused, and he looked for excuses to justify his resentment. Solange conveniently came forward with accusations and Chopin siezed them because he needed them. They made his anger seem reasonable and right.

Thus in the closing act of the Sand family drama George was worsted by her daughter and her friend. After her first explosion she withdrew in silence and let Solange talk and Chopin write as they pleased.

Chopin, certainly, had no idea that his intimate letters, written in moods of bitter misery, would one day constitute the sole evidence offered to the public of a family quarrel in which he had taken a somewhat officious part.

But Solange's defamation was deliberate. Wherever she went she made enemies for her mother. Although George sent her six thousand francs a year, Solange told everyone that her mother refused to give her a sou. Although George sent long letters encouraging her daughter to write fiction, Solange excused her own laziness by complaining to her acquaintances that her mother's persistent discouragement accounted for her failure to become an author. Perhaps the best explanation of Solange's filial animosity was given by Henri Fouquier, who quotes her as confiding to him that she hated being the daughter of a genius and wanted to be a genius herself.

If the mother's nature had been more like the daughter's she would have been better equipped to meet the situation she encountered. George was singularly free from jealousy and vanity. Finding neither of these motives in herself, she never looked for them in others. When they appeared she was ineffective. Her most signal failure in human relationship was her inability to recognize or cope with jealousy and vanity. These were the emotions which animated her daughter and her friend.

12

Sand and Chopin, the two who had been so closely related and who had grown so widely estranged, met once again—March 4, 1848, on the stairs of Madame Marliani's house in Paris. On this occasion Chopin announced to Madame Sand that she had become a grandmother. Solange had not sent word to her mother of the birth of her child.

It was this baby and not, as Chopin fondly maintained, his efforts at playing peacemaker, that reconciled George to her daughter. On the death of the child a week later George sent Solange a loving letter ignoring the past.

But she never trusted Solange again. And Chopin, in illness, loneliness and homesickness for Nohant, never surrendered his allegiance to Solange. Since George would not sacrifice Maurice to Chopin, he retaliated by clinging to Solange.

Was Solange to Chopin but the symbol for his bitterness of spirit? Was that bitterness the expression of his need for more love? Suspicion, distrust and jealousy were his way of saying that he wanted George to abandon all others and devote herself to him alone.

From the time of his rupture with George, Chopin composed no more music. His friends said that his heart was broken. During the three years that followed his departure from Nohant he was slowly dying. He did not write to George or ask her to come to him. George did not write to him or offer to go. But as soon as she heard of his serious illness she sent a letter to his sister Louise, who was in Paris, asking for news of him. Louise never answered her letter. Realizing that her presence would be unwelcome to Chopin's family, George remained at Nohant. Her first successful play "François le Champi" was produced. But she was not in town to attend the rehearsals or the opening night.

During that autumn while Chopin was dying, many stories were circulated to prove that George was heartlessly enjoying life in Paris. She did not go to Paris until December.

Chopin died October 17, 1849.

Two days before his death his friend Franchomme, leaning over his bed, heard him murmur, "She told me that I should not die except in her arms."

VIII

LOVE OF HUMANITY

DURING the fatal summer of 1846 there came a day when George knew that she had reached a crisis in her emotional life. She went into the woods and sought out the spot where once she had offered sacrifice to Corambé. As she looked back upon the child who had built the altar, her twelve-year-old self seemed lost in distance. It came over her that she was now forty, more than forty, she was forty-two years old.

Seating herself upon a stone, she yielded to a mood of introspection, letting memory retrace the crucial experiences of her past.

She did not admire the part she had played, neither did she condemn it. She reproached herself for many stupidities. As she summed up her qualities, it seemed to her that she had been faulty in judgment, often absurd, always sincere, never little or vindictive, and entirely oblivious to evil things and evil people.

Her chief difficulty, she realized, was that she had never been able to make her theories harmonize with her emotional nature. In the effort to do so she had changed her ideas many times.

Facing her mistakes, she knew that she had vainly striven to follow a path that had been lost when she fell in love, found when she recovered, and lost when she fell in love again. In a flash of insight she saw the futility and misdirection of her love life. She saw it the more clearly because she thought of it as a thing of the past. She did not, on this day, say to herself, I shall never love again. She accepted it as a certainty that required no words.

The dream of love was over. Then life itself was over. She could not go on. She knew herself, she could not live without love.

Before her stood a heavy stone. Impatient at the sight of it, as though it were a symbol of the weight that oppressed her, she lifted it and pushed it from her. As it fell to the ground she heard herself exclaim, "Good God, I may have forty more years to live!"

She saw the years stretch ahead of her, long years of inescapable work without the consolation of love.

Age, old age and loneliness!

Throwing herself to the ground, she twisted and rolled in the grip of a terrible emotion such as she had felt but twice before in her life. As she had wept for her mother, as she had wept in her first passion, she now found herself weeping for lost love, lost youth, and dead illusions.

During two hours the yearning for happiness tortured her. Then came reaction. She fell into a trance-like state in which she was able to draw from the roots of her being a mysterious strength with which to combat despair. Her egoistic longings were overcome, slain by the sheer will to kill them and live on.

In this mastery of instinct by will and intelligence she was something more than a middle-aged woman; she became a mature soul. Outgrown was the aspiration for an ideal love such as no human being can hope to deserve. Outgrown was the passionate woman who could not live without love.

Turning from her past, for two or three hours she meditated upon her future. She resolved to face the hostility of life without hatred or resentment, to fight disillusion with faith in human nature, never to make any ambitious plan for herself, never more to dream of personal happiness.

Resignation? No; the word repelled her. She was not resigned to age and loneliness, she was victorious over them.

She felt a vast tenderness toward others. In the new serenity which came to her she was content to give without receiving in return. She could live without being loved but she could not live without loving. One can live without happiness, she argued, but one cannot live without making use of one's life, and one must do this according to one's nature.

She then formulated the principles which were to guide her for the rest of her days:

Henceforth I shall accept what I am and what I am not. With my limitations and my gifts, I shall go on using life as long as I am in this world and, as I believe, afterwards. Not to use life— that alone is death.

Thus George abandoned the search for personal love, and in so doing became a greater woman. But she could not live in and by herself alone. She wished to give devotion, if not to a person, then to a cause or an idea. The fundamental force that welded together her many selves and gave them identity was her need of mystic union with something not herself.

The greater George, determined to use her life according to her nature, was impelled to lose herself in impersonal love.

2

The Second Republic was proclaimed in February, 1848. It was the result of a revolution of fear. Louis Philippe had run away to England, leaving a group of idealists to usurp his power. These men formed a government called provisional because it professed to exist without self-interest until, by a general election, the people could choose their representatives.

During the period of this peaceful upheaval George Sand was in Paris, and from the window of Guizot's former office she watched the great parade by which the people manifested faith in the Provisional Government.

The parade headed for the Town Hall. In the procession each trade, business and profession was represented by appropriate symbols. The hastily organized laborers carried spades, axes or hoes, while the more dignified businesses displayed gay banners and flags. Conspicuous among the marchers were women and children bearing huge baskets of flowers, to be offered as gifts to their disinterested ministers.

In this moving spectacle a novel manner of celebrating freedom was shown by groups of laborers on their way to the planting of trees. Some of the men marched twelve abreast, supporting a heavy pine tree, the emblem of liberty. If the tree were too big to be carried abreast, it was borne on the shoulders of men marching in a long line. George thought she counted fifty men carrying one tree. The sound of tamborines and the cheering of crowds added to the excitement. At intervals in the line of march a band was heard playing. The stirring refrain of the Marseillaise floated to the window of ex-minister Guizot.

Hour after hour George watched the marchers. Four hundred thousand men and women passed from the church of the Madeleine on toward the column of July. And they were Republicans converted to self-government! At least George considered them Republicans, and believed they were able and ready to govern themselves.

She saw the people of France as a harmonious family. The aristocrats, she believed, would surrender their privileges, the bourgeoisie their riches, the workers their resentment. All groups would unite to realize the social ideal of which she had dreamed. For this glorious dream, it seemed to her, all men would live and, if necessary, die.

Forgotten were the personal demands she had made on life. Her enthusiasm now was for the happiness of humanity. Forgotten were her sorrows, physical ills and disappointments. She was well, strong, and intensely alive. She felt herself twenty years old.

And so, as her heart went out to the people and her imagination was set on fire, George fell in love again, this time without desire for any return. The object of her worship was the young Republic.

Early in March expressions of her love began to appear in the form of public letters addressed to the children of the Republic, her own by adoption. She taught them their rights as citizens, their duties to one another. These letters were published in pamphlet form and sold on the streets for ten centimes. The proceeds, so it was stated on the cover, were to go to the unemployed.

Her first pamphlet was a *Letter to the Middle Class.* Their duty, she told them, was to set a good example. In establishing a better order of society, the rich, she said, should take the initiative. They must have confidence in the poor and give them opportunity for work and means of existence. Unless the middle class sided with the workers in their just demands, she urged, the cause of liberty would be lost.

Then followed a *Letter to the People,* expressing her faith in them. Her emphasis, again, was on the necessity of union between the workers and the bourgeoisie. The word classes, she hoped, would be erased from the book of the new humanity.

In a further *Letter to the Rich,* she made an effort to calm their fears of a red terror. She used her gift as a writer to defend the Republic. She tried also to reconcile the rich to the thought that others besides themselves had rights and privileges.

Meanwhile the men who comprised the self-constituted cabinet had aroused hopes they could not satisfy. Not only were they unable to organize Utopia, they failed to relieve the prevailing condition of industrial distress. Even though they had been qualified by experience as statesmen, failure was inevitable. France was in the throes of a financial crisis that had thrown thousands of men out of work.

Discouraged by this situation, in a second *Letter to the People* George was less enthusiastic in her defense of the Republic. Her passionate love seemed to have yielded to calm affection, that recognized, but was tolerant of, the faults of youth and inexperience.

"Some time has passed," she wrote, "and my dream is not yet realized." In this later letter she acknowledged the existence of suspicion, fear and egotism, admitted that the people were calumniated, and concluded, "I have seen things which I could not prevision because I cannot understand them."

She did not anticipate and could not understand the petty

meannesses of human nature. In the large family of the state, George did but repeat her experience in the small family of Nohant. The classes behaved as her son and her friend had behaved. Each wanted to be first. And the world was full of Solanges who set people against each other and fanned the flames of jealousy.

In the large family as in the small, George's attitude was that of the dreamer and idealist. But her adopted children did not share her confidence and trust. Their hearts were full of bitterness and hatred. On March 17th there was an uprising in Paris and several people were killed. After this shock the brief period of exaltation passed. George descended from the clouds and began to demonstrate her practical usefulness.

She recommended to the Minister of Interior that able workingmen be sent into the provinces to organize and educate their fellow workers. The suggestion was accepted by the Provisional Government, and a hundred thousand francs was appropriated for a campaign of the workers.

Assisted by her right hand man, Victor Borie, George next started a weekly newspaper of her own. Its sympathies were shown in the title, *La Cause du Peuple*.

Among her writings for the Republic George's masterpiece was a history of France prepared for the peasants and simply told in Berrichon patois or *langue d'oil*. As the author of this history she signed herself Blaise Bonnin.

Overwhelmed as she was by political activities, her capacity for work and ease of production stood her in good stead.

On one of her hasty trips to Nohant she organized a celebration of welcome to the new Republic. The festival proved so successful that she felt inspired to offer the idea to the public for use in other villages. On her return to Paris the next evening she hurried from the train to her apartment intending to write an article advocating the new form of propaganda. She rang the bell of the huge door barricading the apartment house from the street. No one answered the bell. Her concierge had also entered politics and was attending his club. Turning away discouraged, she spent some time hunting for a furnished room in which to spend the night, after which she was too tired to write. But this discomfort in no wise disturbed her, nor did she allow it to delay her article.

The next morning she went to a restaurant and, while eating breakfast, composed a long description of the patriotic festival. By the time she had finished her coffee the article was done. It appeared in *La Réforme* two days later.

3

It was soon evident that George Sand's political writings, like her novels, had an emotional appeal that reached people of all classes. Her numerous contributions to the journals of the day, as well as her privately published pamphlets, were widely read and discussed. They attracted the attention of the Provisional Government.

The men in power were undertaking the publication of the *Bulletin of the Republic,* a periodical whose purpose was the education of the nation in the principles of self government. Bulletin number three contained a page of George Sand's *Letter to the People,* bulletin number four included a long passage from her *Letter to the Rich*.

Beginning thus, by quoting from Madame Sand, the men of the cabinet, whether moderates, socialists or radicals, united finally in asking her to write officially for the government. They needed her skill as a writer, so they ignored their prejudice against a woman in politics. George was commissioned to prepare unsigned, unpaid articles for the *Bulletin*.

She accepted willingly, and with her usual facility wrote six numbers of the *Bulletin of the Republic* in three weeks.

The busy ministers found it convenient to turn to their gifted collaborator for further literary services. George was glad to put her pen at their disposal.

Late in March she wrote to Maurice: "Here I am busy as a

statesman. Today I wrote two government circulars, one for the Minister of Public Instruction and one for the Minister of the Interior."

Two days later she wrote again to her son: "I have written number 7 and 8 of *The Bulletin of the Republic*. I have asked to be excused from doing number 9 because I haven't time."

She was pressed for time because she was composing a prologue for the first public performance of the Théâtre de la République, which in the old days, that is, a month earlier, had been the Théâtre Français.

The period of her devotion to the Republic was a thrilling interlude in George Sand's life. Perhaps no woman had ever lived through a similar experience.

The public attitude toward a woman politician was shown in cartoons of the period. In one caricature Madame Sand was sketched in men's clothes smoking a cigarette. The legend beneath read: "If this portrait of George Sand leaves the mind perplexed, it is because genius is abstract and has no sex." In another cartoon she was depicted as an attractive woman carrying a big whip to the crack of which men were jumping and dancing. Her figure, in comparison with the men, was as big as Gulliver among the Lilliputians. Some of the men were hiding beneath her skirts.

George's political prominence surrounded her with a new set of admirers. An English visitor to Paris, Mr. Monkton Milnes, afterward Lord Houghton, was one of her hero-worshipers. In May he gave a literary breakfast in her honor. Prosper Mérimée was present, also Victor Considérant and the historian, Alexis de Tocqueville.

"I had a conversation with the celebrated Madame Sand," wrote Tocqueville in his *Souvenirs*. "Milnes was infatuated with her. . . . A friend of mine had asked her one day what she thought of my book on America. 'The only books I read,' she answered, 'are those that have been given me by their authors.' I had a strong prejudice against Madame Sand because I detest women who write, especially those who systematically conceal the weaknesses of their sex instead of trying to interest us by showing themselves in their true characters.

"In spite of this prejudice," continued Tocqueville magnanimously, "she pleased me. I thought her features rather heavy but she had a fine, expressive face. All her spirit seemed withdrawn into her eyes, leaving the rest of her face to go the way of the flesh. What struck me most was that I felt in her the natural attraction that belongs to great minds. Her manner and language had a true simplicity, to which she added what was perhaps an affectation of simplicity in dress. I confess that more elaborately dressed she would have seemed to me more simple.

"Madame Sand was at that time a sort of man of politics. What she said impressed me greatly. She painted in great detail and with singular vivacity the condition of the workers of Paris, their organization, their number, their arms, their preparations, their thoughts, their passions, their terrible plans. I thought the picture exaggerated but it was not. She seemed to take greatly to heart the fate which awaited us."

This meeting occurred early in May. It was evident that George was then fully aware that her country was on the verge of civil war.

After the general election by which a National Assembly had taken the place of the Provisional Government, a new group of conservative Republicans came into power. George and her friends were now called "reds," "communists," and other terrifying names.

On May 15th an effort was made to overthrow the National Assembly. This revolt was followed by severe repressive measures. Paris was filled with armed guards.

George disapproved of the insurrection, and it did not spring from the group with which she was affiliated. Nevertheless all radical Republicans were now suspects. Their houses were searched and some of them were threatened with arrest. During this period of panic George burned her papers and destroyed the intimate journal in which she had narrated the events of the last three months. She refused to take the advice of friends who urged her to fly to Italy, and decided instead to escape the persecutions of Paris by returning to the peace and quiet of her unmolested country home.

But in Berry, as in Paris, those she had exhorted to love one another were full of hatred and fear. Berry had been thoroughly propagandized by the opposition. The people had been taught that the program of the radicals was to abolish marriage and religion, kill off old people and young children, and institute community of wives. Moreover, her neighbors were persuaded that it was the intention of the radicals to take away their lands and vineyards and give them to the woman they knew as Madame Dudevant.

Inevitably, therefore, George's welcome home to Nohant was a recurrence of the popular hysteria which had greeted Aurore at the age of seventeen. The peasants forgot her lifelong love and service and believed all the stories they had heard.

Passing beneath her windows they shouted, "To the lamp-post! Down with Madame Dudevant! Death to communists!"

In June there was a counter-revolution, and the young Republic received its death blow. Hundreds of workers were killed in the streets of Paris by the government-owned National Guard.

George was heartbroken by this tragic dénouement of her dream. The lofty impersonal love begun in service for the people's cause ended like her personal loves, in disillusion and despair. But her letters continued to express the faith and hope she tried to feel. The future belonged to the people, she protested, the cause of liberty was not destroyed, it was deferred.

To relieve the despondency that continued throughout the summer, George wrote one of her most successful novels, *La Petite Fadette*. This was fourth in the series of pastoral stories of which *Jeanne, La Mare au Diable,* and *François le Champi* had already been published.

La Petite Fadette not only added to her reputation as a writer, it brought her what she needed more than increased fame,— money with which to pay her debts. Her stay in Paris had cost her thousands of francs. During the money panic of the last year George had been on the point of selling Nohant, when two of her friends came to her assistance with a temporary loan. She had also tried in vain to save the property she had worked to preserve for Solange. But the financial crisis made it impossible for her to negotiate a large loan. The Narbonne house had been seized by Clésinger's creditors.

Fortunately, before the Revolution of February she had finished two volumes of her autobiography for which, late in the winter, she had been paid eleven thousand francs. No more money would be forthcoming until she produced more books.

4

Clearly it was George's duty to herself to stay at home and devote her attention to her own affairs. But in 1851 circumstances in the outside world again compelled her to forget herself for others.

After their downfall the radical Republicans had been left unmolested by the Moderates, who were in power, and Louis Napoleon's election to the presidency had apparently put an end to party conflicts. But on December 2nd, 1851, Napoleon dissolved the National Assembly and, supported by public opinion, made himself sole head of a government that remained a republic in name alone.

As a result of this *Coup d'Etat*, punishment was meted out to all who might possibly be supposed to resist his ambitious plans. Yielding to the advisers by whom he was surrounded, the would-be emperor allowed a wholesale arrest and deportation of those whose principles were opposed to an empire. Eighty-eight members of the reactionary Assembly were exiled. More than 26,000 men were deported, some for no other reason than that they belonged to harmless organizations. A decree was enforced whereby any man known to belong to a secret society was sent to Algeria.

When this catastrophe happened, George's brothers in the cause of liberty were scattered to the four winds. Some escaped to Belgium, England or more distant countries; others, for lack of passports, were in hiding. The greater number were among those seized and deported to Africa or the Colonial Islands of France, where they were thrown into wretched prisons which often meant slow death. No class was immune. Lawyers, doctors, curés, farmers, all became political prisoners.

For a time George lived in daily expectation of exile or imprisonment. Soon she was informed that her personal safety was assured. But she could not stay at home in peace and security until her friends were free. If one could free them! If one could persuade the Bonapartist Government to declare a general amnesty! Everyone told her that it was impossible to succeed in such a mad attempt. So George attempted the impossible.

She went to Paris and camped on the trail of men who had power over the fate of her friends. She boldly asked for an audience with Napoleon.

The Prince President, as he was then called, had often professed esteem and admiration for the character and opinions of Madame Sand.

Their acquaintance dated back to the days when the obscure nephew of Napoleon the Great had been the prisoner of Louis Philippe in the desolate fortress of Ham. There the unhappy man had occupied his leisure in setting down the democratic theories that embodied his love for mankind. His brochure on the *Extinction of Pauperism* attracted the attention of Madame Sand. She praised it to a friend, who repeated her praise to Napoleon. The lonely Napoleon was pleased.

At that period the luckless conspirator was unpopular with the people of France. He had no influential friends, and his pretensions to the throne were regarded as ridiculous. In the isolation of his prison he needed sympathy, and naturally his need appealed to George. So when, through a mutual friend, the forlorn man begged the illustrious author to write to him she graciously complied. Napoleon answered. She wrote again, and a desultory correspondence was established.

"You who have the qualities of a man without having his faults," Napoleon had written George, "could not be unjust to me. I care for the esteem of men, but I care especially for yours."

Now that the neglected prisoner had become dictator of France, he could scarcely ignore the woman who had been to him a friend in need. The request for an audience, therefore, was graciously granted.

As Louis Napoleon took her two hands in his and expressed his high regard for her, George straightway made her position plain. "I am as much of a Republican as you have ever known me to be and I shall never change," was her forthright announcement. She then presented a little list she had brought along. It contained the names of her friends in exile. To guard their dignity she stated frankly, "They will not retract their opinions." She pleaded eloquently for the right of liberty of conscience, concluding with her entreaty, "Amnesty, immediate amnesty, my Prince!"

But amnesty was unthinkable to her Prince. As for Madame Sand's friends, Napoleon looked over the list and promised every man his freedom.

"You see," George wrote triumphantly to a friend, "it is not necessary to commit the cowardice of denying one's opinions in order to be esteemed by people of intelligence."

George soon accumulated another list. Her demands were now carried to the Minister of Interior. Her friends were again exonerated. Then she came back with more names and presented them to the Prefect of Police.

She was a nuisance and she knew it. She was importunate,

pestiferous. She preferred to make herself hated rather than leave her friends unhelped.

For three months the indefatigable Madame Sand did nothing but run back and forth between ministers and secretaries. When the officials were indifferent or forgetful she wrote a letter over their heads to Napoleon, and with few exceptions, those she pleaded for were set free. Sometimes a sentence of death was commuted to one of exile. Most of the men were sent back to their families. Now and then a man was freed on condition that he live in Berry or at Nohant, so that Madame Sand could be held responsible for her protégé.

In February she was granted another audience with the Prince President.

As soon as her power was known, George was deluged with letters from the families of prisoners. Not one letter was left unanswered, not one request ignored. She interceded for all victims. Workmen and intellectuals were equally in need of protection and therefore equally dear to her heart.

Among those in hiding was Alphonse Fleury, her old-time friend. She secured a passport which enabled him to escape to Belgium, where he stayed until the period of vengeance was past. As he needed money and George had none, she borrowed 1000 francs for his benefit.

During her stay in Paris she secured the aid of Prince Jerome Bonaparte, who became her devoted friend. Through Prince Jerome she obtained pardon for a group of prisoners in Africa.

Her labors in favor of the accused were long drawn out and fatiguing. She was exploited on all sides. The Bonapartists published her former letters written to Napoleon as far back as 1844, when the prisoner of Ham had been a staunch upholder of democratic principles. The cordiality of these letters affronted loyal Republicans. The foreign press was filled with articles against her, contributed by exiles who were forced to live abroad. But the pigeon-holes of her desk were bursting with letters of gratitude from those who through her efforts were enabled to return home.

In these peons of praise she was hailed as "our lady of protection," "savior of political martyrs," "the saint of Berry." Other phrases from the letters sent by liberated men show the excessive admiration she awakened at this time. "I am happy to call you my friend."—"You are a great soul."—"I am prostrate before you as before a divinity."—"Let others admire your genius, I bow before your great heart." A large group of prisoners wrote in a collective letter: "We bless your name, your goodness, your devotion."

Count d'Orsay, moved by George's resolute defense of the unfortunate, wrote to her: "You are a very dear woman, besides being the first man of our times."

As a nurse or savior George was always popular, however much she was hated as a woman of ideas. The general amnesty was not declared, but her efforts in the direction of pardon did not seem futile to those whose lives she saved.

When she attempted the impossible George did not succeed, yet she never wholly failed. In striving to attain her end she went a long way, while those who laughed at her stood still. Her imperviousness to criticism or derision enabled her to live her life without the sustaining approval of public opinion. This spiritual arrogance was, in part, the secret of her resilient power. It helped her to recover from the blows of her enemies and the harder blows of her friends.

5

George's brief political experience taught her that there are only two classes, workers and capitalists, and that the future of society will be determined by the conflict between these two groups.

Having reached this conclusion, it seemed to her of very little importance whether the people of France lived under a monarchy or a republic. Therefore she saw no reason for hating the Bonapartes. Instead of agreeing with Victor Hugo that Louis Napoleon was a monster, she regarded him as the victim of circumstances. The ex-prisoner of Ham, together with Prince Jerome and Princess Mathilde, seemed to her like other people. Often George, with one or two friends was received informally by Princess Mathilde, while Prince Jerome became an intimate friend, dancing attendance on Madame Sand in Paris and visiting her in the country. In order to avoid talk—this was certainly his own idea, not George's—he made his first visit to Nohant incognito. But his presence there soon became known, and some of George's Republican friends were indignant. Alphonse Fleury, who owed his safety to George's efforts, showed his disapproval by ceasing to call on her.

There was no trace of narrow-mindedness in George. She liked people individually and not according to social classification. As her love of peasants was considered vulgar by snobs, so her friendly relation with the Bonapartes was considered snobbish by the bourgeois; she was accused of choosing her friends outside of her class. But George belonged to no class. She liked the common people best, and she found common people among the rich, even among aristocrats. Wherever men and women were simple, unpretentious and sincere, she felt at home.

Surrounded by prejudices she did not share, the inflexible George went her own way, allowing others an equal liberty of opinion. Though she often aroused hard feelings she cherished none herself.

Not even toward Casimir did George harbor resentment. According to the terms of their judicial separation, Maurice never failed to make his stipulated yearly visit to his father at Guillery, where he enjoyed the hunting season. George carefully refrained from prejudicing her son against her husband. But while she forgave and forgot, Casimir resented and remembered, as an event in his later life proved.

In his old age Baron Dudevant wanted to belong to the Legion of Honor. True, he had done nothing to deserve this reward. All the more did he crave the outward symbol of merit he did not possess. Sitting at home and nursing his grievances, Casimir composed a formal epistle to Napoleon urging his claims for recognition. First he mentioned his father's military standing; next he brought forward, rather apologetically, his own services as mayor of his little town. Finally he reached the chief reason why he believed he should be honored by his country:

"Far more than this," wrote Casimir to Napoleon, "I make bold to plead my domestic unhappiness, which belongs to history. Married to Lucile Dupin, known to the world of literature by the name of George Sand, I have been cruelly wounded in the affections of a husband and a father, and I believe I deserve the sympathetic interest of all those who have followed the sad events which have shown this side of my existence."

No doubt Baron Dudevant did deserve some kind of medal for being George's husband. But Napoleon thought otherwise and Casimir's affliction was not officially recognized.

IX

THE THEATRE

A YEAR after the *Coup d'Etat*, Napoleon's deep-laid plans culminated in a carefully prepared plebiscite by means of which his claim to the throne was placed before the people. They voted for an empire. The very men who had taken part in the great parade of 1848 abdicated in favor of a master. Inheritors as they were of the kingly tradition, the people of France remained monarchist at heart. The struggle for a republic was indefinitely postponed.

Rather than succumb to depression George moved on to a fresh enthusiasm. The theatre became her new interest in life. If people refused to be reformed they could at least be amused.

François le Champi, produced in 1849, a year after the revolution, was her first stage triumph. This play succeeded because it was original. Melodrama was the fashion, and *François le Champi* offered a simple story of peasant life. The Berrichon folk songs and costumes, manners and speech, delighted the volatile Parisians. The peasant play became the sensation of the hour. For a time it was the fashion to admire whatever was rustic. Every vaudeville sketch of that time was an attempt to imitate George's play.

François le Champi was followed by *Claudie* in 1852. During this reactionary period there was a widespread fear of subversive theories. The police were not concerned with morals. They censored *Claudie*, not because the heroine had wandered from the path of virtue nor because the lost girl was allowed an honorable and happy end, but solely because the play was written by George Sand. The censors feared that somewhere in the text there lurked a menace to private property.

For the protection of society, therefore, the following dangerous sentence was expurgated: "Justice will be done. God has promised it, and he will keep his word." Another phrase cut out from the play was: "The sheaf of wheat is the pillow of the people." After these incendiary speeches had been eliminated, *Claudie* was allowed to appear and it proved a huge success.

In a parody of the play which appeared a few weeks later, a more discriminating sense of conventional moral values was shown. The parody was entitled *Claudine, or the Advantages of Misconduct.*

In the excitement of the censorship fight George wrote to Augustine: "Happily I take these conflicts with a great deal of calm. Nothing astonishes me any more."

In her plays, as in her life, George protested against convention and tradition. She maintained that the subtleties of emotion offer sufficient motive for drama, without the aid of artificially induced dramatic incidents. This new point of view was unpopular with the critics, but her plays were welcomed by the public, as was proved by the fact that during the five years between 1850 and 1856 twelve plays by George Sand were produced in the leading theatres of Paris. Meanwhile the indomitable George continued her usual output of two novels a year. Of more enduring fame than her pastoral plays, two society dramas, *le Mariage de Victorine* and *Le Marquis de Villemer,* were for a long time included in the repertoire of the French stage.

Yet George was not considered a great playwright. She lacked humor and was not skillful in dramatic construction. A knowledge of psychology and a direct appeal to the emotions compensated for these obvious deficiencies.

Zola, who disliked both Madame Sand and her writings, said of her in his *Dramatic Artists:* "George Sand must be recognized as a playwright. She triumphs in the theatre by her honesty, by the calm and tender feeling with which she interprets the passions."

As a dramatist George exhibited the same amazing facility she had shown as a novelist. At one time she submitted the five-act play *Nanon* to M. Chilly, director of the Odéon. He objected to the second act and pointed out certain necessary alterations. "I understand," George answered with her usual economy of words. The next day she showed M. Chilly an act, not merely altered but rewritten. Then she handed him another version. During the night she had written two entirely new second acts that he might choose between them.

2

The young actress, Sarah Bernhardt, appeared in three of the Sand plays and professed great affection for Madame Sand. She has recorded her memories of George, the playwright, attending the rehearsals of her two plays, *Le Marquis de Villemer* and *François le Champi,* in which the divine Sarah played, in turn, when she was twenty-one years old.

"Madame George Sand," wrote Madame Bernhardt, "was a sweet charming creature, extremely timid. She did not talk much, but smoked all the time. Her large eyes were always dreamy, and her mouth, which was rather heavy, had the kindest expression. I watched her with the most romantic affection, for had she not been the heroine of a splendid love experience!

"I used to sit down beside her, and when I took her hand in mine I held it as long as possible. Her voice, too, fascinated me.

"Prince Napoleon often came to George Sand's rehearsals. He was extremely fond of her. Madame Sand introduced me to him. I scarcely replied to his compliments and went closer to Madame Sand.

" 'Why, she is in love with you!' he exclaimed laughingly.

"George Sand stroked my cheek gently.

" 'She is my little Madonna,' she answered, 'do not torment her.' "

On another occasion when Bernhardt had tried to commit suicide George went to see her, and, forgetting the suicidal moods of her own youth, preached to the reckless woman the beauty and value of life.

George had always felt a friendly affinity for actors, and since the days of her theatrical successes in the convent she had adored the stage.

"I like actors," she said, "and this has often scandalized my conventional friends. I have also been criticised for liking peasants, among whom I have passed my life. As peasants labor in the light of the sun to give us our daily bread, so actors, toiling at night by gaslight, give us the food by which our imaginations are nourished. And this food is needed by our minds, so often wearied and worried by the realities of life."

Through her plays George made new contacts with the men and women of the stage, many of whom became her friends. They visited Nohant, where they enjoyed private theatricals in which they often took part.

Theatricals at Nohant had become a family institution. As soon as guests arrived, a play was put in preparation, and during luncheon and dinner nothing was talked about but the play. George, who disliked gossip and small talk, was happy in this impersonal social atmosphere which provided an interest everyone could share. She wrote plays for Nohant as well as for Paris, and her public performances were tried out on the family stage.

In the midst of these new activities George wrote to Madame Viardot: "Nohant is no longer Nohant, it is a theatre. My children are no longer my children, they are dramatic artists. I am no longer Madame Sand, I am a distinguished leading rôle. We have all the amusement and none of the burdens of art."

3

Maurice had inaugurated a theatrical venture of his own. His enthusiasm was a Punch and Judy show, which he operated on a large scale. His theatre was provided with scenery, footlights, and an elaborate lighting system. It reproduced in miniature, sun,

moon, stars, waterfalls, thunder and lightning, and every acces-
sory of the real stage.

Maurice carved the puppets and used his art as a painter to
give their faces the illusion of life. George spent her evenings fab-
ricating tiny costumes out of bits of chiffon and silk. In this co-
operation Maurice carved and George dressed over one hundred
marionettes. While her fingers were busy sewing, George's
thoughts were occupied in the preparation of appropriate sce-
narios for blood-and-thunder Punch and Judy plays.

George's big stage and Maurice's small stage used the same audience hall, a large room on the ground floor. The stage for real
actors occupied one end of the hall, while the Punch and Judy
theatre had been built into the wall at one side of the room.
While seeing one of George's plays, the audience faced the big
stage. Then they turned sidewise or moved their chairs half way
around, to witness a performance of Maurice's marionettes.

The audience comprised intimate friends, together with the
servants and peasants of the neighborhood. Augustine, now Madame Bertholdi, was leading lady, Maurice or Lambert leading
man; George took various rôles, either of a woman or, quite as
often, of a man. She liked to play dukes or villains, but when,
in the absence of Augustine, she was sometimes inveigled into the
rôle of leading lady, she was miserable and ill at ease. She was not
enough of an actress, she explained, to forget her appearance and
assume the personality of a young girl.

At the age of fifty George's figure was matronly, her face was
heavy, and she had developed a double chin. However, most of
the men who had been friends of her youth were bald and fat,
so she casually recognized that she shared a common fate. She
was middle-aged and unashamed, regarding herself as a human
being made for achievement rather than as a woman born to
please.

But when strangers met her they ignored her human qualities
and looked for the feminine attributes of beauty and fascination.

George made no effort to charm or dazzle. If the conversation did not happen to excite her interest she had nothing to say. She never dressed to decorate the room. Her clothes were plain and dark. Her hair was parted in the middle and coiled on the back of her head. She did nothing to improve her appearance, except that for the sake of neatness she wore a hair net.

Many a man who also had lost his figure and who dressed as plainly as George, nevertheless felt incensed, when he found her no more beautiful than himself.

The impressions of Charles Dickens on meeting George in 1856 were confided to the actor, William McCready:

"Day before yesterday," wrote Mr. Dickens, "I dined with the admirable Madame Viardot in order to meet, as a special favor, the very great, very illustrious, very celebrated George Sand. Alas! One more illusion shattered by cruel reality. The author of so many brilliant works does not in the least resemble the romantic portrait I had made of her. . . . There is nothing of the blue-stocking about her, unless it is in the little tone of finality with which she includes your opinion in her own. Her mind is said to be very brilliant, but I could not judge it as she did not condescend to let it appear. She is just a good woman, very ordinary in face, conversation and manner."

X

THE SAND-MUSSET CONTROVERSY

IN 1857 occurred the death of Alfred de Musset.

George and Alfred, after their romance ended, had met occasionally to discuss the disposition of their letters. From the romantic point of view, which both shared, it seemed fitting that such exalted expressions of love should be saved for posterity. They agreed, therefore, that the letters should be published, and for this future purpose the correspondence was left in the care of a mutual friend. Alfred handed over his letters with the admonition that they must never be shown to his brother Paul.

George found these meetings with Alfred rather painful. During his later years, Musset was usually under the influence of absinthe. When he last called on George he was intoxicated, and, true to his character of old, he wept.

Beginning with his poem *"La Nuit de Mai,"* written three months after their rupture, Musset had for many years been making literature out of their love affair. Whenever he needed money he turned his thoughts backward, reopened his wound, and watched the blood flow while he composed a poem. Not that he ever mentioned George's name. He merely referred to "those eyes," and everyone understood. On one occasion a mistress with blue eyes took exception to his constant reference to the dark eyes that haunted him, so in his next poem he apostrophized blue eyes; still everyone understood, and as the poet continued to appeal to the public for sympathy it was liberally given.

George met these poetic effusions with silence.

Less than six months after the break between the lovers appeared Musset's *La Confession d'un Enfant du siècle.* In this book the poet created two heroines. On one he vented his bitterness and vengeance, the other he idealized and defended. This device enabled him to give full expression to all his emotions about the woman who had been the chief passion of his life.

Seven years after the rupture Alfred published *l'Histoire d'un Merle Blanc,* in which he chronicled the sufferings of a wholly exceptional male blackbird born with white plumage. According to the story, this gifted being met a female blackbird who appeared to be white like himself. The deluded male took her for his mate. But after the manner of women she gave him occasion for weeping. He wept over her so often that the white on her feathers was washed away by his tears. Alas, she had painted herself to pretend to be his equal. She was just a little female bird like all the rest.

As he continues his story, Musset's professional vanity is unconsciously revealed:

"At first I did not know that my beloved was an authoress. She told me about it after a while. I shall leave you to imagine how pleased I was over this charming discovery. From this time on we worked together. While I composed my poems she scribbled over reams of paper. I recited my poems to her aloud, which did not in the least prevent her from continuing her own work.

"She composed her novels with a facility which almost equaled my own, always choosing the most dramatic subjects. Then, as a side issue, she took care in passing to attack the government and to preach the emancipation of female blackbirds. Before setting herself to work she never sketched any plan or bothered her head about construction. She was the typical literary lady blackbird."

This little sketch was extremely popular. It expressed the resentment felt toward George by other authors.

When the fable appeared George still remained silent. With unfeminine restraint, in the face of Alfred's exploitation of their love affair, she maintained her silence during twenty-four years. But in George's nature silence, if too long sustained, was apt to prove as dangerous as a slumbering volcano.

When Alfred de Musset died it was generally supposed by those who read his poems that George Sand had broken his heart and caused his untimely end.

George then decided that it was time to give her version of the love affair. Two years after the death of the poet she wrote with considerable detachment what has been described by John Oliver Hobbes as "the sanest account of a sentimental experience ever written."

This novel, entitled *Elle et Lui,* appeared in the *Revue des Deux Mondes.* The editor, François Buloz, wrote to her concerning it: "It is an elevated work, a beautiful picture of a man of genius in conflict with vice, but not a work of vengeance. Certainly you did not kill the poet, as has been said. On the contrary you gave him his most beautiful inspirations, which have not always been very well veiled."

Elle et Lui was answered by *Lui et Elle,* written by Alfred's brother Paul de Musset.

Lui et Elle, though in the form of a novel, was merely a pamphlet of hate. Whereas George had written out of her own experience, Paul had nothing to write from except his memories of Alfred's bitter words. There were nights when Alfred had come home somewhat overstimulated and had poured out incoherent ravings against the woman he still hated and had never ceased to love. Did not Alfred always talk to Paul when he hated George? These ravings were put in Paul's book as "dictated statements" from Alfred.

"It is Alfred de Musset speaking," wrote Paul authoritatively, beginning his accusations against George. Considering Musset's mental unbalance, if he did speak why should anyone take his words seriously?

The world at large, loving his poetry and supposing him as soulful as the poetry he wrote, did take seriously every word in Paul's book and regarded George as a vampire. That legend, with its Pauline amplifications, took the place of history.

Separated from the credulous public by an intimate knowledge of Musset's idiosyncrasies, was one superior and intelligent woman who sympathized with George.

Madame Allen-Despeaux was the gifted actress who had put Musset's plays into the theatre and created for him his vogue as a playwright. She also became his mistress. In 1849 Madame Allen wrote a confidential letter to her friend Madame Sampson-Toussaint, explaining the strange moods of her lover Musset:

"He has attacks of nerves which lead to brainstorms, he has hallucinations and deliriums. Merely to let oneself be loved by him is drudgery. In this stormy character doubt and suspicion are inseparable from a long train of bitter memories which, to tell the truth, are those of an ex-libertine. I have never seen a more striking contrast than that which exists between the two beings imprisoned in this single individual. The one being is sweet and tender, weeping at any trifling emotion. Turn the page and examine the other side, you have to do with a man possessed by a demon. He is mad, hard and petty. He is distrustful to the point of insult. He blasphemes everything."

It was the man thus described by a wise, observing woman who was held up to the public as one whose diatribes and blasphemies should be believed.

Lui et Elle disclosed also that Alfred had betrayed George by showing Paul her intimate journal intended for her lover's eyes alone. This journal was a complete exposure of the trance-like obsession George lived in for a brief period when she was, as she expressed it, the "slave of passion." During her slavery she identified herself with Alfred and took over his point of view.

As long as they were living together Alfred was denied all knowledge of this self-annihilating confession. George had sent her journal to him after their separation, hoping that the story of her suffering would soften his anger and enable them to regard each other with feelings of sympathetic friendship. She had written Alfred of her unbearable fear that their love and tenderness might end in anger and resentment.

On receiving George's journal, Alfred, so Paul declared, had laughed at the pitiful history of George's love for him and had criticised her phrases as well as her actions. Since, according to Paul's own statement, the brothers thus discussed George's journal, Alfred certainly showed it to Paul, and after Alfred's death Paul had the manuscript, or a copy of it, in his possession or he could not have quoted from it in his book.

Paul de Musset was an author whose works had made no lasting impression, whereas Alfred's poems had given prominence to the Musset name. Alfred's reputation was Paul's only claim to fame. He naturally made a cult of his brother and tried to present him to the public as a faultless man driven to ruin by a woman.

George made no direct reply to Paul's attack on her. But in the preface to her next novel, *Jean de la Roche,* she referred to the fact that a certain poet would speak for himself one day. This reference was to Alfred's letters which contradicted Paul's statements.

The two books, *Elle et Lui* and *Lui et Elle,* created a sensation. As a result of the widespread interest they aroused, their theme was to become "the great love affair of the century," "the classic love affair of literature," "a love as well known as that of Abélard and Héloïse or Romeo and Juliet."

But along with the fame of the Sand-Musset love affair went the noise of the Sand-Musset controversy.

In the course of time the literary public was divided into Mussetists and Sandists. The famous love affair was debated in colleges, discussed at dinner tables, and set forth in books, pamphlets, articles and poems.

All because Alfred told the public of his sufferings, and George answered by telling hers, and Paul answered back again claiming greater suffering for Alfred.

Which suffered more, George or Alfred? Everyone helped to decide the important question.

During George Sand's lifetime the amazing thing about the controversy was the attitude of George herself. She let Paul's legends circulate and grow, without publishing the letters from Alfred which would have vindicated her name. On one occasion when she was tempted to publish them she took counsel of Sainte-Beuve.

"Three horrible things," she wrote to him, "do not weigh on the conscience of your friend; the exhibition of a new love before the eyes of a dying man; the threat, even the thought, of shutting him up in a madhouse; the effort to attract him and get him back again, in spite of himself, after he was cured of his love."

These three indictments, included among others in Paul de Musset's book, especially outraged George's sense of justice. Musset's letters disproved these accusations, yet Sainte-Beuve advised against the publication of the letters.

"Your advice is good," George answered, "I shall follow it. The letters will not appear until after my death."

She ended with her usual magnanimity, "Peace and pardon, that is the whole conclusion. But in the future, a ray of truth to throw light on this history."

George Sand, from the crayon portrait by Thomas Couture, 1844.
Engraved by Alexandre Manceau

XI

MOTHER GEORGE

THE older and homelier she grew, the more George was surrounded by young men. Some of them stayed at Nohant for
months at a time, as though they preferred her to their families.
Others from a distance expressed their affection in letters. They
felt that in writing to George they confided their thoughts and
problems to one who was a sort of mother, yet, in her understanding of young men, a sort of father as well.

In their attitude toward George her present friends differed
from her former lovers. Their vanity was not involved in their
affection. From the beginning these young bachelors had accepted
her, not as a maddening woman who outraged their traditions,
but as a superior human being who excited interest and deserved
respect. The years that separated their youthful ambitions from
her mature achievements prevented any feeling of competition.
If George preached to her admirers, they thought it rather sweet
of her to show interest in their affairs. If she spoke with authority, they were interested in the wisdom of her experience.

George's ideas, once unbecomingly large for a beautiful young
woman, were now the fitting philosophy of plain middle age.
She had grown up to her own precocious mind. Her personality
was stronger than it had been a generation earlier, but now no one
tried to dominate her strength, so she ceased to antagonize. Her
power was, as always, painstakingly concealed behind the calm
exterior which she maintained for days or weeks on end. Then,
as it always had done, her repressed intensity burst into eloquence
or expressed itself in unexpected self-assertion. But these so-called
masculine moods were not overwhelming to the new generation.
They were, on the contrary, considered more inspiring than the

monotonous sweetness and continuous small talk of other less exhilarating women.

And George's habitual silences, which so offended strangers, were soothing to her intimate friends. Guests found her a restful hostess, as was proved by the length of their stay.

There was an easy hospitality at Nohant. No limit was ever set to an invitation to Madame Sand's home. People were often invited to "come and stay a year or two," though seldom did anyone, like Eugene Lambert, remain a visitor for twelve years.

The fascination of Nohant lay in the fact that everyone was free to do as he pleased. One read, slept, walked or worked without interference. The mistress of the house gave no more than her early evenings to her guests. Sometimes she came to luncheon and disappeared again for the afternoon. Often she did not appear until dinner time.

When George was in her early fifties, the more or less permanent guests of the family were, besides Lambert, Victor Borie, Fulbert Martin, Emile Aucante and Maurice's friend, Alexandre Manceau.

Manceau, a pupil of Delacroix and a talented engraver, was congenial to Maurice through their common interest in art. George had found him at Nohant on her return from Paris in 1850. After observing him for a few days her first comment on Manceau was, "He helps everyone, thinks of everyone, but himself."

Manceau's unselfishness was shown in his friendship for Maurice. Whatever Maurice started, Manceau finished. When Maurice decided to write a book on butterflies, Manceau helped collect data and took care of the cocoons. When Maurice made sketches to illustrate a book on Napoleon I, then turned from Napoleon to some new interest, Manceau completed the engravings.

The gifted Maurice was too versatile to choose a vocation or even adhere to one avocation. In consequence he remained a greatly admired amateur in many arts and never became a recognized artist.

While Maurice was in a mood of enthusiasm over his marionettes he took them to Paris one winter, and added to his social popularity by presenting his plays in the homes of his friends. Lambert, Borie and Manceau spent several months at Nohant trying to console George for the absence of her son. After a time Lambert and Borie drifted away and Manceau stayed on.

A curious relation developed between George and her son's friend. Maurice's "Damon," as he came to be known, gradually slipped into the life of Nohant and became George's fidus Achates.

George had not brought up her children to wait on her or concern themselves about her work. Fortunately Damon had not been educated by George. Her exhausting literary labors appealed to his sympathies. It seemed to him that someone ought to help her, and since her children were both enjoying Paris he felt inclined to subordinate what he regarded as his small contribution to art for her greater one. With no urge but his own inner compulsion he undertook to classify and assort her manuscript. Then he took over the bookkeeping and paying of bills. Amazed at the volume of her correspondence, he acquired the habit of classifying the mail and answering her formal letters. He also found time to take charge of the renovations that were always going on at Nohant, such as enlarging the theatre and reconstructing a studio for Maurice. Finally, seeing how burdensome George found the housekeeping, he kept house. In short, he surrounded George with the attentions an important man usually receives from his family.

Manceau's feeling for George approached worship. He relieved her of all drudgery, and felt repaid by contemplating the greater number of pages she was able to produce. Tired George found to her surprise that for the first time in her life she was regarded as a hero in her own home.

Meanwhile the industrious Manceau continued to support himself by his excellent engravings. He even had money to lend

George when, as not infrequently happened, she found her purse empty. But, like a woman working at home, Manceau considered his own work a side issue. When George did not need him, he engraved.

At night when George retired to begin her writing she found her desk made ready with everything necessary for her work. Nor did Manceau ever forget the glass of sweetened water or light wine she was accustomed to sip while she wrote. In the evening when she sat down in her favorite armchair in the salon, Manceau handed her cigarette paper, her pouch of tobacco and matches. Then he placed paper, pen and ink on the table by her side, in case she might feel in the mood to write.

The Goncourt brothers, after visiting Nohant, reported this assiduous devotion with a fine sense of humor. It did not seem to these two old bachelors either dignified or appropriate that attentions usually described as feminine should be received by a woman from a man. Yet judged as a worker, George deserved feminine attentions if ever a man did.

But how could George, who had asserted a life-long independence, consistently become, as she did, helplessly dependent on Manceau? She had protested against, and indeed her nature was incapable of, feminine dependence. She did not want to be provided for, or protected, guarded and guided. But she found it natural to lean on Manceau as a strong self-reliant man leans on a daughter or a wife. She liked the lesser attentions of sympathy and service that helped, without attempting to direct, her own self-expression.

Her helplessness was husbandlike. And Manceau's place in the home was a wifely one. When George made an occasional trip to Paris, Manceau looked up the train, packed the trunks, engaged a carriage to drive them part way, and arranged every comfort for the journey. At Paris he helped her with her shopping, accompanied her to the theatre, was taken along on all her calls, and was received with her by Princess Mathilde. When George, in turn, entertained callers in her apartment on Rue Racine, it was Manceau who opened the door and welcomed the visitors while George remained seated in an armchair smoking her ubiquitous cigarettes. If the conversation languished, as it usually did under George's uninspiring silence, Manceau animated it with anecdotes about George. According to the Goncourts, Manceau's attitude toward George was that of "the proud exhibitor of some great phenomenon."

2

Trips to Paris were few and far between. Hero and hero-worshiper lived in the country winter and summer for the sake of George's work. And while Manceau at Nohant was doing his best to lighten George's burdens, Maurice in Paris was adding to them by turning to his mother for means to continue his bachelor existence.

Maurice, at thirty, had not yet decided whether to be a novelist, a playwright, a painter, an engraver or an entomologist. George awaited this momentous decision with maternal patience. But she was distressed because her vacillating son turned from one interest to another instead of preparing himself for a life work.

In a letter written late in April, 1852, George came nearer than ever before in her life to scolding her adored son.

"I wish that while you are in Paris you would think about working, if not at painting, at least at drawing, which will always be useful to you. I do not believe you would be wise to renounce painting if you can study it in Paris. Can you? And will you? The question has never been decided. For this purpose you do not need to spend five or even four hundred francs a month. That means an income of six thousand francs a year which is quite impossible. We haven't as much as that. You ought not to rent an apartment with a studio for seven or eight hundred francs unless you use it for serious work. All this you alone can determine. I will co-operate with you as much as you wish, but if at the end of several months, I find that you continue to loaf and these sacrifices are made to no purpose, you are too reasonable to ask me to go on working like a negro in order to help you waste your time. I leave all this entirely to you. I will do whatever you wish, however unhappy I am in being separated from you."

In a letter written a week later she described the quiet life at Nohant:

"In the evening we read Cooper, with Martin and Manceau, while I embroider tapestry for the mantelpiece. We go to our rooms at half past ten and I work until three o'clock, continuing my work in the daytime from one o'clock until six.

"I think I spoke to you of my play and told you I was writing a novel. I finished the first volume in fifteen days and am now writing the second volume, which will be completed by the middle of May. Immediately afterwards I shall return to my play."

This letter was dated April 28, 1852. George's state of mind at the time is explained by the fact, concealed from her son, that five days earlier she had received a disturbing letter from her daughter.

Solange was living in Paris awaiting a decision in her legal proceedings against her husband. The bond between these two violent natures endured scarcely a year. Frequent quarrels, followed by reconciliations, had culminated in a suit for judicial separation. George had stood back of Solange through all her troubles, helping her unfortunate child with money and sympathy, though Solange was difficult to assist. George in her younger days, and in a similar situation, had found refuge in work. Solange sought consolation in amusement. She sent her mother a letter full of insinuations and accusations. She felt lonely and abused, she wanted to enjoy the gay life of Paris. "It takes a great deal of courage for me to keep straight," Solange confessed.

In a long letter answering her daughter's complaints George

pointed out that Solange pushed away her friends and then pitied herself for being deserted. She found everyone detestable yet wanted to be loved. "Are you the victim of general injustice," George asked Solange, "or of your own character, which is disdainful and capricious and which exacts everything from others without giving anything in return? You complain of those who abandon you, without understanding that you have repulsed or wounded everyone.

"And now in order to console yourself you want money, a great deal of money. In luxury, idleness and excitement you wish to forget the emptiness of your heart. But to give you what you need I should be obliged to work twice as hard, which would mean, since the work I am now doing exceeds my strength, that I should die in six months. And if I should die you would not long remain rich. My death would do you no good because my heritage will not make you rich at all, you and your brother. I cannot do double the work I am doing now and live for any length of time. Besides, is it proved that it is my duty to you to make myself a horse in a treadmill in order to keep you in luxury and pleasure? No, it has not been demonstrated to me that this is true, and permit me to believe that it is not merely 'the fear of disturbing my own little comforts,' as you put it, which prevents me from consummating this stupid suicide, it is a truer sense of justice. The idea of killing myself in order to keep you amused goes contrary to my other duties in this world.

"Now let us consider my financial situation and yours. For the three of us we have an income of seven thousand francs. The rest comes out of my brain, my toiling nights, my burnt-up blood, and my strained and tired nerves. I will give you more than I can afford, but I refuse to be influenced by useless complaints.

"I know that in your eyes I shall always be the cause of your misfortunes. I shall never be rich enough to decorate your life by giving you equipages and expensive clothes. You will always confide your grievances to others and they will circulate your stories that you are the victim of my neglect. Well, I shall let them talk and you will not be any richer or better befriended because of the stories you circulate.

"The reflections in your letter on the 'women of heart and judgment' who, 'like girls with no education' sometimes succumb to 'pleasure and vice,' make me think that your husband did not always lie when he said you made certain threats to him. My poor child, there are moments when you do not know what you think or what you say. It was in one of those moments that you wrote me the strange paradox which is in your letter. No, women of heart and judgment never succumb to the attractions of vice. For vice has no attractions and no seductions except for those who are without judgment and without heart. A mother reads such words with pity, but a husband cannot hear them without fury or despair.

"Do you really find it difficult to be poor and isolated and not fall into vice? Is it really hard for you to keep straight because for twenty-four hours you have been between four walls and have heard women laugh and horses gallop outside? True unhappiness is to have a brain capable of conceiving such reasoning as yours, 'I must have happiness or vice.'

"I have seen young women fight against passions of the heart or senses, in fear of succumbing to involuntary attractions. But I have never seen one brought up as you have been, in an atmosphere of dignity and moral liberty, who was afraid of privations. A woman of heart and judgment, no matter how strong she is, may fear lest she be led astray by love but never by cupidity. Good night, my daughter. Read this letter not once but three times. It will make you angry the first time, but at the third reading you will agree with me and you will not revert to your bad dream. Just the same I kiss you, and tenderly.

Your mother.

Take your courage in both hands."

But it was in vain to try to dissuade Solange from "falling into vice," as she bluntly expressed it. After her separation from her husband she attached herself to men who could provide her with the luxuries she craved. George never deserted her daughter. Even while Solange was living with a wealthy foreigner of title, George continued to send her six thousand francs a year, so that in case Solange wished to return to a normal life she would find means at her disposal.

The difference in viewpoint between George and Solange was shown in one sentence in George's letter: "A woman of heart and judgment may be led astray by love but never by cupidity." George distinguished between a disinterested union of love and a loveless union of self-interest. But her critics made no such distinction. They summed up the history of Solange's life in the phrase "like mother, like daughter."

Two women were never more unlike than George and her daughter of the flesh but not of the spirit. George threw away her reputation but clung to her self-respect. And she was so exceptional in strength, goodness and achievement that she did not need what she had thrown away. George was able to live down mistakes and compel the respect of others, while poor Solange, having thrown away both self-respect and reputation, had no great qualities or achievements with which to reconstruct her life. When youth was over, the embittered woman turned her thoughts to the mother whom, perhaps, in spite of hatred and jealousy she had always inconsistently loved. At the death of Baron Dudevant Solange inherited one-half of his little fortune. She bought a country place near Nohant and continued to afflict the family by her presence during the remainder of her days.

3

When George hardened her heart against exploitation, she never succeeded in sustaining her mood of self-defense. Temporary revolt was sure to be followed by an affectionate letter enclosing a cheque. Theoretically, she did not believe in futile self-sacrifice but resistance to the demands of others was merely a part of her thought processes and did not reach her instinctive being. Her instinct to give was more than the normal outgoing. It was a leak in her heart and the hole could not be stopped.

It was her fault that people took advantage of her kindness. She invited imposition and they imposed. Thus it followed that she was surrounded by protégés sent to her by intimate friends. If a young man needed patronage, someone was sure to say, "Get Madame Sand interested in him," "Let Madame Sand help him," and he was provided with a letter of introduction, and sent to Nohant.

In Berry also, innumerable families depended on Madame Sand to get their sons "placed." This placing of sons was a friendly service that cost George time and worry. She was often annoyed by importunate people. In response to their need she was persuaded to write letters to those of her friends who had influence and position. Thus she herself was obliged to become importunate. Like a chainless letter, pleading and begging brought to George had often to be passed on by her to others. Her appeals were gentle and appreciative, seldom indeed were they left ignored.

Having allowed herself to become the victim of her own generous impulses, she sometimes experienced moods of reaction in which she felt an impulse to run away. But she controlled or repressed her longing to travel and found change of scene by living outside of herself. Her mind thus acquired a fine detachment. She fell into the habit of speaking of herself as "she" or more often as "he." From some vantage ground outside of, or above herself, she looked at "the individual called George Sand" and found her rather ordinary and dull. "I would not be interested in myself," she said, "if I had the honor of meeting me."

Between the ages of fifty and sixty George's vocabulary changed. The words happiness, passion, ecstasy, despair, suicide, passed out of use. In their place were substituted serenity, tranquillity, peace, and, more especially, the world escape. In letters of consolation and advice, she urged others to escape from self, in study and work. Her heroines of this period were often depicted as seeking escape from self.

George learned many ways of "escape from me," as she expressed it. She forgot herself for hours at a time in the study of nature. Her library was filled with books of information on birds, trees, flowers and stones. One side of the room was fitted with shelves for the various specimens she had accumulated. The study of nature became a new love-life which absorbed the affection and interest of her later years. Several of her heroines were also addicted to the study of natural history.

But since her running away was always subjective, she continued to long for an actual, material place of retreat. She expressed this desire to her friend Charles Poncy, in a letter written July 1856.

"I am always aspiring toward *absence*. To me, absence means a little corner where I can rest from all worldly affairs, all worry, every relation that is boresome, all domestic bother, and all responsibility for my own existence. That is what I found last year at Frascati, for three weeks. That is what I ask the good Lord to find again for me, for six months, in some place where the sky is soft and nature is picturesque; a very modest dream, but it has floated before me for ten successive years and has never allowed itself to be caught."

This longing for absence was further incarnated in a vision by which she had long been haunted. For many years George had dreamed intermittently of a solitary house given her to inhabit alone or with one or two friends. Now, more than ever, the imaginary house occupied her thoughts. As though to rid herself of the obsession she wrote an article, *La Maison déserte*, and because it contained her intimate reveries, she published it anonymously.

While George dreamed and wrote her dream, Manceau set about

fulfilling it. George felt she must not spend money for herself, so the devoted Manceau spent his own money for George. He bought a cottage in a place she loved. The place was Gargilesse.

George had once visited Gargilesse with a friend who was a naturalist. She had fallen in love with the little village situated in a deep valley surrounded by mountains. Although only thirty miles from Nohant, the village was so hidden and barricaded from the world, it seemed to George an ideal retreat.

Manceau's cottage, repaired and furnished by him with meticulous care, provided her with an escape from the importunate. Maurice and an occasional close friend were often invited to "the Villa Manceau." In *Promenades autour d'un village* George described their sorties into the surrounding neighborhood.

In the winter of 1858, George was writing *L'Homme de Neige*. The scene was laid in Sweden, a country she had never visited. George prepared for her novel by reading several books on Sweden. Nevertheless, as she confided to Manceau, she doubted her ability to do justice to the scenery.

Manceau rose to the emergency by arranging a visit to Gargilesse, so that George could observe the winter landscape. Having reached the village, he drove George up and down the hilliest roads he could find. But the trip seemed wasted, as the scenery was hidden behind heavy fogs. Soon George, soothed by the motion of the carriage, fell asleep. As they drove around the snowcapped, fog-wrapped mountains, Manceau allowed his revered friend to continue her nap.

At night, thoroughly rested, George's mind became active. As she looked from her window, where there was blackness and fog, she seemed to see vast cañons of northern Scandinavia. Exalted by the gorgeous view, she described what she imagined.

When *L'Homme de Neige* was published, the Swedish critics marveled at Madame Sand's intimate knowledge of their country. They praised especially the descriptions of scenery, in which, they said, she had been accurate to the most minute detail.

But there was nothing unusual in Madame Sand's achievement. An imagination great enough to make a god of Michel, a saint of Musset, and an angel of Chopin, could easily create the magnificence of Sweden from the foggy village of Gargilesse.

4

In her journal dated May 29, 1858, at Gargilesse, George noted: "I have finished my novel commenced May 4, 620 pages in twenty-five days. I have never worked with greater pleasure than at Gargilesse." This leisure for work George owed to her faithful Achates.

Manceau was more insignificant than any man with whom George had been intimately associated. In spite of this fact, or perhaps because of it, his influence inspired her to prodigious accomplishment. During the six years between 1857 and 1862, that is, from the age of fifty-three to fifty-eight, George wrote seventeen books and two plays, which considerably exceeded her usual abnormal productivity. But her work was badly paid, her expenses were heavy, and she was obliged to postpone indefinitely her extravagant desire for travel. She had set her heart on a trip to Africa. "But," she wrote to Charles Poncy, "there is always that sad word *but!* We can only hope."

Instead of realizing her ambition to see foreign countries, George fell ill of typhoid fever. For several weeks, Maurice and Manceau, who watched over her, despaired of her recovery.

While she lay unconscious, her sick brain, so long habituated to work, went steadily on with the novel she had begun before her illness. During the fever she talked to her characters and went with them into the scenes of their lives. Not one reference to her own life was revealed in her delirium. Year after year she had dominated her body while forcing her tired imagination to work. The habit was so well established that even typhoid fever could not destroy her creative power.

During convalescence, George was taken by Maurice to the

shores of the Mediterranean, at Tamaris, near Toulon. But Maurice was soon bored by the monotony of life at Tamaris, and accepted an invitation from Prince Jerome, to visit Spain, Africa and America. The voyage lasted six months.

It seemed wiser to allow Maurice to do the traveling for the family, because for George to travel cost, not only the expense of the trip, but also the loss of all the money she could make in six months. Stoically, George accepted the fact that her earning capacity curtailed her pleasures and limited her freedom. But she missed her son.

Manceau stayed with her and helped to nurse her back to health. And after all, George, who had always dreamed of seeing America, got something out of Maurice's trip. When he returned, he talked about the countries he had visited and she listened. He wrote the story of his travels and George wrote a preface for the book.

After her illness George was poor again. Expenses of the last year had been heavy. Soon a rumor reached her that her name had been proposed by Sainte-Beuve as the person most deserving a prize of twenty thousand francs offered by the French Academy. Twenty thousand francs! The cottage at Gargilesse, which George was unable to afford, had cost but eight hundred francs. Twenty thousand was wealth. It represented travel, ease, leisure, and the lifting of all economic pressure.

The Academy prize was, of course, awarded for literary merit. The recipient was to be chosen by a committee of twenty-four members. But alas, among the forty immortals was François Guizot, anti-republican and anti-everything in which George believed. Guizot read passages from George's books to prove her influence was a menace to private property. He also contended that her early novels were destructive of the home. Sainte-Beuve defended her manfully, as did Alfred de Vigny and Prosper Mérimée, but out of twenty-four votes George received only six.

The members were unanimous in praising George as an author

but, considered politically and socially, her name was anathema. The injustice of their decision was that a tribunal of literature should condemn opinions. The prize was finally awarded to Adolphe Thiers. Guizot and Thiers, the two distinguished historians, had been opposing ministers under Louis Philippe. Thiers was, therefore, Guizot's ancient enemy. By the irony of fate Guizot had fought against George only to secure an honor for his rival.

The Bonapartes were disappointed by the decision against George. They now offered her an amount equal to the Academy prize, as an endowment. But George had not been friendly with the reigning family for the sake of favors. She wrote a proud decisive letter refusing their generous gift.

A movement was then started to elect George as a member of the Academy. But this presumptuous effort to place a woman among the immortals was quickly and effectively discouraged. In course of time, Maurice Sand was elected to the Academy. This was generally considered a more appropriate recognition of the name George had made famous and of the contribution she had added to the literary glory of France.

XII

GRANDMOTHER GEORGE

GEORGE'S first grandchild, Solange's daughter, born at Guillery, had lived only a week. Her second grandchild, also Solange's daughter, was born before the quarrels between the Clésingers became hatred leading to separation. When Jeanne was two years old, she was left in care of grandmother George while her parents fought for legal possession of her. Jeanne lived at Nohant for three years, while Solange, who hated the country, stayed in Paris. Once when she went to visit Jeanne at Nohant, her absence had been so prolonged that the child did not recognize her mother.

Jeanne became grandmother's "Nini." The fairy-like creature full of spontaneity and charm, was sovereign of the little realm of Nohant, and George proceeded to spoil her as she had spoiled Solange.

But George was a wiser grandmother than mother. Nini had been brought to her in a nervous state that required the entire attention of one person. Under the care of an excellent nurse she became quiet, healthy and comparatively self-controlled. George was able to write to Solange that, instead of daily fits of temper, Jeanne now exhibited tantrums only once every four or five days.

The frequent letters sent by George to Solange, describing Jeanne's fascinating ways, awakened loneliness in the mother's heart. Naturally Solange wanted her own child. But unfortunately, her nature did not permit her to sacrifice herself even for her child. So she appeared suddenly at Nohant, demanded Jeanne, and took her to Paris.

After a brief reconciliation the fight broke out again between the two parents of Jeanne. Clésinger had in his possession incriminating letters addressed to his wife. Armed by these, and aided by his lawyer, he asserted the legal rights of a father, took the help-less baby from her mother and put her in a Paris boarding house. Solange's mad impulses were always mistakes that she regretted too late.

In December 1855 the Clésingers' law suit was brought to a close. The court decided that since Clésinger was not a fit father, nor Solange a fit mother for an innocent child, Jeanne should be reared by her maternal grandmother, Madame George Sand. Both George and Solange were radiantly happy at this victory. They waited impatiently for Jeanne. But Clésinger would not surrender her until the proper papers were served. There were heart rend-ing legal delays.

Meanwhile, deprived of the attentions and surroundings which agreed with her, Nini, poor victim of two selfish parents, sickened, and after a brief illness, died. The child's body was brought back to Nohant and buried in the family cemetery beside her great-great-grandmother Dupin.

After this tragedy George's health collapsed. "I am too old," she said, "to be consoled." Fainting spells and sleeplessness reduced her vitality until, for the second time in her life, she was unable to write. The thought of Nini's unnecessary death became a fixed idea to which her thoughts reverted constantly. But her philosophy did not permit her to yield to sorrow. If only for the sake of others, she felt compelled to fight stubbornly for recovery.

Maurice had been planning a trip abroad. Conscious of her need for an extreme remedy, George straightway arranged for the plan to include herself. Six weeks after the death of her grandchild, she left Nohant to travel in Italy, where change of scene enabled her to escape the melancholy power of her former fixed idea.

Of course Manceau went to Italy with George and Maurice, as did Borie and Lambert. George could not move without her harmonious family. No one wanted to be first, no one was jealous, each of the men was a friend of the other three, and all enjoyed her collective affection. In this atmosphere of brotherly love

George's nature throve. Decidedly, there were compensations in growing old.

After her return home she wrote to a friend:

"I have seen Rome, revisited Florence, Genoa, Frascati. I have walked a great deal in the sun, rain and wind and have lived for whole days out of doors. This for me is a certain remedy and I have come back cured."

George's cure did not include forgetfulness. She talked and thought about Nini, but she ceased to brood upon the past. Once the child came to her in a dream and seemed surprised that her grandmother was weeping, so George grew ashamed of grief and regarded it as weakness. She began to think of Nini as happy. She expressed her affection by making sketches of her in all her remembered attitudes. While George was thus courageously keeping Nini alive before her eyes, Solange appeared with a death mask taken from the dead child's face.

"I don't want to look at it," cried George. "I don't want to think of her in her coffin! We see her." And George held up the sketches of the laughing dancing child. But Solange preferred her death mask and her plaster reproduction of the child's dead hands.

As Jeanne's mother, Solange doubtless felt a deeper despair than George's and she had at her command lesser powers of recuperation. Nevertheless the contrasting natures of the two women was shown in their different manner of bearing affliction. Poor Solange yielded completely to her grief, brooded over her memories and, with a morbid egotism of which she was unconscious, imposed her misery on others. She would not allow her wound to close and took mournful pleasure in celebrating the anniversary of her child's death by doleful pilgrimages to Nohant where she wept on Jeanne's grave.

One January when the Nohant house was closed, and George, with her family, was in Paris, Solange wished to go in the cold and snow of midwinter, to view the little grave that lay alongside of the now desolate empty house. George knew that Solange was deliberately preparing herself for agonies of grief. She wrote to her daughter:

"If only I could dissuade you from this journey. It will exhaust you and will do you no good. The soul of our dear child is with us. Her grave is merely an object of respect. Let us respect graves, certainly, but not make a cult of them. If you take this journey now, not one of us will be with you to share your grief. The visit will mean unavailing suffering for you. If you want to make me less sad on this anniversary day, you will renounce your trip.

"Besides, what significance is there in an anniversary? Must we feel our sense of loss more acutely because time has marked off a certain number of days and hours? Is not every day the anniversary of so great a grief? Deep sorrows have no prejudices and do not arrange for emotional crises at fixed hours."

This appeal awakened no response. Solange made her journey, as she had planned, to the grave of her daughter.

In January of the following year, George was at Nohant. Again she begged Solange not to come. "This *establishing* of an anniversary makes me very unhappy," she wrote. Again Solange made her pilgrimage to the grave.

George never understood her daughter. If she had begged Solange to come and weep at Nohant, she would have stayed away. Whenever her mother offered counsel, Solange did exactly the opposite of that which her mother advised. "She was contrary," said Madame Viardot, "for the love of contrariness."

How could Solange express her ego if she did not resist and resent her famous mother? For a time she tried to emulate George and win fame for herself. She wrote two slight novels which attracted no attention. She then undertook to write a life of Maurice de Saxe. George consumed a great deal of time encouraging and helping her daughter's efforts. Solange began the work with enthusiasm, but when she saw that the task meant long hours in the library, she lost her zest for writing and turned again to pleasure and excitement.

2

George did not wish either of her children to emulate Manceau in devotion to herself. She wanted them to live their own lives. But it was hard for her to see them miss happiness. Solange seemed incapable of either love or work. But George hoped and believed that Maurice would find these essentials to happiness.

Her patient expectation was at last rewarded. When Maurice reached the age of thirty-five he decided to be an illustrator and at thirty-nine he married, as George wished him to do, for love.

Madame Maurice Sand, or as she modestly called herself, Madame Maurice, was the daughter of Luigi Calamatta, the well known engraver. In choosing Lina Calamatta as his wife, Maurice violated established French custom by marrying a girl without a dot.

In a letter written to her old friend Boucoiran, George proudly sided with her son: "The fortune which he would have asked from an unknown person, he does not demand from one who is worth a fortune in herself. He is right, and I am full of happiness and satisfaction."

Lina proved to be a marvelous young woman. She was both intelligent and domestic. Without trying to rival her talented husband, she also showed artistic appreciation and taste. She was unspoiled and gave to George more unselfish devotion than she received from her own children. Before Maurice's marriage George had written to Lina: "I feel that I shall be to you a true mother, because I need a daughter."

In the same way that George had lost a daughter, Lina had lost a mother, not by death, but by hopeless difference of viewpoint. Lina who, like George, refused the practices of the Catholic church, was alienated by her mother's excessive religious devotion. After her husband's death, Madame Calamatta withdrew from the world and became a nun. Thus George took the place of Lina's mother and Lina became the spiritual daughter of George.

Lina often said to her friends: "Oh, I am more married to George Sand than to Maurice Sand. I accepted him because I adored her."

George, who had missed happiness where it was supposed to be found, in romantic love, achieved happiness where it is supposed not to exist, in the love of a daughter-in-law. It was like unique George to make of the despised and ridiculed position of mother-in-law the most beautiful relation of her later life.

In her behavior toward the young couple, mother George showed infinite tact. She left them alone for their honeymoon and for the greater part of their early married life. Maurice was now the head of the house. George encouraged him to feel that he had inherited the family home before her death. And to increase his sense of freedom she stayed in Paris or Gargilesse. Therefore her visits to Nohant were always cause for rejoicing.

In July 1863 George wrote to Sainte-Beuve: "There was born to us, on July 14, a superb wide-awake boy who squalls delightfully. His father is mad about him, and I am as happy as one can be in this world."

As though in celebration of this great event George was overwhelmed a few months later, by the sensational success of her play, *Le Marquis de Villemer*.

On the eve of the première, she wrote from Paris:

"My dear children, to-morrow is the great day. When you receive this letter I shall have had bravos or hisses, perhaps both . . .

"The theatre, from the director to the ushers, one of whom calls me 'our treasure' and to the musicians, the machinists, the troupe, the lamp lighters, the firemen, weep at rehearsals like a lot of babies. They are in the intoxication of a success which is to exceed that of *Champi*. But all this is the night before, we must wait until to-morrow."

On the next day there followed her description of an astonishing first night. Enthusiasm, shouting, applause like thunder, crowds outside who could not find seats and, as the final touch: "Flaubert was with us and wept like a woman."

Grandmother George, on this momentous evening, was the sensation of the hour.

"In the foyer more than two hundred people, whom I knew or did not know, came and hugged me until I could not stand it any longer. If you could see my calm in the midst of all this you would laugh at me, for I felt no more fear or pleasure than as though it had nothing to do with me personally, and I could not explain why. I was prepared for the worst and perhaps that was why the unexpected success, so unconceivable in relation to me, left me stupefied.

"Next week I hope to run back to you and my darling, who is growing a lot, I hope. Write me of yourselves and of him."

After the third night of *Villemer*, she wrote to her children that the success seemed permanent.

"The paying public are commencing to get seats. The first day they took in only seven hundred francs because of complimentary tickets to the ministers and their friends; the second day twelve hundred, to-day three thousand, the box office receipts for to-morrow have already reached four thousand francs, an un-heard-of sum for the poor Odéon, and for Saturday and Monday they have already taken in six thousand francs. . . . *Villemer* will easily pay for your marriage and the baptism of Marco.

"To-morrow I shall run away for awhile to escape visits, letters, cards and bouquets. Everyone is charming toward success. It is always like that. . . .

"The success is such that I cannot believe it has anything to do with me."

While George was staying in Paris during this winter of 1864, the celebrated photographer Nadar, in an effort to perpetuate the illustrious writer by a perfect likeness, took sixteen photographs of her. The final result was the well-known picture of George at sixty, in which her face looks strong, plain and benign, and in which she is wearing the then stylish, but now hideous, striped dress.

During these sittings, Nadar discussed his coming book on aviation. He was considered a crazy man because he believed in the possibility of constructing machines in which man could travel in the air. At that time the law of France absolutely forbade any attempt to fly, either in a balloon or in any apparatus heavier than air. Nadar's book, therefore, was entitled *The Right to Fly*, but he despaired of attracting the attention of readers because his name as a writer was unknown. In response to his appeal for sympathy, George generously offered to lend her name to Nadar's mad enthusiasm by writing the preface of his book.

In her preface George declared that we ought to help and encourage the innovators of great ideas. She contended that the theory of aviation was based on logic and that the fact that the air had never been mastered did not prove the attempt impossible. In the century of steam and electricity she urged further, we ought to have faith in the future triumph of aerial navigation.

For this bold defense of the right to fly, George received a great deal of ridicule. But so many of her ideas belonged to the century ahead of her that she was used to living in an unrealized future. She had ceased to expect understanding from unimaginative friends.

Before he made George's acquaintance, Flaubert asked her to write a preface for one of his books. George modestly refused saying that a preface by her never made a book successful. The true reason for her refusal was that Flaubert did not need her. She saved her name and her assistance for unpopular people and unpopular ideas.

3

After the success of *Villemer*, George stayed at Nohant for a few days with her "dear love" Marco. She then spent several weeks at Gargilesse. At this time she was greatly disturbed over the state of Manceau's health. He had lately developed symptoms of consumption and George realized that she was soon to lose her devoted friend.

While George and Manceau were stopping at Nohant on their way to consult specialists in Paris, Maurice showed that he was bored and annoyed by his former Damon. On some slight pretext of a difference of opinion, a quarrel broke out between the two men. Manceau, deeply wounded in his affection for Maurice, left abruptly for Paris, courageously facing loneliness and death.

George had once again to choose between her son and her dearest friend.

The situation seemed on the surface to parallel the one that had existed between Chopin and Maurice. But fundamentally it differed in essentials. Maurice no longer needed his mother. And Manceau was neither jealous nor suspicious. He trusted her. No one could turn him against her. When people told lies about her to Manceau, he believed in her and disbelieved the lies. Besides, Manceau had given her what she had given Chopin, years of service. She owed him gratitude, as Chopin had owed gratitude to her. For fifteen years Manceau had been with her almost daily, yet no misunderstandings had ever arisen between them. He was by no means a genius but he possessed a loyal heart. And life had taught George that for everyday companionship, the true heart of a friend was more to be desired than gifts of intellect or genius.

For Manceau, George left the home of which she had said, "Nohant is myself." She concealed from her children and intimate friends her reason for departure. At sixty years old, she followed her man to Paris, resolved to devote herself to him as long as he lived. The two went house hunting together like a young couple about to be married and finally decided on a "very little, very pretty, very neat house" in Palaiseau, an hour's distance by train from Paris. There the oddly assorted pair settled down together with George's old time indifference to what people might say.

Her old friends came to call on her. One of the first to appear was Alexandre Dumas, the younger, who on alighting from the train asked directions of one of the natives. At first the man professed ignorance, then "Wait a moment," he said, "Do you mean the lady whose name is in the papers? Her home is over there." "That's the one," said Dumas, convinced that he had found the right house.

Dumas père was an old friend of George's and Dumas fils had known her since he was a young man of twenty-six. He always called her "Mother Sand" and she in turn called him "My son." George as a playwright was said to have prepared the way for Dumas' more famous plays. He confessed that she helped him greatly. Even Manceau had been no more extravagant in admiration for George than was young Dumas. "Madame de Staël kneels before her and Madame de Sévigné kisses her hands," he said.

George was happy, also, to renew her friendship with Sainte-Beuve, who had been antagonized by her radicalism. As soon as she stopped writing novels of social reform he loved her again, and greeted with enthusiasm the series of pastoral novels of which he approved. Before she opened his letters, George always knew by glancing at the envelope what Sainte-Beuve's state of mind was. When he felt displeased he addressed her as "Madame Dudevant." As soon as she was restored to favor she became "Madame Sand."

Whenever George visited Paris she arranged a rendezvous with Sainte-Beuve. Her tiny apartment was at 3 Rue Racine. Just below was Magny's restaurant where she dined every night. It was a favorite resort of writers. In 1862 Sainte-Beuve instituted a fortnightly dinner at Magny's. It was arranged for Monday as on that day he had completed his weekly article. The favorite fortnightly program was one of literary or personal confessions in which everyone was supposed to take part. The new group formed by "Uncle Beuve" included Gautier, the Goncourts, Taine, Renan, Turgenev and Flaubert.

At these dinners George remained silent unless some one attacked what she called her "principles." One day the literary guests agreed that one should not write for the common people. George grew angry and said to them scornfully, "You are gentlemen instead of men."

At one of these dinners Ernest Renan is reported by the Goncourts as saying in the course of a literary discussion, "I find more truth in George Sand than in Balzac. She is the greatest artist of our time. Three hundred years hence the novels of George Sand will be read."

It was at Magny's in 1863 that George met Gustave Flaubert, who, in spite of his reputation for cynicism, lost his heart to plain middle-aged Madame Sand. "I admired you before I knew you. From the day I saw your lovely and kind face, I loved you," he confessed.

4

While George was thus busily engaged with her friends, her work and her new house, Maurice and Lina had departed for the yearly visit to Guillery, the home of Baron Dudevant. Soon after their arrival George received news that Marco had suddenly died of some childish disease caught at Gullery. She hurriedly journeyed to Nérac, where she accepted the compulsory hospitality of her former husband, whom she had not seen since Solange's wedding. George and Casimir together attended the funeral of their grandson, who was buried at Guillery beside Solange's first child. In deference to Casimir the name on the tombstone was inscribed, Mark Anthony Dudevant-Sand.

Having persuaded Maurice and Lina to assuage their grief by travel in the south of France, George returned to her invalid at Palaiseau.

For a year she endured the crucial experience of watching her friend Manceau slowly die. During the last three months of his life he was difficult to care for. "I alone have nursed him for three months. My servants would have lacked patience," she wrote to her nephew Oscar, the day after Manceau's death. "I have lost the companion of my life for fifteen years, the prop of my old age."

After Manceau's death, it was expected that George would return to Nohant and make her home with Maurice. But to everyone's surprise she decided to live on at Palaiseau alone. The independence built up during the last fifteen years had become a spiritual necessity. She did not propose to surrender it. "I love my solitude," she protested. She also admitted, "I am sad here, nevertheless."

George missed Manceau. He had become a habit, and he had relieved her loneliness without encroaching on her freedom. His attitude of distance and deference had emphasized her sense of belonging to herself.

In the autumn following Manceau's death, George was persuaded to spend a few days in Brittany with Maurice and Lina and afterward to visit them at Nohant. They begged her to remain with them. But, true to her resolution, George returned to Palaiseau, where, in apparent contentment, she continued to live alone. Flaubert came often to see her, as did other devoted friends. She enjoyed the leisure which enabled her to feel aloof from human ties yet one with humanity. Solitude did not close her heart. She loved a million men and women, some of them dead and some as yet unborn. "I cannot separate myself from humanity," she said, "because it is myself; because the evil it does strikes me to the heart; because its shame makes me blush; because its crimes gnaw at my vitals; because I cannot understand paradise in heaven or on earth for myself alone."

George had a genius for loving. She also had a fear of personal possessive love. She had yielded to it and broken away from it. Now, in her old age, she was afraid of it because she knew herself, knew her weakness, knew how easily she allowed herself to be possessed.

In 1866, George being then sixty-two and Flaubert forty-five,

George was persuaded to visit her friend in his home at Croisset, where he lived with his mother and sister. From the time of this visit the misanthrope and the lover of humanity continued an active correspondence.

From the beginning George made her position clear. "You don't have to write to me when you don't feel like it. There is no real friendship without absolute liberty," she proclaimed.

"Impersonality, a sort of idiocy which is peculiar to me, is making noticeable progress," she wrote to Flaubert. "If I were not well, I should think it was a malady. If my old heart did not become each day more loving, I should think it was egotism. In short, I don't know what it is, and there you are."

"To love, in spite of everything, I think that is the answer to the enigma of the universe. Always to grow, to spring up, to be born again, to seek and will life, to embrace one's opposite in order to assimilate it, to receive the prodigy of blendings and combinations from which emerge the prodigy of new forms,—that is the law of nature."

"Life where one does not play a rôle, is such a pretty performance to look at and listen to," concluded George.

5

After remaining in her retreat for considerably more than a year, grandmother George agreed to celebrate the New Year of 1867 with her family. On her way to them she was taken ill in Paris and was delayed there for two weeks.

While her illness continued, she was conscious of mental conflict. She realized that as soon as she reached Nohant her children would recommence their argument that she was too old, or too ill, to live alone. Would they try to persuade her to live at Nohant? Did she secretly hope to be persuaded?

She wrote Flaubert from Paris, "I am too alone at Palaiseau with a dead soul; not enough alone at Nohant with the children. I love them too much to belong to myself."

Poor George! It was the conflict of her life, between theories and emotions, between the desire for freedom and the need of human ties. How many times she had surrendered to personal love while her mind preferred detachment! Now she had taken her last stand. If she yielded, it would mean the end of the much-prized independence for which she had so often struggled in vain.

Maurice and Lina were inexpressibly dear to her. And she was once again a grandmother. As she thought of the year-old baby who awaited her, she was eager and anxious to know her new grandchild. Love called to her again. But George was no longer a dependent woman afraid of loneliness, she was a self-reliant human being reluctant to be engulfed by family life.

When she reached Nohant, her children, alarmed by her illness, would not permit her to speak of leaving them. Lina, who secretly wished to care for her, showed her understanding of George by declaring that Maurice needed a mother and the baby needed a grandmother.

It was a relief to George to postpone decision and spend the winter at Nohant. When spring came she wrote to a friend, "I did little work all winter, I have felt too unsettled."

Maurice and Lina then insisted that George must remain for the summer. Again she consented. Her stay was indefinitely prolonged, but for some time she regarded it as a visit. It was not until two years later that she sold her home in Palaiseau.

After she had definitely settled at Nohant she ceased to resist the tranquil pleasure of a harmonious family life. Her proud assertion of independence was almost, though not entirely, forgetten. It cropped out occasionally in what appeared to be an inconsistent mood.

On one occasion when she was ill, she wrote to Flaubert, "If I do not get cured here I shall go to Cannes where some friends are urging me to come. But I have not mentioned it yet to my children. When I am with them it is not easy to move. There is passion and jealousy. All my life has been like that, never my own!"

Then as though ashamed of her outburst, she concluded her letter with these contradictory words:

"Pity yourself then, you who belong to yourself."

George was determined to convince herself that what remained of her mental conflict was unreasonable. She did this by trying to convince Flaubert that he ought to take a wife or adopt a child. She constantly scolded him for his isolation and independence. If she protested overmuch it was because she had moods in which she envied him. These moods expressed the part of her nature she had once called masculine. The conflict that had formerly been waged between her masculine self and her feminine self, now seemed to exist between her personal and impersonal desires. The psychology remained the same but her vocabulary had changed.

When Flaubert confessed, "I am of both sexes," George replied, "Here is something for those who believe in the importance of anatomy. *There is only one sex.* A man and a woman are so entirely the same thing that one can scarcely understand the subtle reasons for sex distinctions with which our minds are filled. I have observed the childhood and development of my son and daughter. My son was myself, therefore much more woman than my daughter who was an imperfect man."

Maurice was always considered by George "a comfort and a blessing." She had once said, "Of the two children God has given me, only one was for myself." She wrote of Maurice to Flaubert, "He is the soul and life of the house. When he is depressed we are dead."

After his marriage Maurice lost his indolence but his energies were dispersed by the diversity of his gifts. He worked as an engraver and illustrated many of George's books. He also wrote nine novels which were only fairly well received. His chief interest remained entomology. His book, *Le Monde des Papillons* illustrated by himself, contained the researches of years.

These achievements, however, did not go far toward increasing the family exchequer and George continued to maintain Nohant by her writings. In spite of the interruptions of family life, she produced, during the last ten years of her life, from one to three novels a year.

6

After George's return to Nohant, a second granddaughter was born. And now George was indeed needed by her family. How could Maurice and Lina travel, but for grandmother? How could Lina manage when the children were ill? Who but grandmother could teach the children's lessons, tell them stories at night, and answer the thousand and one childish questions for which a busy mother lacks time?

The children never troubled their Bonne-Maman. Her study was their favorite place of play. George did her writing with one child in her lap and one leaning on her shoulder, or with both sitting at her feet, playing dolls and chattering out loud. To the minds of the children, mother often seemed occupied, but grandmother was never busy. She belonged exclusively to them.

Maurice's elder daughter received the family name Aurore, that had been handed down through several generations. First had been Aurore Koenigsmark, mother of Maurice de Saxe; next came Aurore de Saxe, Madame Dupin; then followed Aurore Dupin, who was George Sand; and Aurore the fourth was Aurore Sand.

Aurore Sand was George Sand's last passion. No greater love had ever held sway over her heart. Scattered through her letters were expressions of devotion that became more intense as the child grew older.

"Aurore is a treasure . . . that Aurore is a wonder . . . Aurore is a love . . . little Aurore promises to be very sweet and calm, understanding in a marvelous manner what is said to her and *yielding* to *reason* at two years of age. It is very extraordinary. I have never seen it before."

Then followed references to the second grandchild. "Gabrielle is a big lamb, sleeping and laughing all day; Aurore, more spiritual, with eyes of velvet and fire, talks at thirty months as others do at five years, and is adorable in everything!"

When George put on her new play, *Cadio,* at the Odéon she wrote, "If Cadio succeeds, it will be a little dot for Aurore; that is all my ambition. If it does not succeed, I shall have to begin over again, that is all."

The fond grandmother thought of her grandchild even in her sleep.

"This morning I woke up saying this strange sentence, 'There is always a youthful first part in the drama of life. First part in mine: Aurore. In fact it is impossible not to idolize that child. She is so perfect in intelligence and goodness, that she seems to me like a dream."

Before the baptism of her two grandchildren she wrote, "Our friend Napoleon is the godfather of Aurore and I am the godmother. My nephew is the godfather of the other."

In the absence of Maurice and Lina, George noted with pride: "Aurore has not asked a single time where they are. She looks in my eyes to see if I am sad or anxious. I laugh and she laughs, I think we must keep her sensitiveness asleep as long as possible."

Then followed the final conclusion of George's expanding love: "My dominant passion is my Aurore. My life depends on hers."

Aurore was two years older than her sister Gabrielle and therefore more companionable. She became her grandmother's pupil. George's method of teaching was exceedingly original for those days. She made lessons seem like story telling and play. Aurore the fourth, like Aurore the third, adored mythology. They read together the Iliad and the Odyssey. Then they "exchanged opinions" on what had been read. George sided with the Trojans while Aurore, who had a mind of her own, preferred the Greeks. Grandmother asked her to explain her preference.

"Because Pallas Athene was with them, so they must have had

justice on their side. But why, Bonne-Mère, do you like the Trojans?"

"Because they are to be pitied," was George's answer. "However, you are right to choose justice. But some day you will see
that above human justice there is something greater and better
still."

When Aurore suffered from whooping cough, George held the
child in her arms day and night and ended by catching the disease herself. The doctors advised quiet and an even temperature,
but George defied them and continued her daily swim in the river
Indre where there was a cascade as cold as ice.

"Boiling hot" from her walk to the stream, George with her
sixty-eight years and her whooping cough plunged in, and believed that her cough was cured by her glacial bath.

The doctor called it madness. But George answered, "I am like
the grass; sun and water are all I need."

George reached the age of permanent impersonality. "I accept
everything," she said. She spoke of "the great calm, continually
growing calmer, which exists in my formerly agitated soul. What
presents itself to my eyes when I awaken is the planet. I have considerable trouble in finding there the *me* which used to be so interesting and which I begin to call *you* in the plural."

When friends called in the evening, and brought the neighborhood gossip, George listened as though half asleep. But if the
conversation turned to the last play by Dumas, she had something
to say, or if there was talk of the new books by Darwin and Renan
she became eloquent.

Each evening, in the midst of these discussions, George would
hear a tip-tap on the ceiling. Little Aurore in the room above had
been told to knock on the tiled floor as soon as she was made
ready for bed. In answer to the summons grandmother slowly
mounted the long flight of stairs to Aurore's bedroom, where she
told the fascinating history of the fairy who lived in a palace
under the sea. The story continued for weeks at a time. It was, in

fact, a serial novel like the story told between four chairs. So the cycle of a life of imagination was completed, and Aurore Dupin returned to her first fairy tales.

When she was sixty-five George Sand wrote to her friend M. Louis Ulbach that her letter writing taxed her time and strength since she was obliged to write an average of a dozen letters a day. "After my death," she added, "I hope to go to a planet where they do not know how to read or write.

"If you wish to know my material position," she continued, "I have earned a million by my work—I have given it all away except twenty thousand francs which I set aside two years ago— Keep the secret for me so that I may guard this sum as long as possible."

As M. Ulbach was intending to write her biography, he asked her a number of questions, the answers to which seemed to her unimportant.

"I am merely a good woman," she explained, "on whom they have fastened ferocities of character which are altogether fantastic. They have accused me of inability to love passionately. It seems to me that my life has been full of tenderness and that they might be satisfied with that. At present, thank God, nothing more is asked from me and those who are good enough to love me in spite of the lack of brilliancy in my life and mind, do not complain of me—

"I must have grave defects. But I am like others and do not see my own faults. Neither do I know whether I have good qualities and virtues. I have spent a great deal of time trying to understand what is true, and in this seeking after truth the consciousness of self is more and more effaced every day."

7

As she approached seventy, George's life was full of serene happiness. Several friends of her youth had died but their places were taken by others. And many of her old friends who remained came to her with their children and grandchildren. Those who loved her now belonged to three generations. George was no longer criticised, she was venerated and adored.

Her pleasures were many. The garden she had cultivated for years was a wealth of bloom and perfume. The flowers had become her friends to such an extent that she never allowed them to be cut.

The cats and dogs and birds on the place were also her very dear friends. She always had several special pets among them. During the last few years the dog Fadet was her favorite. She wrote a story about him called *Le Chien et la Fleur Sacrée*. In the story Fadet goes on to larger existence and becomes a man. But in life he outlived his mistress and was buried by her side.

George was sixty-six when the Franco-German war devasted France. Her journal written from September 1870 to January 1871 gave a vivid impression of the effects of war. Although Prussians were quartered all about them, George viewed approaching calamity with philosophic calm. While her friends went mad with anger and despair she wrote in her journal: "It will pass like a squall over a lake."

She lived through the war, through the Commune which followed, and on into the Third Republic.

In May 1876 George was approaching her seventy-third birthday and in honor of the event a family festival was being arranged. For a long time she had been ill and had concealed the fact from her children. For several days she had suffered acutely and was now almost too weak to move. Nevertheless she was able to write with her usual facility. The novel *Aldine* was well under way. She had reached Chapter VII.

On May 29th a doctor called to see Maurice, who was troubled with neuralgia. Having reached the last stage of endurance, George sent Aurore to ask the doctor to come upstairs.

"As I entered her study," he related, "I saw Madame Sand seated at her writing table. A cigarette was at her lips and she held a pen in her hand."

Thus she faced him with a smile that lingered in her kind eyes. It was the last day on which she was able to remain upright.

A few days later, in the intervals of pain, she asked to see her grandchildren and her dog Fadet. On June 8th, at about nine o'clock in the morning, knowing the end had come, she asked for her grandchildren again.

As they were brought to her, "Look at me, my darlings," she entreated.

The two little faces were upturned to hers. George then knew all the agony of separation.

"I love you, I adore you!" she cried.

At the moment of dying she was still ardently alive, and living still meant for her, loving;—

"Good-bye, Maurice, good-bye, Lina, good-bye, Aurore," the generous heart stopped beating.

Magnificent, impossible George, adoring to her latest breath, had ended her life-long search for love.

BIBLIOGRAPHY

ADAM, MME. EDMOND. *Mémoires des hommes du temps présent.* (Figaro, 10 septembre 1893.)

ALLEM, MAURICE. *A. de Musset.*

ALLEN, PERCY. *Berry: The Heart of France.* 1923.

AMIC, HENRI. *George Sand, Mes Souvenirs.* 1893.

    La Défense de George Sand. (Figaro, 2 novembre 1896.)

BARINE, ARVÈDE. *Alfred de Musset.* 1893.

BERTAUT, JULES. *Victor Hugo.*

BOREL, PIERRE. *Trois lettres inédites de George Sand à Pagello, publiées per Pierre Borel.* (Candide, April 1926.)

BRANDES, GEORGE. *The Romantic School in France.* 1904.

BRISSON, ADOLPHE. *Les Amours de George Sand.* (Le Temps, 25 octobre 1896.)

CABANES, DR. *Une visite au docteur Pagello. La Déclaration d'amour de George Sand.* (Revue hebdomadaire, 24 octobre 1896.)

CARO, ELME. *George Sand.* 1887.

CLOUARD, MAURICE. *Alfred de Musset et George Sand.* (Revue de Paris, 15 août 1896.)

COLET, LOUISE. *Lui.* 1880.

COUBERTIN, BARON PIERRE DE. *France since 1814.* 1900.

DONNAY, MAURICE. *La Vie Amoureuse d'Alfred de Musset.* 1926.

DOUMIC, RENÉ. *George Sand.* 1922.

FILON, AUGUSTIN. *Mérimée et ses amis.* 1894.

GANCHE, ÉDOUARD. *Frédéric Chopin.* 1926.

GIRARD, JEAN. *Alfred de Musset.* 1912.

GONCOURT, EDMOND ET JULES DE. *Journal.*

GRIBBLE, FRANCIS. *George Sand and Her Lovers.* 1907.

HAUSSONVILLE, VICOMTE DE CLÉRON D'. *George Sand.* 1879.

HEYLLI, GEORGES D'. *La Fille de George Sand.* 1900.

HUNEKER, JAMES. *Chopin: the Man and His Music.* 1901.

JAMES, HENRY. *French Poets and Novelists.*

JANZÉ, LA VICOMTESSE DE. *Alfred de Musset.* 1891.

KARÉNINE, WLADIMIR. *George Sand, sa vie et ses œuvres.* (4 Vol. 1899-1926.)

LEROY, ALBERT. *George Sand et ses amis.* 1903.

LOVENJOUL, VICOMTE DE SPOELBERCH DE. *La Véritable Histoire de "Elle et Lui."* 1897.

Galerie des Femmes de George Sand. 1843.

MARIÉTON, PAUL. *Une Histoire d'Amour.* 1897.

MAURRAS, CHARLES. *Les Amants de Venise.* 1903.

MUSSET, ALFRED DE. *Premières Poésies.*

Poésies Nouvelles.

La Confession d'un Enfant du siècle.

Contes: Le Merle blanc.

MUSSET, PAUL DE. *Lui et Elle.* 1860.

Biographie d'Alfred de Musset. 1877.

NIECKS, FRIEDRICH. *Frederick Chopin as a Man and a Musician.* 1882.

PALACHE, JOHN GARBER. *Gautier and the Romantics.* 1926.

PLAUCHUT, EDMOND. *George Sand à Gargilesse.* (Le Temps 13 août 1901.)

POURTALÈS, GUY DE. *Polonaise. The Life of Chopin.* 1927.

PRÉVOST, MARCEL. *La Simplicité de George Sand.* (Les Annales politiques et littéraires. Paris 1900.)

George Sand, sa vie son œuvre. (La Contemporaine, mars 1901.)

RAVENEL, FLORENCE L. *Women and the French Tradition.* 1918.

REVUE DES GRANDS PROCÈS CONTEMPORAINS. (1897, mars Nos. 3 et 4.)

REVUE ILLUSTRÉE. *Lettres de femme.* (Letters from George Sand to Michel de Bourges. 1890. Nos. 118, 119, 120, 121 et 123.)

ROCHEBLAVE, SAMUËL. *George Sand avant George Sand.* (Revue de Paris, 15 mars 1896.)

Fin d'une legende. Preface aux Lettres de George Sand à Alfred de Musset et Sainte-Beuve.

George Sand et sa fille. 1905.

RODAYS, FERNAND DE. *Le Procés en separation de corps de George Sand.* (Supplement du Figaro, 2 novembre 1876.)

SAINTE-BEUVE. Article sur *Valentine et Indiana.* (le National 5 octobre et 31 decembre 1832.)

SAND, AURORE. *Le Roman d'Aurore Dudevant et d'Aurélien de Sèze.* (Revue des Deux Mondes. April-August 1926.)

Journal Intime de George Sand. 1926.

Souvenirs de Nohant. (Revue de Paris, septembre 1916.)

SAND, GEORGE. *Histoire de ma Vie.* 4 Vol.

Correspondance. 6 Vol.

Correspondance de George Sand et d'Alfred de Musset. 1904.

Correspondance de George Sand et Gustave Flaubert. 1892.

Lettres à Alfred de Musset et à Sainte-Beuve. 1897.

Un Hiver à Majorque.

Lettres d'un Voyageur.

Souvenirs et idées.

Souvenirs de 1848.

Impressions et Souvenirs.

Elle et Lui.

Indiana.

Valentine.

Lélia.

Léone Léoni.

Jacques.

Jean de la Roche.

Lucretia Floriani.

François le Champi.

Marquis de Villemer.

SANDEAU, JULES. *Marianna.* 1885.

SÉCHÉ, L. ET BERTAUT, J. *George Sand.* 1909.

SEILLIÈRE, BARON ERNEST. *George Sand mystique de la passion, de la politique et de l'art.* 1920.

STERN, DANIEL (COMTESSE MARIE D'AGOULT). *Histoire de 1848.*

THOMAS, BERTHA. *George Sand.* 1889.

VUILLERMOZ, ÉMILE. *La Vie Amoureuse de Chopin.* 1927.

INDEX

THE

JOHN DAY

COMPANY

INC.